MW01617980

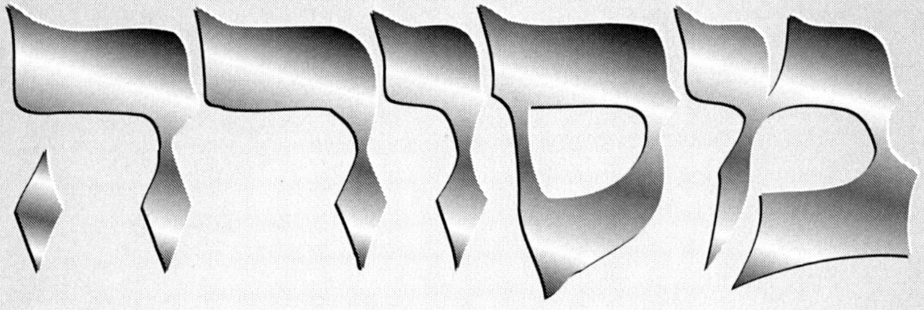

ArtScroll® Series

Rabbi Nosson Scherman / Rabbi Gedaliah Zlotowitz

General Editors

Rabbi Meir Zlotowitz ז״ל, *Founder*

Published by

ARTSCROLL
Mesorah Publications, ltd

ANGEL OF MERCY

MRS. MIRIAM LUBLING

PIONEER OF BIKUR CHOLIM, MEDICAL ADVOCACY, AND CHESED IN AMERICA

SHOSHANA FRIEDMAN

FIRST EDITION
Three Impressions ... June 2025 — August 2025
Fourth Impression ... September 2025

Published and Distributed by
MESORAH PUBLICATIONS, LTD.
313 Regina Avenue / Rahway, New Jersey 07065

Distributed in Europe by
LEHMANNS
Unit E, Viking Business Park
Rolling Mill Road
Jarow, Tyne & Wear, NE32 3DP
England

Distributed in Australia and New Zealand by
GOLDS WORLDS OF JUDAICA
3-13 William Street
Balaclava, Melbourne 3183
Victoria, Australia

Distributed in Israel by
SIFRIATI / A. GITLER — BOOKS
POB 2351
Bnei Brak 51122

Distributed in South Africa by
KOLLEL BOOKSHOP
Northfield Centre, 17 Northfield Avenue
Glenhazel 2192, Johannesburg, South Africa

ARTSCROLL® SERIES
ANGEL OF MERCY

ITEM CODE: MERCYH
ISBN 10: 1-4226-4447-2
ISBN 13: 978-1-4226-4447-8

Typography by CompuScribe at ArtScroll Studios, Ltd.
Printed in the United States of America
Bound by Sefercraft, Quality Bookbinders, Ltd., Rahway, N.J. 07065

לזכר נשמות

הרה״ח ר׳ יעקב

בן הרה״ח ר׳ חנוך העניך ז״ל

נלב״ע כ״ד תמוז תשמ״ח

והאשה החשובה מרת מרים לאה

בת הרה״ח ר׳ יונה ע״ה

נלב״ע י״ח אדר ב׳ תשע״ד

ולזכר נשמות משפחותם

שנהרגו על קדושת השם

תהא נשמותיהם צרורות בצרור החיים

Table of Contents

PHOTO CREDITS:

Mrs. Lubling's personal archives
David Nachman "Ding" Golding
Dr. Etti Hadar, granddaughter of Esther Malka and Yitzhak Levin, Shechunat Maccabi
Epstein Family archives
Hamodia
Israel Government Press Office
Joe Shlabotnik
Ajay Suresh

Acknowledgments

By the Lubling Family

As children growing up with the last name "Lubling," or as new *chassanim* or *kallahs* marrying into the family, we knew that the name carried a certain prestige. It felt almost like a badge of honor, a distinct privilege to be related to Mrs. Miriam Lubling, the legendary medical advocate and paradigm of *chessed*. We felt (and still feel) a constant gratitude to Hakadosh Baruch Hu for the *zechus* of having Bobby in our lives, and for gifting such a uniquely productive activist to Klal Yisrael.

Bobby Lubling possessed a heart that overflowed with compassion. She also possessed outsized measures of grit and gumption, and an unrelenting persistence to pursue her goals no matter what others might think or say. For some people, those traits could have drawbacks, but Bobby's twin compasses of *yiras Shamayim* and *ahavas Yisrael* channeled them toward an astounding *chessed* enterprise.

Back in the days before there were established *frum* medical advocacy organizations and activists, Bobby built relationships with prestigious doctors and their secretaries, arranged life-saving surgeries literally overnight, liaised with politicians and philanthropists with grace and confidence, and raised millions of dollars without any apparent speck of angst. She made it all look so easy, never focusing on setbacks or challenges. But it surely couldn't have been simple for her to overcome language barriers and navigate unfamiliar, intimidating processes and institutions. She must have experienced significant disappointments along the way, but that never stopped her from focusing on the positive and trying another channel, another direction, another method.

Bobby worked quickly and efficiently, but she wasn't one of those stereotypical "big-picture" people who neglect the small details, dismissing them as minor and insignificant. If something was important to a patient, it was important to her, and she invested time, thought, and effort into ensuring that all those little details were arranged — even checking in with her patients afterward to verify that all their ongoing needs were met.

Throughout her long decades of *askanus* and *chessed*, Bobby remained a proud student of Sarah Schenirer. Regal and refined, she was a model *bas melech* with exemplary *tznius*, *kavod haTorah*, and deference to *gedolim*. The prestigious company she kept, the influence she wielded, and the tremendous respect she earned from some of New York's most powerful doctors and administrators — none of it diluted her sweetness and approachability, or her adherence to the *yesodos* of Yahadus.

At the end of the day, she was still our Bobby: a mother, grandmother, and great-grandmother who could relate to all ages and stages with overwhelming affection. She kept a connection with every one of us and radiated love and interest in our lives. And that love was mirrored in her devotion to all Yidden in need, no matter their stripe or type.

As the family of the famous Mrs. Miriam Lubling, we knew that we were living with a legend who played a vital public role, someone who literally saved lives throughout the night and day. But we never felt shortchanged. Bobby Lubling managed to do it all, running from her kindergarten to the hospital to the *simchah* halls, all while never missing a grandchild's siddur play or graduation. She managed to be everything to everyone.

With the publication of this book, we once again have the chance to share her with others, and retell the story of a woman who wouldn't accept a "no" in her quest to help her brothers and sisters in need. Bobby never sought acclaim, but her story is important and very relevant to so many people seeking role models who remained true to Yiddishe values while actualizing their talents and abilities. We hope that the biography of this modern-day Angel of Mercy will serve as an inspiration, and that it will encourage readers to emulate her ways.

We are grateful to ArtScroll/Mesorah Publications for their enthusiasm about this book, and for their professionalism throughout the process of preparing it for publication.

We are also indebted to all of Bobby's friends, volunteers, and admirers who contributed to this project and assisted her in her *avodas hakodesh*. We feel privileged to call them family. Most importantly, we would like to express our deep appreciation to Mrs. Shoshana Friedman, not only for the beautifully written book, but for the way she interfaced with family members with outstanding *middos tovos* and *eidelkeit*. She put her whole heart into the book, as well as her physical *kochos*, as we often received correspondence from her well into the night. Her talents and capabilities, as well as her incredible gift with words, led to a masterpiece that far exceeded all of our expectations.

Mrs. Friedman did not know Bobby personally, but by the time she finished her initial manuscript, she knew her very well. In fact, the family was very touched that on the day of Bobby's recent *yahrtzeit*, Mrs. Friedman visited Bobby's *kever* on Har HaZeisim.

May she and her husband be *zocheh* to much *nachas* from their family, מתוך הרחבת הדעת ושמחת החיים לאורך ימים ושנים טובים.

The extended Lubling family

Author's Acknowledgments

"Would you be interested in writing a biography of a very special woman?" That's how this project started: with a vague email.

To be honest, I wasn't sure. I had never written a full-length book; it sounded very intimidating. Plus the phrase "a very special woman" is, for better or worse, a nebulous and clichéd description that can be applied to almost anyone. But my interest was piqued when I learned who would be the subject of the biography: the famed medical advocate and bikur cholim pioneer Mrs. Miriam Lubling.

I didn't know Mrs. Lubling personally, but I'd read about her and I was aware that the story of this *heimishe* Boro Park grandmother — a European immigrant who never fully mastered English, yet won the respect and obedience of New York's top doctors — held so many threads that were novel and unexpected. I wanted to hear more.

Then I met her children, who extended the warmest welcome. Mrs. Nechama Frankel, R' Chanoch and Rachel Lubling, and R' Aharon and Peshi Drillick maintained that warmth and helpfulness throughout the very long process of researching, writing, reviewing, correcting, and producing this book. Every single interaction with them and their extended families, throughout what was at times a challenging and protracted journey, was unfailingly pleasant and positive.

It quickly grew clear that none of Mrs. Lubling's children are comfortable in the limelight; they learned from their parents that the people who do the most *chessed* are the ones who speak about it least. It took them years to grow comfortable with the idea of sharing their mother's life story with the wider public. But after so many explicit requests of *mechanchim* and other public figures, they realized that Mrs. Lubling's story holds too many valuable messages to keep private.

As we worked to bring that story into written form, R' Chanoch Lubling served as "captain" of the project, reaching out to sources, providing contact information for interviewees, resolving discrepancies between varying accounts, and carefully reading and correcting the manuscript — moving the book forward purposefully, but without any pressure or tension. As the extended family pitched in to bring the book to the finish line, they worked with the same purposeful yet pleasant attitude. It has been a privilege and learning experience to work with such special people — no clichés intended.

At one big family gathering of Mrs. Lubling's grandchildren and great-grandchildren, I asked if anyone in the room could be considered the successor of their legendary matriarch. "No, no one's like Bobby," they told me. "None of us can do what she did." But even if none of Mrs. Lubling's descendants can order a doctor out of his pajamas and into the operating room, all the family bears her mark — unbending fealty to bedrock values, an *ayin tovah* and easy manner, the ability to get things done quickly and efficiently, and a constant desire to do good for others. May they enjoy continued *nachas* and *simchah* from their beautiful families, and may Hashem grant R' Chanoch, his wife Rachel, and his sister Nechama *refuos* and *yeshuos*.

I've worked together with acclaimed writer R' Yisroel Besser for many years. It was his recommendation that brought me from the magazine arena to the book world. But he didn't stop once he'd made that initial "*shidduch*"; he kept offering encouragement and wise advice at many different junctures through the writing process. I'm grateful for the many times he put his own work on hold to answer my questions, locate sources, explain the minutiae of book publishing, or even hunt for old photos from his own archives.

R' Yonoson Rosenblum, a former boss and still-mentor, encouraged me to take on this project and gave me valuable guidance early on.

Malky Heimowitz is a longtime colleague in the world of Jewish writing, editing, and publishing. More importantly, she's a faithful friend who's offered support and smart advice at crucial moments — including the early stages of writing this book.

Dovi Safier and Yehuda Geberer helped clarify historical details, generously availing me of their extensive knowledge, research skills, and personal libraries.

The team at ArtScroll welcomed me with warmth and professionalism. Rabbi Gedaliah Zlotowitz was always available — be it in the early mornings or late evenings — for every question and concern. Rabbi Nosson Scherman offered encouragement and advice when I was feeling very lost and unsure; his feedback was a generous and tremendously helpful boost. Mrs. Miriam Zakon has been the best possible guide to the world of book writing, holding my hand throughout the process. I am grateful for Mrs. Judi Dick's precise edits, Mrs. Tova Finkelman's exacting proofreading, for Estie Dicker's careful and artful pagination, to R' Mendy Herzberg for shepherding the project from a dizzying collection of hundreds of small details to a final seamless product, to R' Avrohom Biderman for lending his professional knowledge and interest, and to R' Eli Kroen and Aviva Kohn for the beautiful cover design.

My bosses at *Mishpacha* Magazine, Mr. Eli Paley and Mr. Yehuda Nachshoni, gave me the go-ahead to take on this project, knowing it would cut into my time, energies, and focus at the magazine. I am grateful for their support and for the trust they demonstrate every week in our team at the English-language edition. It's a privilege to work for a company with elevated goals and integrity, and that ethos comes straight from the top.

During my work on this book, Nomee Shaingarten and the team at *Mishpacha* filled many holes graciously and willingly. They never voiced any complaints, only encouragement and goodwill. Their dedication to the readers is evident in every edition the magazine publishes. What readers may not know is how dedicated the team is to one another. I'm so grateful to work with such talented teammates whom I can also count as true friends.

~

This book primarily tells the story of one very special woman, but it also relates the stories of so many others who came along for the ride (or, in some cases, provided the ride). Even before the Rivkah Laufer Bikur Cholim was established, Mrs. Lubling had a gift for enlisting others for her *chessed* pursuits. As her activities expanded, she drew in a large circle of friends and partners. Many of those friends and partners — or in some cases, their children — helped me in the quest to capture Mrs. Lubling's personality and lifework.

Mrs. Lubling's Israeli cousins, the extended Albert family, invited me into their homes to tables set with homemade cheesecake to share their personal memories of a Tel Aviv that no longer exists. Those conversations overflowed with warmth, nostalgia, and strong family ties. They were a testament to Mrs. Lubling's magnetism and beloved character, but also a testament to a family that cherishes its bond with every relative.

Esther Chaviva (Zucker) Svei was the subject of my first full-length interview for this book. I was intimidated by the scope of the project, and she eased me into it in the most pleasant and natural way. She came to my home, pulled out a photo, and brought me into the world of Mrs. Lubling with color, detail, and so much heart. She was available during the entire process to clarify details, ensure the dialogue was true to Mrs. Lubling's manner of speech, and iron out any inconsistencies. She even sketched a map of the hospital to help me visualize Mrs. Lubling's daily routine. I'm also grateful to her sister Sima Zucker, another devoted volunteer.

It was a privilege to speak to the legendary Morah Chevy Kramer, my former teacher whose lessons and songs still resonate in my home, about her own memories of driving and accompanying Mrs. Lubling. She also helped me track down interviewees and provided a treasure trove of journal clippings, additional source material, and even an entire book with background information.

As I interviewed and researched, I met more of the incredible women (along with some men) who drove Mrs. Lubling to the hospital, visited patients alongside her, hosted patients from abroad, and/or ran the yearly fundraising parties. They painted their adventures with Mrs. Lubling in vivid detail, taking me into the car or hospital corridors along with them. It was a true inspiration to hear from this cadre of women who have made bikur cholim and *chessed* an integral part of their lives. And it was especially moving to hear that many of their children learned from their example, and are perpetuating their mothers' *chessed* among the next generation.

I know that Mrs. Lubling's circle of givers includes some women whom I did not manage to reach, and I sincerely apologize to anyone who was inadvertently left out.

Several doctors and medical professionals shared memories and stories of Mrs. Lubling; they are all extremely busy, but when they heard the name "Mrs. Lubling," previously closed doors miraculously opened and they suddenly found time to speak to me.

I feel especially fortunate that Dr. Yashar and Mrs. Perie Hirshaut carved out some of their very precious time to share their personal memories. Dr. Hirshaut provided a valuable perspective on the mindset of the modern-day medical professional. Mrs. Hirshaut's storytelling skills and spot-on impersonation brought Mrs. Lubling to life with wit and affection. Her encouragement during the approval and editing process was so uplifting that I should have bottled it for the long, late nights still ahead.

Mrs. Pearl Pinter opened her home to me, along with her husband R' Mordechai *a"h,* and walked me through the history and inner workings of the Rivkah Laufer Bikur Cholim with precision and great sensitivity. When I needed some missing details for a crucial story, Mrs. Pinter quickly and efficiently hunted them down in the RLBC records. The *chessed* that emerges from this organization is staggering, but there is zero fanfare or self-acclaim: just quiet efficiency and unpretentious dedication. Chazal tell us that *berachah* rests where publicity is absent; when you see the RLBC's humble center of operations, you learn yet another reason why the organization has seen so much success.

My family has always been my bulwark. Though we live far away from them, my parents, Dr. Reuven and Miriam Cofsky, and my in-laws, Rabbi Nosson and Toby Friedman, are a tangible presence in our lives. They radiate constant encouragement and support for all of our family's endeavors, and provide a valuable listening ear when the going gets tough.

Throughout this project, my husband and children were the best cheerleaders. They accommodated my flights and road trips, my erratic interview schedule, and my late-night writing sessions with flexibility and grace. They were an enthusiastic audience, always eager to hear another story about Mrs. Lubling. Some of those newly unearthed tales became our bedtime stories and Shabbos talk, adding a rich dimension to our conversations and aspirations.

Most of all, I am grateful to the Divine Scriptwriter for carrying me through this venture, for arranging that I "meet," as it were, the amazing and indomitable Mrs. Lubling, and for assigning me a project with such a valuable takeaway. The years spent researching, discussing, and writing the story of the Angel of Mercy brought me and my family a new appreciation for what a single determined person can accomplish when they're fueled by a desire to help their fellow Jew. And that, I hope, is the lasting message of this book.

Prologue

It was Friday afternoon in the emergency room at New York University Medical Center, and no one was in a rush. The surge of adrenaline that accompanies an ambulance ride had long since tapered down for the many patients now settled into cubicles, in their introduction to the most commonly performed hospital activity: waiting.

The critical emergencies had immediately been redirected to the cardiology ward or the operating rooms. Here in the ER, everyone else had to wait — for blood pressure readings, test results, referrals for scans, results of scans, consultations with doctors, and finally, the decision whether to be admitted, transferred, or released.

In one cubicle, a man kept glancing back and forth from his son, who was seated on the bed, to the watch on his wrist. As a nurse passed, he stood up. "Excuse me?" he asked, his voice tinged with anxiety.

"Yes?" the nurse responded.

"I was wondering... I was wondering how long it will take for you to check the results of my son's CT scan," the man said. "The doctors said that if it looks okay, then we can go home."

"You heard what he said," the nurse said. "When they read the scan, then we'll know what to do."

The man swallowed. "Yes, but how long will it take? Because it's Friday afternoon, and our Sabbath is starting soon. I want to get back to Brooklyn."

The nurse shrugged. "It's busy here," she said, then walked away.

The man's shoulders sagged. He returned to the plastic chair and sat back down, pulling out his phone and dialing home.

"It looks like we're going to have to spend Shabbos here," he said despondently. "I hear there's a fully-stocked bikur cholim room here at the hospital… so we'll have food. But what about you? Are you sure you'll manage without us?"

Suddenly there was a voice from the ER entranceway.

"Who is waiting to go home?" It was a woman speaking in Yiddish. "Who needs to leave before Shabbos?"

The man stood up and followed the voice. Standing near the nurses' station was a petite, elderly woman who looked like she'd just stepped out of a Boro Park *simchah* hall: dressed all in black with fresh lipstick, bouffant *sheitel*, gleaming pearls, and high heels. She met his eyes, taking in his quiet desperation with a quick, appraising look.

"What are you waiting for? You're waiting to leave?" she asked.

He nodded. "I'm not sure. My son was hit by a car, and they said we had to come here for a scan, to make sure the brain is okay. He seems fine, but I'm still waiting for the results. Until we get them, we can't go anywhere."

The woman turned to the nurse. "This man, he is my cousin. He needs to leave now," she commanded. "Let's get his results."

She slipped off her fur coat and draped it over the nurse's chair, then leaned over the computer and waited expectantly.

The nurse looked at the woman in black. She sighed. Then she turned resignedly to the man. "What's your son's name?" she asked.

Within ten minutes, the boy's discharge form had emerged from the printer.

"Here," Mrs. Miriam Lubling snatched the papers and handed them to the waiting man. "You see, the scan is good. Your son, he will be fine. Take your papers, take your son, and have a good Shabbos."

Mrs. Miriam Lubling, the indefatigable medical advocate who shepherded thousands of Jews through medical treatment in America's leading hospitals, had many nicknames. Rav Avrohom Pam called her "The Queen of *Chessed*." Rabbi Moshe Sherer called her "The Angel of Mercy." Famed pediatric neurosurgeon Dr. Fred Epstein called her "The Boss." Nurses called her "The Queen of NYU." Her bank teller called her "Hurricane Miriam." At least one doctor called her a pain in the neck. "But," he added, "if I were sick, she's the one I would want advocating for me."

Wherever she found herself, Mrs. Lubling's heart pulsated with concern for Jews in need. With her quick mind, capable hands, and unmatched powers of persuasion, she acted on that concern. Along the way, she built effective organizations, inspired a cadre of volunteers, empowered a new generation of activists, and saved too many lives to calculate.

Although she never quite mastered the English language, everyone understood her promise: "I take care." They understood that here was a woman who could meld the softest of hearts with the steeliest resolve to assure them a better present and future.

With time, she became the inspiration and mentor for an entire network of advisors, advocates, fundraisers, and donors who are hard at work to this day, connecting their fellow Jews to the best medical care and easing the overwhelmingly painful and frightening process of hospital treatment.

This virtual army uses the most up-to-date technology to guide patients and maintain relationships with doctors and other hospital personnel. They wield databases and instant messaging and sophisticated fundraising methods. But years earlier, when Mrs. Lubling was the universal address for sick Jews seeking a helping hand, there was just a phone number, a pocketbook, a yearly fundraising luncheon, and a planner stuffed with Post-it notes.

And that was enough, because the persona behind them had something more valuable than any database: she simply would not take no for an answer. When faced with a closed door, she knocked so insistently that people had no choice but to allow her entry. And if they refused to open the door, she found a window instead.

A rotation of young women used to drive Mrs. Lubling to NYU Medical Center every afternoon, and accompany her as she made her rounds of the hospital. "If there was a DO NOT ENTER sign," one of those women remembers, "it may have been meant for other people — but not her. She went right in."

"Excuse me," a nurse once said as Mrs. Lubling opened the door to a doctor's private office, "don't you see the sign? You can't come in."

The doctor looked up, took in the familiar figure, and waved away the nurse. "Come on in, Mrs. Lubling," he said.

If one of "her patients" needed surgery, she wanted it to be the first surgery of the shift, when the doctor would be at his best — and the patient not overly weakened by the mandatory fasting. She'd call the scheduling desk at the Operating Room and say, "My cousin [every Jew was her cousin] is having surgery tomorrow; we need the 7:30 a.m. slot."

"Someone else has it already," she'd be told.

"How old is he? My cousin is older, she needs to go first."

"We can't change it."

"It's a piece of paper," she would say. "I can change it for you."

To the Jewish doctors who could be moved by a *heimishe* lexicon and message, she urged, "*Zai ah gitte yingel*, be a good boy, and just do what I say."

When she arranged an immediate appointment so a neighbor could see a top Manhattan doctor with a long waiting list, the doctor pointed at Mrs. Lubling and told the patient, "You know why we listen to her? Because we're going to end up listening to her in the end anyway."

After Mrs. Lubling passed away, a distant relative visited her grieving family. "Growing up," he said, "we had no claim to fame, no money, no connections. But when my wife got sick, we had the magic key to get the best care, the best doctors, the finest hospital. You know what we had? We knew Miriam Lubling."

CHAPTER 1
Pioneering Spirit

Just past midnight one Tuesday in June of 1995, a car pulled up at 1369 51st Street, in the heart of Boro Park. The proprietors of the shops lining 13th Avenue had lowered the aluminum grates over their storefronts hours earlier, and the rumbling yellow school buses had long retired for the day. Boro Park's constant chorus of honking cars, school buses, and delivery trucks had finally dissolved into the muted hum of a neighborhood settling down to sleep. But the woman who emerged from the car was fully alert.

She was nearing the end of her eighth decade, but she moved with the energy and ease of a much younger woman. Dressed in a dark two-piece suit with elegant silver beading on the lapels and cuffs, earrings glinting in the darkness, she hoisted a heavy black handbag from the passenger seat. "It was a beautiful wedding, wasn't it?" she said, pulling herself to her full height — just a bit under five feet, if you disregarded the patent-leather high heel shoes propping her up.

"Beautiful," the woman in the driver's seat agreed. "And it meant so much to the Frieds that you came to dance with them."

The elderly woman nodded. "I promised them, when their Heshy was so sick, that one day I would dance at his *chasunah*. You

Mrs. Miriam Lubling looked like the classic Boro Park grandmother — but possessed the stamina and drive of someone much younger.

see? I told them to keep hoping, and the *Eibeshter* helped." She looked at her watch. "But it's late now! You have to go home! Tomorrow is a busy day for you. Thank you so much, I'll see you next Tuesday at three o'clock, yes?"

"Yes. My pleasure, Mrs. Lubling," the woman said. "Good night."

The car glided down the dark, quiet block, and Mrs. Miriam Lubling pushed open the door to the red brick two-family residence. With her handbag over her shoulder and her heels clicking rhythmically, she began climbing the two flights of stairs to her apartment.

She took the last few stairs quickly, because the insistent sound of a ringing phone was growing steadily louder. She opened the door, hurried through the immaculate dining room with its matching mahogany dining table and chairs, breakfront, and buffet, and headed to the kitchen, where she grabbed the receiver.

"Hello?" she said. Her voice was slightly raspy, and even that one word carried the imprint of an Eastern European childhood. But it carried unmistakable warmth, too.

"Is this Mrs. Miriam Lubling?" came a tremulous response. Then, in Hebrew, a flood of words. "I don't know you and you don't know me, but everyone said we must call you. It's about my daughter. She was fine, she was healthy, and then a few months ago the headaches started. We thought she needed glasses, but that didn't help. Then we tried the local neurologist here at our neighborhood health clinic in Bnei Brak. He said it was nerves, that she was just too tense about her schoolwork. But the headaches kept coming. So we tried a different doctor, a big professor in Hadassah-Ein Kerem. Finally, they sent us for an MRI. And now the doctors are saying that she has a tumor."

"*Oy*," Mrs. Lubling said. Something in the man's Hebrew recitation prompted her to switch to Yiddish — she sensed he would feel more comfortable that way. "How old is your daughter? Where is the tumor? Which doctor found it?"

She listened attentively as the details came, occasionally interjecting with a question. Then she spoke, broadcasting a blend of empathy and authority.

"I know the right doctor for your daughter, and I will speak to him tomorrow morning to schedule a surgery right away. How soon can you bring her to New York?"

"To New York?" the man stammered. "We don't have passports. And we'll need visas too."

"Here, take this number," Mrs. Lubling responded. "This is an *askan* who can help you with the passports and visas. And I need you to send the doctor the MRI reports and scans of the tumor, and any bloodwork that you did. Can you fax it to this number?"

The man dutifully took down the details.

"Good, good," Mrs. Lubling said. "Call me back when you have a flight scheduled, and I will have someone pick you up from the airport and bring you straight to the hospital. We don't want to waste a minute."

The man was quiet. Mrs. Lubling sensed it wasn't just the overwhelm of all the duties on his to-do list.

"You are wondering about the money, yes?" she asked softly.

"Yes," he admitted.

And you are wondering how a chassid from Bnei Brak who doesn't know English will communicate with the staff in a bustling, impersonal New York hospital, she thought. *And how your daughter will find the courage to face a surgeon's knife and the stamina to endure the grueling rehab to follow. And where you will find kosher food in the heart of Manhattan. And how long you can last without the familiar sounds of davening and Krias HaTorah connecting you to your Source. And whether Shabbos will bring any serenity when you are surrounded by the constant beeps and alerts of the Intensive Care Unit.*

She had answers to all those questions — answers won through years of determined and persistent lobbying, relationship-building, trial and error and trying again. But for now, she focused on the sole doubt he'd conceded.

"You don't have to worry about the money," she said firmly. "We have an organization here in Boro Park with money for cases exactly like this one."

"Are you sure?" the man choked out the words. "I don't have to raise any money on my own?"

"Yes," she said. "You work on the passports and travel arrangements, and I will take care of the rest. Make sure to call me as soon as you have the flight number. Day, night, it doesn't matter what time."

Mrs. Lubling hung up the phone. She made a mental note to begin her to-do list the following morning with phone calls to the hospital, to three favored *baalei tzedakah* in her network of donors — almost all of whom had been won to her cause after seeing her in action when their own relatives benefited from her advocacy — and to a local family that often hosted hospital patients who'd traveled from afar for medical care.

Then she thought of that faceless girl about to be wrenched from her family, her community, from everything familiar.

Miriam Lubling was a woman of action, not a woman who analyzed emotions. She radiated practicality and purpose as she maneuvered through the intimidating kingdoms of New York's leading medical centers. But even though she rarely talked about her early life, she acted with a certain empathy that can only come from personal experience.

She knew what it meant to leave behind everything familiar and journey to a strange new land.

She knew what it meant to face the frightening possibility that serious illness might snatch away the people you love most.

She knew what it meant for a hospital patient to taste warm, homemade food. To hear the sounds of *Megillas Esther* in a sterile hospital room. To know that a network of caring brothers and sisters are standing at the ready, opening homes and wallets to carry a patient through the bewildering process of medical treatment.

She may have been the president of the trailblazing organization and a fearless medical advocate, an indomitable woman with unflagging energy and an always-perfectly styled wig. But for all that influence she wielded and all the doctors who obeyed her commands, Mrs. Miriam Lubling still remembered how it felt to be vulnerable — and how a helping hand could make all the difference for a Jew in need.

Krakow, Poland, 1939

"There is no future for the Jews here!" the strange man screamed. There was passion on his face and fire in his voice. "Anyone with eyes in his head can see that. You want a future, you have to leave!"

Among the curious Jews who had gathered in Krakow that day in the late 1930s to hear the stranger's address was a young woman named Miriam Albert. Strong-minded, bright, and confident, Miriam wasn't deterred by the unfamiliar or untested. Others may

Miriam (upper left) with her family in Konskie. Strong-minded and confident even as a youngster, she made the hard decision to leave everything she knew.

have been intimidated or repelled by the doomsday message, but she internalized it instead.

Born in the summer of 1917 two days after Shabbos Nachamu, Miriam grew up in a Gerrer family in the Polish town of Konskie (referred to by its Jewish residents as Koinsk or Kinsk). Most of her childhood memories were cloaked in shadow: her father, Reb Yonah, was diagnosed with tuberculosis when she was a very small child, and spent the remainder of his short life in a sanatorium.

Her mother, Pesia, bravely tried to rebuild her family while feeding her homemade food to local children who'd fallen ill. Those early experiences with illness must have left a mark on young Miriam, but she kept the memories locked deep inside and rarely spoke about her early life or the father who'd been snatched away so young.

There was one bright memory she did share: When Miriam was a teenager, the pioneering educator Frau Sarah Schenirer visited Konskie to recruit students for her fledgling Bais Yaakov. Frau Schenirer spent that Shabbos at the Albert home, and Miriam was privileged to bring her *negel vasser* in the morning.

Young Miriam (bottom row, center) with her fellow students back in Poland

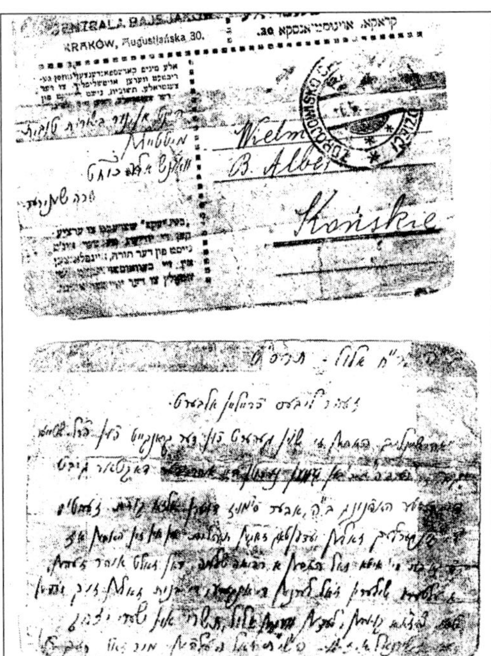
KRAKÓW, Augustiańska 30.

B. Albert

Konskie

"To my beloved Miss Albert." Throughout her life, Mrs. Lubling held on to the precious postcard she'd received as a girl from her earliest mentor, Frau Sarah Schenirer.

Something in Miriam must have caught Frau Schenirer's eye: she saw confidence, initiative, and charisma in her teenage host, and encouraged her to start a Shabbos Bnos group in Konskie. Miriam rose to the challenge, and maintained a correspondence with Frau Schenirer.

Throughout the many stations of her life's travels, she held on to a postcard from her mentor. On that postcard, Frau Schenirer asked Miriam to arrange for the older girls to teach the younger ones, and to gather the Bnos groups each evening to learn a *sefer* and to read the *Bais Yaakov Journal* together. Perhaps most important were the words right at the beginning: "To my beloved Miss Albert."

A few years later, Miriam was able to tap into that affection in person when she attended the central Bais Yaakov in Krakow. A bright student who learned and absorbed quickly, she mastered the formal curriculum and absorbed the passion for Yiddishkeit that was an equally vital aspect of the Bais Yaakov education.

Passing the torch. Miriam Albert (far right) taught the young girls of her *shtetl*, Konskie, sharing what she had learned in Bais Yaakov.

In the late 1930s, a wave of idealism stirred Poland's Jews to consider *aliyah*. Some of those who listened to the call were secular Zionists who aimed to build an irreligious Socialist paradise in the land of their fathers. But many of the potential *olim* were religious Jews who hoped to transplant their Torah-based values to their ancient homeland, drawn by both the promise of Eretz Yisrael and the darkening situation for Jews in Europe.

The chassidim of Gur had in their Rebbe, the Imrei Emes, a model of love for Eretz Yisrael and the determination to make it home: the Rebbe himself journeyed to the Holy Land on five occasions. On his final trip, in Elul of 1935, he moved into an apartment that had been prepared for him in Yeshivas Sfas Emes in Yerushalayim. That Succos, he followed the custom of Eretz Yisrael and did not observe the *yom tov sheini shel galuyos* — a very public declaration that Eretz Yisrael was now his home.

With her family's Rebbe now living in Eretz Yisrael, Miriam had an additional motivation to undertake the journey. And when, in her early twenties, she heard a recruiter exhorting the Jews of Poland to join a ship leaving from the port of Constanta in Romania, the message resonated. She must have been a bold and decisive

The Imrei Emes of Gur granted a blessing to young Miriam Albert before she embarked on her courageous journey to Eretz Yisrael.

young woman, because she sent a telegram to her family informing them of her decision to leave Poland. But she was also fueled by *emunas chachamim*; before leaving, she obtained the blessing of her family's Rebbe, the Imrei Emes of Gur.

On July 13, 1939, Miriam boarded the *Parita*, joining 849 other *"ma'apilim,"* the name given to European Jews who dared to defy the British authorities and attempted to enter Mandate-era (also known as Mandatory) Palestine without the necessary certificates.

It was a very risky proposition. In sole charge of what they called Palestine, the British severely restricted the number of Jewish immigrants allowed into the country, using force and incarceration to prevent Jews from immigrating. In 1937, they reduced the number of entry certificates from 61,900 to just 10,500 — this as Europe's Jews felt increasingly unsafe in their homes. Chaim Weizmann, the Russian-born scientist and Zionist leader who later served as Israel's first president, famously stated that for Europe's millions of Jews, the world seemed to be divided into two sorts of countries: places where they could not live, and places they could not enter.

The ill-fated *Parita* brought hundreds of hopeful emigres from a darkening Europe to the Promised Land — only to be attacked by the British upon arrival.

In defiance of those onerous quotas, a group of Zionist activists decided to arrange illegal sea passage for groups of immigrants. For their first transport, they hired the Greek-owned vessel *Parita*. An initial group of immigrants boarded near Marseilles, France, and then the *Parita* continued to Romania, where the remaining immigrants boarded.

The plan was for the *Parita* to travel as far as Cyprus. There the passengers would transfer to small fishing boats to complete their journey to Palestine. The fishing boats were much less likely to be spotted by the British forces, and hopefully their passengers could slip undetected onto the Jaffa (Yaffo) coast after nightfall.

But reality did not go according to the plan. The vessel had never been meant to carry anything near the eight hundred fifty passengers who crowded on. Food and fuel supplies ran out early for the overloaded ship, and hunger and illness set in.

When the *Parita* reached Cyprus, the promised fishing boats never materialized. The journey — which should have lasted just a week — extended over forty parched, miserable days, as the ship limped toward Izmir, Turkey, where local authorities quarantined it for some time.

Decades later, Miriam would recount every detail of the horrific trip. At some point the passengers were given tomatoes to eat, but Miriam was unfamiliar with this vegetable and wasn't sure it was kosher. She remained hungry rather than risk eating forbidden food.

But worse than the hunger and thirst was the loneliness. The ship was packed with people, but Miriam had never felt so alone. In that swell of humanity, she had no family. No friends. No one rooting for her to make it to the other side. She was just a tiny speck in an endless sea, lonely and vulnerable and wondering what her future would be — if she even had a future.

Finally, on August 23, the crew sighted the Holy Land on the horizon. The exhausted passengers cheered as the chief mechanic pointed and said, "You see that beach over there? That's Tel Aviv. You're almost home!"

But then a ripple of fear went through the crowd. As the *Parita* neared the shore of Tel Aviv, the crew discerned the telltale uniforms of the British authorities waiting to apprehend them on the shore. This was a "specialty" of the British Mandate: intercepting boatloads of Jewish refugees and refusing to allow them into their homeland.

The British used the forbidding Sarafand detention camp to house illegal immigrants. It was Miriam's first "residence" in the Promised Land.

The *Parita*'s captain and the chief mechanic refused to move any farther; they knew better than to steer directly into danger. Sure enough, their fears were realized. When the *Parita* was about fifty yards from the shore, British artillery struck and disabled the ship.

The doomed vessel began to fill with water. The passengers had no choice but to enter the sea and swim to the trap awaiting them at the shore. Miriam had never learned to swim, and one of her fellow passengers pulled her through the Mediterranean waters by her hair. For the rest of her life, she would never willingly enter the ocean.

Once they reached land, the shivering Jews were arrested by the waiting British soldiers and transferred to the Sarafand detention camp. This camp had been established by the British in the 1930s to jail members of the Jewish Underground and to house illegal immigrants (and thereby deter other Jews who might attempt to follow their example). It was a forbidding place, complete with barbed wire and watchtowers, spartan barracks, and forced separation between men and women. This was Miriam Albert's welcome to the Promised Land.

But feisty young Miriam wasn't one to be deterred by a rocky start. Ten days later, the prisoners were released and Miriam was invited to the home of her uncle, Reb Yitzchak Shaul Albert, who had immigrated to Mandatory Palestine several years earlier and now came to collect her from the camp. During her incarceration in Sarafand, she learned, Hitler's forces had invaded Poland. There was no going home now.

"From now on," her uncle told her, "you will be part of our family, and your home will be our house in Tel Aviv."

Tel Aviv was at the time a magnet for European immigrants who were drawn to the swiftly burgeoning coastal city that offered electricity and plumbing — not to be taken for granted in the still-developing country — along with a growing assortment of shuls and chassidic courts.

Among those European immigrants, Reb Yitzchak Shaul Albert stood out. Like Miriam, he was a chassid (later to become a *mechutan*) of the Imrei Emes of Gur. As a youngster back in Poland, he had been privileged to participate in a *melaveh malkah* at which the Rebbe declared, "*Kinderlach*, we are ascending to Eretz Yisrael!" Back then, the boys didn't dream that his words could be taken literally — but in fact, every person in that room did indeed merit to live in Eretz Yisrael.

Trailblazing educator Rav Yitzchak Shaul Albert took Miriam into his rickety home and shared his passion for uncompromising *chinuch* with his young niece.

Not that it was easy. Reb Yitzchak Shaul entered Mandatory Palestine on a tourist visa in 1924. When his visa expired, he was formally expelled from the country. A good friend from his yeshivah days, Reb Shlomo Birnbaum, gave him the requisite one thousand lirot sterling to remain.

Reb Yitzchak Shaul then sent for his wife Shprintze and their three children (others would be born in Tel Aviv). In order to finance their journey, they agreed that Shprintze would sell her jewelry and Yitzchak Shaul his precious Vilna Shas. The newly reunited family was awarded a plot in the Maccabi neighborhood of Tel Aviv. Despite the bravado of the name, it was a far cry from their comfortable home in Poland.

The Maccabi neighborhood was a jumble of ramshackle wooden shacks in close proximity to Jaffa. The tin roofs sweltered in the summers, and all too often, fires ignited and spread among the wooden homes. A two-story building served as a watchtower for the British authorities, so they could keep an eye out for Arab marauders from nearby Jaffa.

Tel Aviv's Maccabi neighborhood was a far cry from the Alberts' comfortable home in Poland — rain dripped through the roof in the winter and the tin roofs baked in the summer.

The Albert family's plot had a palm tree at its center. Reb Yitzchak Shaul, who never compromised on halachah, refused to cut down a fruit-bearing tree; instead he built his home around it. When the winter rains came, the moisture collected on the wide palm branches and steadily dripped down into the crowded, rickety house.

But for Miriam, the oft-sodden home was a true haven. The family embraced her warmly and concocted a fond nickname for her — "Miriam Parita," after the ill-fated ship that had brought her to Eretz Yisrael. Their three daughters — Pesia, Chaya, and Tziporah — treated Miriam as a beloved sister. They cheered her on as she picked up modern-day Ivrit and they delighted in her boundless energy and wit.

Not only did Miriam become part of the family, she also became part of their single-minded mission to provide pure Torah *chinuch* to the children of Tel Aviv. That venture had begun a few years earlier, when Reb Yitzchak Shaul — a spiritual warrior who would lie down on the street to prevent buses from traversing his neighborhood on Shabbos — realized that the Torah-observant immigrants of Tel Aviv did not have a suitable kindergarten for their children. Children are the future, and with so many alien secular winds blowing through the rapidly expanding city of Tel Aviv, its religious identity was at stake.

So in 1937 he opened a network of kindergartens for *chareidi* children, called Chorev (not to be confused with the Jerusalem school of the same name), and a Talmud Torah system that eventually educated thousands of children, including many prominent *marbitzei Torah* and even several chassidishe Rebbes.

The Chorev playgroups — one on 68 Rechov HaKishon and the second on 50 Rechov HaChalutzim — were a revolution in Mandatory Palestine's nascent educational landscape, because Reb Yitzchak, a skilled pedagogue, infused every educational decision with his abiding *yiras Shamayim*. And he had the best possible support staff: one daughter, Chaya (later Bleier), taught the *gan* on Rechov HaKishon, and another daughter, Tziporah (later Kehan), taught the *gan* on Rechov HaChalutzim.

The Albert girls were just teens when they began teaching in the kindergartens, alternating their hours at work with high school classes. They poured their creativity into their young charges, creating routines and songs that are still taught in kindergartens today. (Tziporah Kehan's "*Achalnu v'Savanu*," "*Paam Hayah Tzaddik Gadol*," and "*B'Chag HaShavuot*" are beloved kindergarten classics.)

They also strove to convey how everything in the *mesorah* has a source and root: the weekly *parashah* was taught from an open Chumash, and even a truncated davening for four-year-olds was led from a siddur. Along with the fun and finesse, color and creativity, the children learned the sacredness and gravity of their heritage.

When Miriam took her place on the kindergarten staff alongside her cousins, it was a perfect fit. She loved children and had a natural exuberance that made her a magnet for the little ones. She also possessed a deep loyalty to the education she'd received in Sarah Schenirer's Bais Yaakov, and even though this Mediterranean city with its sandy beaches and pastel-colored buildings was worlds away from the red brick of Krakow, she was determined to instill in a new generation the same faithfulness to Torah she had learned there.

On Simchas Torah of 1941, Uncle Yitzchak was davening in the local Gerrer *shtiebel* at 33 Rechov HaKishon, known as the Kishon *Shtiebel* or simply *Drei un Dreizig*. The *shtiebel* was a gathering place for the Gerrer chassidim of Southern Tel Aviv, a shul where everyone knew everyone (and their grandfather from back in the *heim* too).

But that night Reb Yitzchak noticed an unfamiliar face. It was a chassidishe young man, a newcomer who possessed an obvious refinement, even shyness. But when the dancing began, he was seized by an otherworldly exuberance. He sang and spun, stamped his feet, and when he was given the *Sefer Torah* to hold, he got up on the table and kept on dancing as he clutched it tight.

Rabbi Albert looked at this young man. "That's it," he said. "I found a *shidduch* for Miriam Parita!"

After Yom Tov, he made some inquiries and learned more about the fellow. His name was Yaakov Lubling, and he was a fellow Gerrer chassid who had also left his family behind in Poland for the Holy Land. In time Reb Yitzchak would also discover that Yaakov actually had a quiet, reserved persona — it was only on one day of the year, Simchas Torah, that his emotions spilled over for everyone to see. But from his glimpse of Yaakov's unbridled enthusiasm as he danced on the table, he sensed the *bachur* could be a suitable spouse for his spunky, determined niece.

When Miriam met the young man, she learned that they had quite a bit in common.

Yaakov had grown up in the southern Polish town of Zawiercie. His parents, who owned a small retail store, sent him to learn in the Kesser Torah yeshivah in Sosnowiec, a branch of the Radomsker yeshivah network. Young Yaakov quickly gained a name as a leading student — both for his achievements in Torah learning as well as his unbending adherence to chassidus.

Those years of intense Torah learning left an indelible mark;

no matter where life took him and no matter the challenges it threw at him, he remained a yeshivah student at heart, seizing every available moment to learn Torah in depth. And he remained a devoted Gerrer chassid as well, nourishing and cherishing close relationships with its Rebbes.

Shy, reserved Yaakov Lubling as a *bachur*. His once-yearly show of exuberance sealed his *shidduch* to feisty Miriam Albert.

In Zawiercie, the local Jewish boys faced the risk of being drafted to the Polish army, which posed both physical and spiritual threats. Yaakov's older brother amputated his trigger finger to avoid the draft. Yaakov took a different route. He was advised by the Imrei Emes to leave Poland and go to Eretz Yisrael instead.

In order to qualify for an *aliyah* certificate, Yaakov enrolled in a *hachsharah* training program in Lodz, where he learned the rudiments of agricultural labor and committed to working the land for six months after his arrival. Then, in 1938, at the age of twenty-four, he bid his family goodbye and embarked on a boat journey to Eretz Yisrael. He didn't know that they would be decimated by the Nazis, and he'd never see them again.

True to his promise, he spent his initial months working the land, tending the fields at Kibbutz Tirat Tzvi, a religious kibbutz in the Bet Shean valley where the fierce heat nurtures copious orchards of date trees.

Though he'd spent his youth in the *beis midrash* and Gerrer chassidic court, Yaakov went out to the orchards every day, braving the heat to keep his commitment — and he joined the security detail, too, helping protect the vulnerable Jews during the Arab uprisings of 1936-39, when the entire country was effectively the front line and innocent Jews found themselves targets of barbaric violence.

Even as he worked the fields or wielded arms, he never changed an iota of his chassidic lifestyle and values. Soon Yaakov Lubling gained a name as a staunch defender of sacred tradition.

Once he had fulfilled the terms of his commitment, Yaakov left the kibbutz and moved to Tel Aviv, where he felt at home among the many Eastern European chassidic immigrants. There he was introduced to Miriam Albert. Their modest wedding took place in 1940 in a Tel Aviv apartment. A small group of relatives and friends attended, and Rabbi Yitzchak Yedidya Frankel — then the rav of Tel Aviv's Florentin neighborhood — served as *mesader kiddushin*.

The young couple settled into an apartment at 44 Rechov Wolfson, in the Florentin neighborhood of Southern Tel Aviv not far from the citrus orchards of Jaffa.

The small stucco buildings of Florentin drew many immigrants, a mixture of Sephardim from North Africa, Turkey, Greece, and Bukhara along with a growing stream of Eastern European arrivals. It was far from luxury living — the apartments were cramped and cheaply constructed — but Florentin offered other advantages. In the hodgepodge of newcomers, it was easy to find friends who understood one's struggles and growing pains. And then there was the famously warm neighborhood rav, Rabbi Frankel (later to become chief rabbi of Tel Aviv and the father-in-law of Chief Rabbi Yisrael Meir Lau).

Miriam continued to teach in her uncle's kindergarten. It was a strange time to be a Jew in Eretz Yisrael: she and her new husband were busy building a new home and future, while at the same time desperately worried about their families back in Europe. There were ominous rumors, but reliable information was painfully absent.

Eventually both Reb Yaakov and Miriam learned that their families had been wiped out, every last one murdered by the Nazis, with just two exceptions: Miriam's sister Chana Albert, who escaped before the war, married her cousin Shaul Albert, and settled in Netanya; and Reb Yaakov's sister Tziporah Okrent, who survived the Nazi devastation and found a new home in Tel Aviv. The Lublings maintained very close relationships with these sisters; family took on heightened value when there was so little of it.

When their three children were born — Nechama, Chanoch, and Peshi — the little ones, who carried the names of their murdered grandparents, called Reb Yitzchak Shaul Albert "Saba Yitzchak." In the aftermath of the Holocaust, that was the closest they would come to having a grandparent.

During the early years of her marriage, Miriam quickly found a social circle among the European immigrant women of Tel Aviv. One of her close friends was Rebbetzin Miriam (Goldman) Weitz, a fellow Polish immigrant whose scholarly husband — a friend of Reb Yaakov's from their days in the *heim* — was now a *R"M* in the Gerrer Yeshivas Chiddushei HaRim of Tel Aviv.

The Weitzes' daughter Shoshana — presently Rebbetzin Shoshana Alter, the Rebbetzin of Gur — was a very bright student. As an eighth-grader, she was one of only seven girls in her class who passed the very challenging national exam for exceptional academic ability.

Young Shoshana became a close friend of the Lublings' eldest daughter Nechama, and Mrs. Lubling took great pride in her achievements. Rebbetzin Alter still remembers how Mrs. Lubling hurried over to their home when she heard that Shoshana had passed the national exam, and her overflowing excitement as she proclaimed, "Mazel tov! Mazel tov! Today Tel Aviv celebrates for Shoshana!"

Rebbetzin Alter also remembers Mrs. Lubling's enthusiastic participation in community initiatives such as *shiurim* and gatherings for women. "She had this presence," she remembers. "She came into a room and brought smiles, jokes, and positivity with her."

Reb Yaakov basked in that positivity and in the blessings of his three lively children — but like most young *chareidim* in Tel Aviv of the late 1940s, he struggled to provide for his family in the raw economic landscape. At first he found employment as a laborer and set out every morning to build roads. Eventually, he saved up enough money to purchase a liquor store and then a restaurant before finding success with a dye factory.

Soon the family was on sounder economic footing and Miriam, who possessed an abundance of energy and passion, began devoting her considerable talents to the Poalei Agudas Yisroel organization, known as PAI for short.

At the time, Tel Aviv was not yet the cosmopolitan high-tech and cultural mecca it is today. Some of the area streets were surfaced by sand instead of sidewalks, and there were none of the steel towers associated with its modern skyline. Instead, there was a profusion of *shtieblach* affiliated with Gur, Belz, and various Ruzhiner branches, and the sounds of davening and Yiddish conversation filled the streets.

Many of these European immigrants affiliated with the PAI movement, an idealistic social-religious force that would later become a political party. The movement had been established back in 1922 in Lodz, Poland, under the umbrella of Agudas Yisroel. Much of its initial platform concerned fair treatment of workers — with the distinction, unlike the Socialist movements of the era, that PAI was faithful primarily to the Torah and that it would not recognize any union or group that did not conform to Torah principles.

The Israeli branch of PAI was established in Mandatory Palestine in 1933, and from its base in Tel Aviv, it sought to help its members find housing, employment opportunities, and social services such as absorption assistance for new *olim*, a money-lending fund, and health services.

PAI expended significant effort to develop kibbutzim that fully observed halachah. The most famous of these is Kibbutz Chofetz Chaim, which heroically observed *shemittah l'chumrah* in 1938 according to the directives of the Chazon Ish. (The kibbutz also consulted Rav Yosef Tzvi Dushinsky as to whether young female laborers could sleep there at night — he ruled that until there were married couples living on the kibbutz, the young women should sleep elsewhere, which they did.)

PAI also initiated social and cultural events true to Torah values,

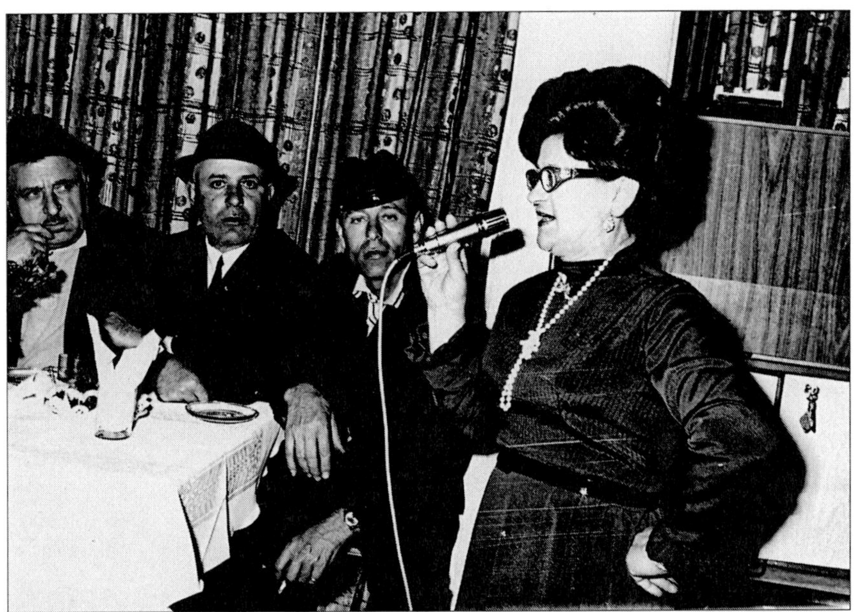

Mrs. Lubling found a worthy cause for her ambition and drive in PAI, the Poalei Agudas Yisroel organization. Fundraising and lobbying came naturally to her.

such as *shiurim*, lectures, lending libraries, and an independent publication named *Shearim*. And after the Holocaust, the organization became a major resource for survivors, finding them jobs in religiously supportive environments and arranging government benefits and funding for members. Once the State was formed, it transitioned to a political party that represented religious Jews in Israel's Knesset.

Miriam Lubling must have been born with a fire inside her. Other women considered their days full running a home, bringing in some additional income, and creatively overcoming the limited resources of the fledgling state. But she wanted to do more. In PAI, she found a worthy cause for her ambition and drive.

During those years, she found time to drum up support and rally voters for PAI. She founded a women's branch of the movement known as Nshei PAI, of which she would later serve as president. (Her good friend Mrs. Raizel [Besser] Abramczyk, upon moving to America, led the American sister branch of Nshei PAI. These determined women eventually raised enough money to support six

An early Nshei PAI event in the United States, at which Golda Meir served as guest of honor. Mrs. Lubling appears on the far right.

children's homes and villages in Israel, with a combined population of over two thousand children.)

Recognizing the power and potential of women to both raise money and conduct outreach, in early 1955 Mrs. Lubling formed, along with Mrs. Gross-Hamburger, a women's election committee committed to recruiting voters for the new party.

A fairly new immigrant herself, albeit one who had gained confidence and familiarity with her new country, she connected easily and effectively with the new immigrants who'd arrived after the war. She understood their language, background, and needs, and helped them navigate a strange new country with her fluent Hebrew and refusal to be cowed by bureaucracy — or leftist ideology.

She spoke often at public gatherings for women about the struggle for the religious character of the newly forming State, and she impressed upon them their role in preserving traditional Torah values in their new land.

During the postwar period, a huge influx of approximately seven hundred thousand immigrants from Europe as well as Arab countries swelled Israel's population. With insufficient housing available for the new arrivals, by 1951 there were over two hundred thousand immigrants housed in transit camps known as *ma'abarot.* The *ma'abarot* consisted of tiny, unstable shacks for the families, usually constructed of tin or flimsy wood that baked in the hot

The *ma'abarot* transit camps for new immigrants offered housing in the form of flimsy huts or tents. For many Jews, the only way out was to abandon tradition and commit to leftist ideology.

summer sun and barely kept out the winter rains. Additional shacks provided basic services such as kindergartens, grocery stores, infirmaries, and some sort of structure for a shul. Running water was available only from central faucets, and it was not reliable.

It was a time of strong currents and passions, and the secular, leftist streams of the newly formed State had an upper hand in virtually every sphere of influence. Government, labor unions, schooling, the legal system — all were dominated by secular leftists. From their vulnerable position in the transit camps, many of the newly arrived immigrants were convinced that their only ticket to integration and self-sufficiency was abandonment of their ideals. But Miriam Lubling fought back.

So she made it part of her routine to visit the camps, meet the immigrants, and encourage the religious arrivals to maintain their traditional lifestyle and values.

Some of the newly arrived immigrants were confused by the school options — the secular schools of the irreligious left made a concerted effort to attract immigrant families — and she directed them to religious institutions. Some were bedazzled by the campaign promises of the irreligious parties, and she invested time and effort to win votes for the PAI party.

There was another danger: the lure of Christian missionaries in nearby Jaffa.

Christian missionaries had a far-reaching historic footprint in Israel, but the establishment of the State inspired them to invest even more energy and manpower in the region. Tragically, the newly formed state did not ban missionary activity; perhaps this was an attempt to broadcast tolerant liberal values (it took until 1977 for Israel's penal code to forbid proselytization via means of material benefit or proselytization of minors). Whatever the reason, the government's toleration of missionary activity left cash-strapped immigrants vulnerable to the efforts of local missionaries, who offered free education along with many tantalizing perks to struggling parents.

While Tel Aviv is a city devoid of churches (in fact, it is said that this is why many of Europe's chassidic Rebbes initially chose to transplant their courts there instead of to Jerusalem), its sister-city Jaffa is a Christian stronghold, dotted with churches and Christian icons. And the missionaries who lived there saw potential prey among Tel Aviv's immigrant children.

An advertisement in the PAI publication *Shearim* dated September 17, 1954, informed readers that Mrs. Miriam Lubling would be available at 39 Montefiore Street in Tel Aviv on Sunday and Thursday, from the hours of 9-12, to see anyone concerned about rescuing children from "foreign education."

In another article dated September 27 of the same year, writer Menachem Label described a survey of the numbers of immigrant children placed in religious institutions — a prime goal of PAI and of Agudas Yisrael — and gave special mention to forty-five children who had been rescued from the clutches of the missionaries and placed in Torah institutions, thanks to a task force led by Mrs. Miriam Lubling.

"Without question, it is possible to save even more children," the article continues, "but bitter experience has shown that merely removing them from the Christian institutions is not sufficient, and it is foolhardy to rely on a father's promise that he won't send his daughter back there [ostensibly due to the many tantalizing benefits promised by the missionaries to the struggling immigrants]. What is needed here is a full rehaul of the absorption process."

Clearly, young Miriam Lubling had her work cut out for her in the Holy Land. And with her unceasing energy and unflagging spirit, she was poised to continue her trailblazing efforts. But the Divine Scriptwriter was preparing a different role for her to play.

It was a role that would become apparent only after she experienced the shattering toll of a medical emergency, a prolonged period of loneliness, doubt, and worry — and the uprooting of the vibrant life and home that she had built with sweat and tears.

CHAPTER 2
Angels in the Hospital

On Erev Succos of 1953, Yaakov Lubling was taking a shower when his family heard a loud thump. Alarmed, they hurried to help and discovered that he had slipped and banged his head. It seemed like a simple injury, and the family waited for him to recover. But at some point, they realized he wasn't getting better; in fact, he was steadily, terrifyingly losing his vision.

The local doctors did their best to treat what they realized was a traumatic brain injury — a blood clot had formed in Yaakov's brain as a result of the fall — but in the early days of the State of Israel, high-level medical resources and expertise were scarce. After escaping Poland, slaving over the fields and primitive roads of a new country, and building a new life and family, Yaakov Lubling seemed destined to spend the rest of his days as a sightless invalid.

Near Tel Aviv, in the fledgling *chareidi* city of Bnei Brak, lived a frail *talmid chacham* whose reputation as one of the generation's greatest Torah authorities was swiftly spreading. Yet even as Rav Avraham Yeshayah Karelitz, known as the Chazon Ish, effectively shaped the policy and character of Eretz Yisrael's *chareidi* sector, he was also widely recognized for his incisive medical advice.

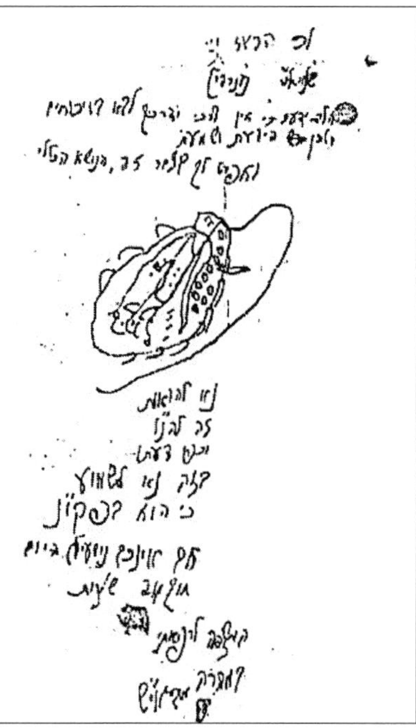

The Chazon Ish, Rav Avraham Yeshayah Karelitz, gave the Lublings the crucial guidance to seek medical care in New York. The instructions he provided the doctor were similar to these (inset) that he prepared for a different patient, complete with a diagram for the neurosurgeon.

The Lublings approached the Chazon Ish and described Yaakov's worsening condition. "Send him to America for treatment," he said. "There is a neurologist there named Dr. Morris Bender. Tell him not to excise the clot in one surgical procedure; instead he should perform a slow, multi-stage process to drain the buildup of blood through a series of procedures targeting the spinal cord." The Chazon Ish wrote a note with instructions for the doctor.

As they left, the Chazon Ish cautioned them, "Undertake the trip to America *al menas lachzor*, with the intention of returning to Eretz Yisrael." The Lublings would never forget that stipulation.

Miriam was advised to contact Mrs. Kato Kahn, a Hungarian Holocaust survivor who had settled in New York City's Upper West Side. Mrs. Kahn had formed relationships with doctors in several leading hospitals, primarily Mt. Sinai Medical Center. Mrs. Kahn connected Yaakov Lubling to Dr. Bender and assisted in arranging his travel plans, and Miriam enlisted a companion to accompany him during the journey.

And so Yaakov Lubling left his wife and three small children and traveled by plane to New York. He spent the entire flight on a stretcher, his vision shuttered and shadowed by the pressure on his optic nerve.

Miriam and the children hoped their father would return soon, good as new. They remained in Tel Aviv, striving to keep up their spirits and maintain their busy schedules. Miriam remained devoted to PAI and to her various *chessed* initiatives, trying to remain optimistic and productive.

During those months of waiting, she took her family to spend Pesach at one of her favorite PAI projects, the Beit Asher girls' orphanage in Rishon L'Tzion. After spending Yom Tov with the orphaned children, sharing her characteristic warmth and encouragement, she prepared to leave. But a girl who had befriended her daughter Nechama during their stay followed them as they went out the door.

"I want to come home with you," the girl said. "I want to stay with Nechama."

"What's your name?" Miriam asked gently.

"Chaya, Chaya Maltz."

"Chaya, this is your home now," Miriam tried to comfort her. "Here in the orphanage, there's a bed for you, there are friends for you."

"But I don't have a father or mother here!" Chaya cried. "My mother isn't alive, and my father is in Russia. I want a real house, with a mother and a sister!" She clutched Miriam's skirt and started to cry.

"Ima, can't we bring her home?" Nechama pleaded. "We have Abba's empty bed. So we do have room."

Miriam turned to Nechama. "Are you willing to share your things with Chaya and treat her like your sister?"

"Yes, yes, Ima," Nechama insisted.

"If that's the case," Miriam said, "you can go help Chaya pack her clothing. I will speak to the orphanage director and arrange for her to come home with us."

Love from afar. A comical photo of the Lubling children that was sent to Reb Yaakov in far-off New York during his long stay for medical treatment surely made him smile: The "Shabbos tatty" making Havdalah is Nechamah, the "Shabbos mommy" is Chanoch, and the "little *yingele*" is Peshi.

That's how Chaya became part of the Lubling family, where she remained until her father arrived in Israel.

Throughout Chaya's stay, Yaakov's bed was no longer empty, but his absence was still a gaping hole for the little family. Miriam didn't tell her children about the girl in far-off Poland whose father had vanished due to illness and who had never returned. She kept the door to her own childhood losses tightly closed.

But at night, when the children nodded off into dreamland and silence overtook the streets of Florentin, she wondered and worried. Would Yaakov ever recover? Would her children have a father again?

For months, Miriam and her children waited to hear good news from Yaakov in far-off America. But the news was not good. Yaakov's recovery was proceeding very slowly, and his health remained

Miriam and her three young children in a joint passport photo for their journey to America

compromised. There was no way he could make the grueling trip back to Eretz Yisrael. A difficult decision had to be made.

Back in Poland of 1939, before she had taken the fateful step of uprooting herself from the only familiar surroundings she'd known, Miriam asked for the *berachah* of the Imrei Emes of Gur. When she stepped onto the gangplank of the *Parita*, a young girl traveling to the Middle East totally on her own, she was girded by that blessing.

Now, in 1955, she faced a similarly fateful dilemma. And so she sent a messenger to the Imrei Emes's son, Rav Yisrael Alter, the Beis Yisrael of Gur.

"My husband has been undergoing medical treatment in America," she relayed to the Rebbe. "We had hoped he would return to Eretz Yisrael upon his recovery. But he remains weak and ill. It doesn't seem that he will be able to return anytime soon. The only way to keep our family together is for me and the children to move to America.

"But Rebbe, I am afraid of America. I am afraid of how my children will turn out if we move there. Here in Tel Aviv, my son is in a good *cheder* and my daughters are learning in schools that are faithful to our *mesorah*. They have good friends, relatives, and neighbors. How can I uproot them from everything we have here and risk bringing them up in the country where so many Jews have left the path?"

The Beis Yisrael's response was clear and unequivocal. "Right now, you need to go to America," the Rebbe instructed the emissary to tell her. "You should pack up your possessions and undertake the trip with your family, and you should not worry. You will have a beautiful family that follows the path of your ancestors, and you will merit to see *ehrliche* children and *talmidei chachamim* among your descendants."

Miriam grasped that *berachah* with both hands. She took a deep breath and made her decision.

In 1955, nearly two years after her husband had slipped in the shower, she sold the dye factory, packed up the apartment on

"Go to America; you will merit to have *ehrliche* children and *talmidei chachamim* among your descendants." The Beis Yisrael's response gave Miriam the strength she needed to uproot her little family.

MANIFEST OF IN-BOUND PASSENGERS (ALIENS)

Manifest No. 22

on S/S "JERUSALEM" arriving at port of [illegible]

No.	Family Name	Given Name		T	HB	S	PEG	
1	HALPERT	ABRAHAM	I-808162 ISRAELI	-	5	2	1	[illegible]
2	HALPERT	DOROFA	I-808165 ISRAELI	-	- DO -			149 DO -
3	HALPERT	JAFFA	I-808166 ISRAELI		- DO -			- DO -
4	HIRSCH	ABRAHAM	I-808139 ISRAELI	-	2	-	1	412376
5	ICZKOVICS	MIRIAM	I-808161 ISRAELI	-	2	1	-	412389
6	ICZKOVICS	AARON	I-808061 ISRAELI		- DO -			- DO -
7	JUSTEN	LASLO	I-808190 ISRAELI	-	5	-	-	412395
8	JUSTEN	JULIA	I-808191 ISRAELI		- DO -			- DO -
9	JUSTEN	REVEKA H.	I-808152 ISRAELI		- DO -			- DO -
10	KORETH	RUTH	I-808128 ISRAELI	-	5	-	2	412397
11	KLEIN	PNINA	I-808063 ISRAELI	-	3	-	2	[illegible]
12	KHUBASHI-LEVY	HANNAH	I-808062 ISRAELI	-	2	-	-	412416
13	LISS	ARLENE A.	I-380986 BRITISH	-	2	-	1	412439
14	LESCHZINER	RUDOLF	I-808125 ISRAELI	1	3	4	1	412448
15	LESCHZINER	HANNELORE	I 808155 ISRAELI		- DO -			- DO -
16	LUBLING	MIRIAM	I-808086 ISRAELI	-	2	4	1	412454
17	LUBLING	NECHAMA	I-808087 ISRAELI		- DO -			- DO -
18	LUBLING	HANOCH	I-808097 ISRAELI		- DO -			- DO -
19	LUBLING	[illegible]	I-808098 ISRAELI		- DO -			- DO -
20	LEHMANN	SALLY	I-808114 ISRAELI	-	3	-	1	412456
21	LEHMANN	HELENE	I-808113 ISRAELI		- DO -			- DO -
22	MAISIN	ESPHIR	I-808151 ISRAELI	1	2	-	1	412470
23	NUDELMAN	[illegible]	I-808118 ISRAELI	-	2	-	1	412494

The ship manifest listing Miriam, Nechama, Chanoch, and Peshi as passengers traveling to America.

Rechov Wolfson, and said goodbye to the neighbors and friends who had become part of the life she had built in Tel Aviv. She bought tickets to travel with her three young children by boat to America — preparing to be a newcomer once again, with a new language, culture, and environment to master.

An article in *Shearim* dated August 11, 1955, describes the *seudas pereidah,* the goodbye party, that her fellow PAI volunteers held in her honor. It ended with a promise: "You know and I know that I have so much to accomplish here in Eretz Yisrael," Mrs. Lubling told her friends. "Today we say goodbye, but I will come back as soon as I can."

During that period, word got out that Mrs. Lubling, the famed activist, would be relocating to America, and one night there was a knock on the door. Miriam opened it and faced an unfamiliar man. He pulled out a photo of a girl whose posture was horribly contorted.

"This is my daughter," he said. "Her spine is deformed — it's a very bad case of scoliosis."

Mrs. Lubling invited him to sit down and offered him a cold drink, but he only grew more distraught.

"I went through the Holocaust. I lost everything. Then I met my wife. She is also a survivor," he said. Then he began to cry unabashedly. "We tried to start a family, to build anew. We have just one child. You can imagine how we celebrated when she was born. Then she began to grow, and her spine did not develop properly. Every year, it got more crooked and she became more bent over. Now her internal organs are in danger of being compressed as the condition progresses. She will never be healthy, certainly she will never be able to have children.

"The doctor said our only hope is spinal surgery in America. We don't know the language, we don't have money, we don't know any doctors there. What can we do?

"I heard that you will be moving to America soon. I beg you — please help my daughter have surgery in America so she can get married one day and have children. We've suffered enough to have it all end here."

Mrs. Lubling thought for a moment. "Look," she said, "I don't know my way around American hospitals. I don't even know English. But I'm going to try to help you."

The next day she contacted Rabbi Menachem Porush. Rabbi Porush would later serve as a Knesset member, and had already forged extensive contacts among Israel's political elite. Mrs. Lubling told him about the girl's plight. "Come to the Knesset," he said. "I'll introduce you to some of the Knesset members and we'll try to raise some money so this girl can have her surgery."

On the appointed day, Mrs. Lubling dressed carefully, packed a photo of the girl in her handbag, and went by bus to the original Knesset Building on Rechov King George in Jerusalem. Rabbi Porush had assembled those colleagues he thought might be sympathetic — and even a few he wasn't sure about — and Mrs. Lubling made what might have been her first bikur cholim fundraising pitch.

Her language may not have been flowery, but the story of the little girl — the Holocaust survivors' sole hope for eternity after all they'd endured — touched hearts. The politicians took out their checkbooks and donated significant sums.

That evening, Mrs. Lubling went to the local post office and put in an international call to Mrs. Kahn, on the Upper West Side. "I'm not calling about my husband," she said. "I have a different case to discuss." She described the little girl with the crooked spine. "What should we do with her? Where can they fix it?"

Mrs. Kahn, who spent hours every day visiting patients in the hospital and building relationships with the local doctors, suggested a Manhattan physician who specialized in spinal surgeries.

"And where can she stay while she recovers?" Mrs. Lubling asked.

Mrs. Kahn suggested Rebbetzin Rebecca Goldstein, who was the wife of Rabbi Herbert Goldstein, a prominent West Side rabbi, and the daughter of noted philanthropists Harry and Jane Fischel.

Mrs. Lubling along with her three children
Nechama, Chanoch, and Peshi
on the ship that brought them to America

Rebbetzin Goldstein was a gracious and generous woman who often hosted guests, and there was a good chance she could help out in this case.

"I have an idea," said Mrs. Lubling. "Soon I'll be in America, and I can visit her myself."

After a two-week voyage on the *SS Jerusalem*, Mrs. Lubling arrived in the United States in August 1955 with Nechama, age 13, Chanoch, age 9, and Peshi, age 5. Waiting at the pier on Manhattan's West Side to welcome them was Yaakov Lubling.

As the Chazon Ish had predicted, Dr. Bender's treatments had slowly restored Reb Yaakov's vision. After a period of initial treatment in the hospital, he was discharged and instructed to continue weekly treatments on an outpatient basis. During this time, he rented a room in Williamsburg near the Gerrer *shtiebel* and found new friends who hosted him for Shabbos meals — including the Amshinover Rebbe Reb Itzikel, and the Iwaniski family.

But Mrs. Lubling was terribly distressed to hear his account of his hospital stay. It was an excruciatingly lonely experience. His sole visitors were Reb Shimshon Heller, the executive director of PAI in America, who greeted him at the airport upon his arrival in America, escorted him to Mt. Sinai Hospital, and then visited him every morning to help him lay *tefillin*; a few of Miriam's *landsleit* from Koinsk; and the devoted Mrs. Kahn, who visited the hospital regularly along with famed philanthropist Mrs. Necha Golding. With the exception of the solitary bright spots provided by their visits, Yaakov had spent most of his time alone in the ward, unable to communicate with his caretakers, who spoke only English.

"Something is wrong," Mrs. Lubling told herself fiercely, "if a Yid can lie in a hospital for months and barely have any visitors. As soon as I can, I am going to do something to make sure no Jew goes through what my husband did."

But first she had a promise to keep. The image of the young girl with the contorted back looming large in her mind, Mrs. Lubling paid a visit to Rebbetzin Goldstein. In simple but passionate language, she described the plight of the girl and her shattered parents. "We are arranging to bring them to America for surgery, but the family will need a place to stay. Can you help?"

Rebbetzin Goldstein graciously offered her home, driver, and maid to service the girl during her stay. Mrs. Lubling contacted the family and helped arrange their journey to America, where the young patient successfully underwent the surgery and restored her family's hopes for a future after all they had lost.

The event left a deep impression on Mrs. Lubling. With *siyata d'Shmaya*, the right connections, and adequate funding, she realized she could literally save lives. She tucked this awareness in the back of her consciousness, where it quietly took root.

Eventually that incident would spark a calling.

During Yaakov Lubling's lonely stay in America, he had alternated between the hospital and a rented room. Now that his family had arrived, they needed a proper home. Initially, they settled in the Brooklyn neighborhood of Bedford-Stuyvesant, and Miriam found a job at Poznanski's bakery. The job didn't last long; she was let go because at the end of every day, instead of discarding the leftover cookies or bread, she distributed them to elderly, impoverished people. A bakery can't remain solvent when customers know they can get the goods for free, her boss explained.

She then found employment as a kindergarten teacher while taking night classes at the Bank Street College of Education to master English and obtain an official teacher's certificate. Two years later, the Lublings moved to Crown Heights, a graceful neighborhood of

Mrs. Lubling (far right) and Rebbetzin Tziporah Friedman (far left) partnered to form the Ohel Sarah kindergarten in Crown Heights.

tree-lined streets and brownstone residences that attracted a sizable *frum* population. Dotted with *shtieblach* and yeshivos, it was the neighborhood of choice for thousands of Holocaust survivors and a soft landing spot for several chassidic Rebbes who rebuilt their courts in the quiet, peaceful environs.

The Lublings rented a third-floor apartment on Eastern Parkway, a block away from Chabad headquarters. Then, several years later, they moved to a ground-floor apartment in a brownstone on Crown Street.

Along with another survivor, Yaakov Lubling opened a bakery in Boro Park. Miriam partnered with Rebbetzin Tziporah Friedman (later to become the Sadigerer Rebbetzin in Eretz Yisrael) and opened up a kindergarten that became immensely popular. She named it Ohel Sarah, in tribute to her mentor Sarah Schenirer.

The Ohel Sarah kindergarten wasn't a slapdash basement

arrangement — it was located in a two-story building at 771 Crown Street, with a small but proper playground in the backyard. Hot meals were served daily and, just as she'd done in Tel Aviv, Miriam poured her creativity into beautiful craft projects and high-level performances. She taught the children how to eat their food neatly and politely, saw to it that they were costumed as *groggers* in honor of Purim, and even produced a yearbook for the children to bring home at the year's end.

Chanoch was enrolled in Yeshivah Torah Vodaath in Williamsburg ("You'll pay tuition after you get a good job; for now pay what you can," Rabbi Yisroel Kanarek, then the registrar at Torah Vodaath and later the founder of Yeshivah Ohr Hameir, told Yaakov Lubling), and the girls attended Rabbi Meir Levi's Bais Yaakov.

Chanoch spoke only Hebrew when he arrived, and was unfamiliar with the subway system. So Torah Vodaath assigned a student named Kalman Krohn to help him. Every day as Kalman and his brother Paysach made their daily commute from their home in Queens to Williamsburg, the Krohn boys met Chanoch at one of the train stations along the way. Then they escorted him to yeshivah.

In Crown Heights, the Lublings found new family: a kernel of fellow Holocaust survivors, mostly from Poland, who banded together, raised their children together, and davened in the Sosnovtza *beis midrash* together. Only a few members of the *kehillah* had surviving siblings; all their extended families had been brutally murdered by the Nazis. So it was only natural that the little shul at 534 Crown Street became a very tight-knit club.

Rav Avraham Yissachar Englard and his wife, Rebbetzin Sarah, turned the Sosnovtza *beis midrash* of Crown Heights into a haven for shattered Polish survivors.

Just like the *mispallelim*,

the shul's rav, Rav Avraham Yissachar Englard, was a survivor. Born in Sosnowiec (Sosnovtza), Poland, he was a Radomsker descendant who married the daughter of the Radziner Rebbe, Rav Mordechai Yosef Elazar Leiner. Though his wife was murdered during the war, he retained his connection to Radzin and assumed the mantle of Radziner Rebbe in the early 1950s.

In 1954, he opened a little *shtiebel* in Crown Heights. Together with his second wife, Rebbetzin Sarah, he built the Sosnovtza *beis midrash* into a haven for the shattered Polish Jews who had lost everything.

In the unassuming brownstone on Crown Street, these Polish survivors found a built-in social circle of *landsleit* who shared a familiar background and culture. It was a nurturing place where the Rebbe and his unmarried brother Reb Yankele, who lived in a room above the shul, personally prepared coffee every morning for each *mispallel.*

The 1950s gave way to the early '60s, and the good Jews of the Sosnovtza *beis midrash* steadily built new families and businesses as they knit the ties of a new-old community. Together they enjoyed the warm, melodic davening, the regular *shiurim* delivered in a familiar Polish accent, and the *kiddush* every Shabbos, where cholent and kugel prepared by Reb Yankele were served and eaten with wooden forks and spoons, to the children's delight.

As the Englards poured their warmth and energies into their *shtiebel*, the members of their *kehillah* engaged in a side pursuit as well.

Not far away, on the border of Crown Heights and East Flatbush, stood a gloomy brick building known as the Jewish Chronic Disease Hospital (currently Kingsbrook Jewish Medical Center). This hospital on Schenectady Avenue was the country's largest voluntary institution for chronically ill patients of all ages. Its patients suffered from medical conditions ranging from cancer to Parkinson's disease to polio, cerebral palsy, and heart ailments. They also suffered from bleak conditions, abandonment, and acute loneliness in what was considered a hopeless facility. In fact, the institution was widely known as the "Home for Incurables."

Rebbetzin Englard and her brother-in-law Reb Yankele made regular visits to the Jewish patients in this hospital. Reb Yankele, who had no family at home, would even stay at patients' bedsides entire nights. And the idealistic, hardworking women of the shul made their own visits as well. These were dynamic women who had narrowly escaped the Holocaust and were all too acquainted with its atrocities. They knew how fragile life was; their gratitude for what they had was tinged by a constant ache for all they'd lost. Though most worked hard to help support their families and didn't have the benefit of an extended family network, they decided to use their Shabbos afternoons to lift the spirits of Jews facing tough times.

For Miriam Lubling, these hospital visits were the fulfillment of a promise she'd made after hearing of her husband's lonely stay in the crowded ward at Mt. Sinai. But they were also the seed of something much bigger.

In a very real sense, that band of immigrant women laid the groundwork for the vast bikur cholim empire that spans America today. Their initiative was simpler and much, much smaller than today's hi-tech empire, but the principles were laid down in the late 1950s by that small group of women who'd experienced devastating loss yet somehow found time and energy amid their own rebuilding efforts to care for others.

They cooked fresh meals and brought the hot food to the patients along with cheer, encouragement, and solace. Sometimes they helped the patients recite a *berachah*, and when they saw a patient was interested in putting on *tefillin*, they'd ask a man to visit and help the patient fulfill that mitzvah. Soon the occasional visits became a regular part of their lives, and Mrs. Lubling became a "captain" of sorts for their efforts.

"Ess, ess, eat, eat," Miriam Lubling always used to say as she piled food onto the plates of her children, her husband, and her

guests. When her children's friends came to visit, she welcomed them, shmoozed with them — and then set to work feeding them. Nothing seemed to satisfy her more than watching people eat well. She even used to *shlep* a watermelon — her youngest daughter Peshi's favorite summer treat — all the way to the Catskills every year, when she visited Peshi in Camp Chedvah on Visiting Day.

Eating well was so important to Mrs. Lubling that she reversed the order of the Friday night meal, serving the meat course before the chicken soup, so the children wouldn't fill their stomachs with soup and skip the main dish. Sometimes things got a bit intense as she urged Peshi to finish all the food on her plate, and Reb Yaakov mildly remonstrated in Polish, "*Zostaw ja w spokoju,* leave her alone." Soon Peshi knew to appeal to her Abba in a mixture of Hebrew and Polish when she felt too full to finish her plate: "Abba, *tagid l'Ima zostaw ja w spokoju,* tell Ima to leave me alone."

But if her children didn't always appreciate the food she kept piling onto their plates, the patients in the hospital savored every crumb. As an active member of the PAI movement, she enlisted fellow PAI members the Widowskis, who had acquired Schick's Bakery, to donate rugelach to the bikur cholim. The women would pack the rugelach into plastic bags, tie them, and then bring them along to the hospital to distribute to the patients.

Miriam Lubling was a doer and organizer by nature, and she realized that more could and should be done to help the patients. It wasn't long before she decided to get more people involved. Very warmly and persuasively, she began by asking local women to cook hot kosher meals for the patients. In Crown Heights back then, everyone knew everyone, and no one could refuse her requests. Soon a small cadre of women was regularly cooking meals for the Jewish patients at Chronic Disease.

Her next focus was the young generation. Mrs. Lubling encouraged her children to visit the hospital every Shabbos afternoon, and help feed the patients their evening meal. Nechama used to give out electric Shabbos candles to Jewish women spending Shabbos in the hospital. Chanoch and his good friend Yonah Blumenfrucht made their visits after the local Pirchei group activities they led, and Peshi went with her friends Vivian Zupnick (later Garfunkel) and Naomi Freschl (later Dessler). Eventually Mrs. Lubling recruited an army of young men and women to deliver the food and visit the patients.

And it wasn't only for the patients of Chronic Disease. There was a psychiatric ward in Kings County Hospital in East Flatbush, a darkly dysfunctional facility where patients were routinely neglected, mistreated, and subject to invasive procedures. It was not a pleasurable Shabbos afternoon destination, to say the least. But Miriam Lubling knew there were lonely Jews there, so she made it part of her family's routine, and urged other youngsters to join them. She was determined to bring their bright banter and optimism into the dark ward.

One of the young women who visited the psychiatric facility remembers wondering aloud, "Why do these rooms all have bars on the windows?" But it was just a fleeting question in what otherwise was a most natural and routine visit — part of her Shabbos afternoon schedule, along with *kiddush*, challah, and cholent.

During those decades, the pillars of America's postwar *frum* world were being laid and reinforced. Shuls, yeshivos, and chassidic courts were built. Bais Yaakov mushroomed in strength and numbers. And businessmen tapped into the needs of the growing *frum* community, offering goods and services to suit their needs.

As those pillars were put in place, the pillar of *chessed* — already present before the war — was buttressed as well. The young generation growing up in Crown Heights, Williamsburg, Boro Park, and later Flatbush learned that being *frum* meant davening in shul, learning in yeshivah, and caring about your fellow Jew. And Mrs. Lubling, with her floundering English, was one of the prime forces shaping that worldview.

Along with her bikur cholim activities, Mrs. Lubling worked with her friends Mrs. Bella Brodt and Mrs. Bella Weiser to establish a forerunner to the official Tomchei Shabbos organization: each Thursday they purchased food from the local grocery and butcher shops, and assembled food packages for Shabbos, enlisting their sons to clandestinely deliver them to families in need.

Famed Agudah activist and Pirchei leader Rabbi Josh Silbermintz was also involved in bikur cholim, and he encouraged the members of his Pirchei groups to visit nursing homes and hospitals. At some point he connected with Mrs. Lubling, and put the Willowbrook State School of Staten Island on her radar.

Willowbrook was a state-supported institution that housed — and staggeringly neglected — thousands of physically and mentally disabled children. A WABC investigative report would subsequently blow open the scandal of the horrific mistreatment and abuse of the Willowbrook patients. This resulted in the eventual dismantling of state institutions and the establishment of community-based homes for this demographic, such as those run by Ohel and HASC. But back when Mrs. Lubling made her visits, few if any governmental regulators were aware of the horrific conditions.

In honor of Purim and Chanukah, she arranged for Rabbi Josh Silbermintz, her son Chanoch, and Yonah Blumenfrucht to conduct holiday parties for Willowbrook's Jewish patients. She also recruited her good friend Mrs. Raquel Wolf to prepare packages of holiday goodies and gifts for the patients. And she phoned a talented teenager named Yisroel Lamm and asked him to provide the musical accompaniment for these events.

Growing up in Williamsburg in a very musical family, Yisroel had assembled a group of fledgling teenage musicians who enjoyed performing together with the Lamm brothers — Yisroel on the trumpet, Michoel on the flute, and Yitzchok on the saxophone. Every boy in that little band knew Mrs. Miriam Lubling, and everyone listened to her instructions. If she wanted you to perform you knew you had no choice but to pack up your instrument and make the trip to whichever venue she instructed: Willowbrook, Kings County, even the Otisville prison in Upstate New York.

Yisroel often gave Mrs. Lubling a ride to the parties — he could never refuse her requests, made in a Yiddish-peppered version of immigrant English. When they arrived at the venue, Rabbi Silbermintz shared a few words about the holiday they were celebrating, while the members of the amateur band set up their instruments in the front of the room (they never dreamed of a proper stage back then). Then they played the standard hits of the era: "*Yismechu HaShamayim*" for the youngsters, "*Bai Mir Bistdu Shein*" for the older patients, and whatever hits were most current for the *heimishe* Jews in Otisville. There were no professional singers leading the audience — Josh Silbermintz led those present in song as Mrs. Lubling clapped along in satisfaction.

From the vantage point of decades later, as the *frum* world's veteran musical arranger and conductor, Yisroel marvels at this petite woman's unrivaled ability to make things happen. She knew music held a certain power to lift hearts, and she was determined to bring that gift to the forgotten, institutionalized Jews.

His other memories of those concerts are less bright. Back in those days, children with Down Syndrome and other intellectual disabilities were hidden away in institutions. Their existence was viewed as a shameful secret that could tarnish the family name if, G-d forbid, it were revealed to the public. During the parties, he met parents who warned him and his fellow musicians, "Don't tell anyone you saw us here. Don't let anyone know we have a child at Willowbrook."

As Miriam Lubling arranged party after party, as she navigated the wards of these hospitals, as she recruited local teens to cheer up and feed lonely patients, she subconsciously took notes. She noticed what motivated doctors and nurses, and what alienated them. She noticed how crucial it was to have a personal advocate in the impersonal and institutionalized world of medical care. And she noticed how a friendly face, a hot meal, a cheerful melody could improve not just the spirits, but also the health, of a frightened patient confined to a hospital bed.

CHAPTER 3

The Will and the Means

In 1965, the tight circle of women at the Sosnovtza *beis midrash* heard the distressing news: Rivkah Laufer, one of their own, had been hospitalized. She was only fifty-five years old when she was diagnosed with a serious illness. The doctors tried to operate, but when they saw how advanced the disease was, they closed the incision and left the room.

"We're sorry," they grimly told the Laufer family, "but there's nothing we can do. Keep her comfortable and try to enjoy whatever time she has left."

The women were devastated. They included their friend in their list of regular hospital visits, bringing her food and whatever good cheer they could muster. "Now I really understand how important our visits are," Rivkah told them. "I can't wait to recover and get back to visiting the *cholim*."

Sadly, her wish never came to fruition. She never made it back to that friendly circle of giving women. Rivkah Laufer passed away later that year. But her dedication to bikur cholim — and those final visits — left the women determined to build their *chessed* efforts into something bigger, more powerful.

They held an *azkarah* on her *sheloshim*, and together with a dynamic cousin of Rivkah's named Fran Laufer, decided to launch an official bikur cholim organization in her memory. The organization would coordinate hospital volunteers, offer medical referrals, and provide financial aid for those in need of medical treatment.

Reb Itche Laufer, Rivkah's widowed husband, was a *talmid chacham* and *mechaber sefarim* who delivered a *shiur* in his shul. He was also a man of means with a "starter" mindset. All the *mispallelim* of the Sosnovtza *shtiebel* knew that if you were planning to open a new business venture, Reb Itche was your address. At his dining room table, you could share your plans, dreams, and doubts, and he would readily provide a startup loan, delivered along with a generous helping of wise advice.

Now he used some of his means to jumpstart a decidedly more spiritual venture, providing the women of the shul with the seed money to launch the new bikur cholim organization, named Rivkah Laufer Bikur Cholim.

The three women who assumed the most public roles of the organization — Miriam Lubling, Bella Brodt, and Fran Laufer — brought different backgrounds, talents, and personalities to their tasks. But they all knew what it meant to be vulnerable and lonely.

All were Polish Jews who had lost too many friends, relatives, and family members in the Nazi inferno. All had rebuilt families and social circles with sweat and tears. All lived with a constant sense of indebtedness for their salvation and a drive to pay it forward. And so they worked together with respect and shared passion to build a remarkably effective organization.

Bella Brodt, nee Friedman, was born in Mielec (Melitz) in 1925. She was just a teenager when her life changed irrevocably. Shortly after the German invasion of Poland in September of 1939, her father, who was the *rosh kahal* of the community, got a police tip: his name was on a list of prominent Jews soon to be arrested. He knew he had to escape, and quickly.

Rabbi Friedman gathered his family and urged their dear friends, the Brodts, to come along. The two families drove across

Poland in a truck that belonged to the Brodt family business, heading eastward to Sambor.

When the Russians overtook the Sambor region, they pressured the Polish immigrants who'd flooded the area to assume Russian citizenship. Upon the advice of the Belzer Rebbe, Rav Ahrele Rokeach, the Friedmans and Brodts refused to declare their allegiance to the atheist Soviet ideology. Their punishment was deportation to Siberia — a trying experience of hunger and privation that, in hindsight, saved them from the Nazis.

In the barren environs of Siberia, there wasn't much to eat. But even when they were subsisting on stale bread and onions, the Friedmans always invited other hungry Jews to join them. That was Bella's *chinuch*.

After the war, the Friedmans and Brodts traveled to Krakow. There Bella married Shulim Brodt, and soon they welcomed prematurely born twins (one of those twins is widely known today as Reb Abish Brodt, the famed *baal tefillah* and *baal menagen*). But it didn't take long for them to realize that there was no future for Jews in Poland. They would have to rebuild their lives elsewhere.

They relocated to Antwerp, Belgium. After a few years, they journeyed to America and eventually found a new home on St. John's Place in Crown Heights, right near the transplanted court of the Bobover Rebbe.

Though the Brodts did not daven in the Sosnovtza *shtiebel*, Bella quickly became involved in the homegrown *chessed* that typified its women. A quick learner, she mastered English and learned how to drive, and was soon busy delivering food to patients in the local hospitals. But she didn't just drop off the food and leave; she connected with the patients on a personal level and asked each one, "How are you? Why are you here? Which doctor is seeing you?"

Most of the Jewish patients of the era suffered from what was called "Herr Doktor Syndrome" — they were intimidated by the medical establishment and too fearful to advocate for themselves. Bella Brodt was not easily intimidated, though. A confident and aristocratic woman, she had the gumption to stand up for patients who needed another examination, a second opinion, or treatment administered more quickly.

With her empathy, can-do attitude, and considerable experience in the hospitals, she was the perfect partner to launch the new bikur cholim organization.

Fran Laufer brought a different skillset to the venture. At first glance, she looked like the embodiment of the American dream — down to her keen fashion sense, glamorous blond wig, and successful antiques business headquartered in a Manhattan storefront. But Fran was in fact the sole survivor of her family, and she had emerged from the Nazi camps fragile and ill.

Born Frimit Fuchsbrumer, Fran grew up in a religious home in the Polish city of Kazanów (Kyshanov). In 1943, at age seventeen, she was deported from her hometown to a series of labor and concentration camps. She endured two years of forced labor and hunger, culminating in a weeks-long death march that left her ill with typhus. After liberation, she remained in the Displaced Persons camp that had been established in Bergen-Belsen. When Auschwitz survivor Simon Laufer approached her to propose marriage, she turned him down: she was too sickly and too ugly to marry, she thought. And she doubted she could ever bear children.

But Simon nursed her back to health with extra food rations that he obtained by trading coffee and cigarettes. In October of 1945, they stood under the *chuppah*, the first couple to marry in Bergen-Belsen.

At the conclusion of the *chuppah*, Simon leaned toward his new bride and asked her, "So, what do you think we should do? Will we have a religious home or not? After all, where was G-d in the camps?"

"G-d was there. He kept us alive," she answered resolutely.

As for what kind of home they should build, she had a clear vision. "We will build a home that continues the golden chain of our people and our parents," she pledged to her new husband. "With their ashes — and the ashes of so many Jews — spread all over Eastern Europe, we must build a new generation of Yiddishe children."

It took time to realize those dreams, but eventually the new couple received a sponsorship from cousins in America that allowed them to emigrate to the Land of the Free. They worked hard, were blessed with three children, and saw significant financial success. Fran studied interior and fashion design and opened the Fran Laufer Collection, a gallery of antiques and *objets d'art*. True to their values, the Laufers invested the returns in *tzedakah* and *chessed*, building shuls and yeshivos and helping support *chessed* organizations and the fledgling State of Israel.

Now Fran eagerly jumped at the idea of establishing a bikur cholim organization in memory of her cousin Rivkah Laufer. With her extensive social circle, flair for organizing beautiful events, and inner drive to rebuild, she was confident she could help get the new organization off the ground.

But before they took any dramatic steps, Mrs. Lubling had a concern. She feared the organization might be viewed as unwelcome competition to the renowned Satmar Bikur Cholim, which provided fresh, hot, kosher meals to patients in major New York hospitals. So she decided to consult directly with the Satmar Rebbetzin, Rebbetzin Alte Feiga Teitelbaum. Fran Laufer and Rivkah Laufer's daughter Pearl Pinter accompanied her to Williamsburg for the meeting.

"We're a group of women that does bikur cholim in the local hospitals," they explained to the rebbetzin. "We managed to collect a nice sum of money, and we want to know if we should start our own separate bikur cholim organization. Would it be detrimental in some way to the Satmar Bikur Cholim?"

The rebbetzin smiled. "By all means, you should definitely open your own organization," she said. "And if you need help, you can come to me and I'll be happy to help you."

"But how will the *cholim*, the ill people in need of help, know about us?" they asked the Rebbetzin.

"Don't worry about that," she said. "If you have the will and the means to help people, they'll find you!"

The bikur cholim had the green light to move forward.

The very first fundraising event for the newly formed Rivkah Laufer Bikur Cholim was a women's tea, held in Crown Heights in early 1966. Miriam Lubling and Bella Brodt were the signatories on the simple invitation, and fellow Crown Heights resident Gisela Freschl opened her home to host the gathering. Five dollars was considered a generous donation, and by that measure the first event was wildly successful — it brought in two hundred fifty dollars. The bikur cholim was in business.

Next, Fran Laufer hosted a lavish garden party in her Queens home. Many of the donors were Holocaust survivors who identified with the women behind the bikur cholim and the assistance they extended to lonely, frightened Jews. They opened their wallets wide and donated generously to the new organization. (The group of attendees would eventually grow so large — up to six hundred women! — that the Queens luncheons were later moved to the high-end venue Terrace on the Park.)

Then a group of women in Flatbush, headed by Margo Sledzik and Bella Brodt, arranged their own fundraiser — they believed in this cause too. With time many of the women from the Crown Heights community moved to Boro Park, and soon there were

בעזהי"ת

Mrs. Gisela Freschl

invites you to a

* *Tea* *

In behalf of

Rivkah Laufer Bikur Cholim

Monday evening, November 28th, 1966, 8 p.m.

In her home: *1673 President Street, Brooklyn, N. Y.*

Guest Speaker: *Rabbi Abraham Kelman*
Spiritual Leader of Prospect Park Jewish Center

Chairlady: *Mrs. Henny Weiden*

The invitation to the very first fundraising event of the nascent Rivkah Laufer Bikur Cholim, hosted by Gisela Freschl in her Crown Heights home

Mrs. Lubling at an early Rivkah Laufer Bikur Cholim luncheon. The food and décor were homemade, but it was the event of the year for hundreds of local women.

regular fundraising events in Boro Park as well, headed by Chana Mlynarski and later Chani Kofman, who became president of the bikur cholim's Boro Park branch, and chaired by Barbara Handler (later Goldgraben).

Mrs. Lubling appointed Rivkah Laufer's daughter Pearl Pinter, whose husband was an accountant, as financial secretary of the organization. Her office was her kitchen, her filing cabinet a little shoebox, and she took no salary. From those humble surroundings, the Rivkah Laufer Bikur Cholim was soon distributing hundreds of thousands of dollars toward medical treatment for Jews in need.

Decades later, the organization still operates the very same way. Though its ambit and impact grew by leaps and bounds, the headquarters and management style have never changed — it's still a modest, no-frills operation, with all bills tallied and paid from Mrs. Pinter's kitchen table.

Rebbetzin Chaya (Chaychu) Frankel, a neighbor and friend of Mrs. Lubling during the Crown Heights years, shared her passion for bikur cholim. The two women helped one another in their *chessed* work

The Satmar Rebbetzin had promised the hopeful organizers of the Rivkah Laufer Bikur Cholim that the *cholim* would find them, and she was swiftly proven right. The phones in the Lubling and Brodt residences, already quite busy, were soon ringing around the clock. Mrs. Brodt installed a second line just for the *cholim*. In the evenings, when her husband returned home after a long day, the children suggested that they disconnect that second phone line, so he could enjoy a quiet atmosphere while he ate.

"How can you even think of doing that?" he admonished them. "These are people who need help!"

In the Lubling home a few blocks away, Reb Yaakov Lubling had his own approach to the constantly ringing phone: he rarely answered it. "It's for you anyway," he told his wife, and more often than not, he was right.

While her children were growing up, Mrs. Lubling did most of her bikur cholim work over the phone, raising money, making medical referrals, and arranging travel plans and hosts for patients coming for treatment from Israel or Europe. Mrs. Brodt personally accompanied patients to appointments and treatments in a range of hospitals: Columbia-Presbyterian, Special Surgery, Mt. Sinai, and Cornell. She even flew to Boston or Seattle when a patient needed specialized care.

The Brodt children often came home after school to an empty house. But they weren't alarmed; they knew their mother was doing important work. Mrs. Brodt used to call her little daughter Zehavi from the payphone at Mt. Sinai and direct her to cook farfel or heat up the pot of ready supper she had left in the refrigerator.

The Lubling home at 658 Crown Street doubled as a guesthouse for patients who arrived from abroad for treatment (as would their residence at 1369 51st Street in Boro Park in later years). There were just three bedrooms — no guestroom or family room — but somehow, if a bed was required to host a Jew in need, the Lublings managed to find the space.

As the bikur cholim raised and distributed money for medical treatment, the dynamic women at its helm compiled private Rolodexes of New York's top doctors. Each possessed a phonebook dedicated only to medical contacts, and each phonebook was crammed with names and numbers. Mrs. Lubling's phonebook became one of her most prized possessions — she took it everywhere with her and guarded it zealously.

The bikur cholim steadily gained a name — not only among local Jews, but also in Europe and Israel. Patients from overseas called the Brodt and Lubling homes and were relieved when a *heimishe* woman answered the phone and unraveled their medical concerns in familiar Yiddish, Hebrew, or even Polish. Whatever their needs — a referral, an appointment, transportation from the airport, even funding — the women of the bikur cholim reassured them that it would all be taken care of.

Many of the patients who traveled from Eretz Yisrael for treatment did not have insurance coverage, and had to pay out of pocket for treatment. In these cases, the bikur cholim liaised directly with the doctors to arrange payment.

Not only did these patients require funding, they also often needed travel arrangements and housing. So the women of Rivkah Laufer Bikur Cholim began to build an infrastructure of drivers and hostesses along with the financial aid. Soon a team of volunteers was greeting new arrivals at the airport, hosting and feeding them, and driving them to their appointments.

Not only that: during the patients' hospital appointments or treatments, volunteers accompanied them through the process. Volunteers kept tabs on patients in the major New York hospitals as well as Maimonides Medical Center in Boro Park, expediting appointments, finessing bureaucracy, and translating doctors' instructions to bewildered patients from abroad.

Among those volunteers, Mrs. Lubling's reach and influence became legendary. She came to know just about every staff member at NYU — even the nurses and orderlies — and she stayed on top of every case she referred to the hospital. She could conjure empty beds out of nowhere, reschedule surgeries according to her preferences, even summon doctors back from vacation to perform emergency procedures. Jews across the world would phone her at all hours, sharing shattering diagnoses. "Come to America," she would tell them in Yiddish or Hebrew. "I take care."

And so they came to America, with very little knowledge of the doctors, the healthcare system, or how they would possibly cover the cost of their treatment — and just as she'd promised, she took care of it all.

CHAPTER 4
Because She Is the Boss

"I've dealt with a lot of people in hospitals," says a veteran *askan*. "When I walked the halls with Miriam Lubling, her presence commanded a certain awe. People just sensed they had to listen to her."

It would be easy to characterize Mrs. Lubling as a bulldozer, but that would miss her keen perceptiveness. She did push — hard — but she was able to gauge when her pressure made progress, and when it met a brick wall. As long as she sensed ground giving way, she would continue to make her case; if someone balked or resisted or just couldn't give in, she let go and went on to try a different option.

Mrs. Hudi Silber, who managed Boro Park's Khal Chassidim catering hall for many years, and who partnered with Mrs. Lubling on many bikur cholim ventures, often accompanied Mrs. Lubling on her hospital rounds. She watched in amazement as Mrs. Lubling donned surgical scrubs, knocked on the door of the OR and strode right in, even mid-surgery.

"Dr. Cohen," she said, "I have a patient here with me in the hallway. You'll do her next, right when you finish up here."

The doctor looked up from the operating table, startled. "Mrs. Lubling," he sputtered, "are you crazy? You can't just bring a patient into surgery. They need medical clearance, pre-op testing, bloodwork..."

"Okay," Mrs. Lubling said, unruffled. "I take her."

She then marched out of the OR, took her patient to pre-op, and told the technician, "This is my cousin. She's going into the OR as soon as Dr. Cohen finishes. Please give her all the tests she needs."

"But Mrs. Lubling," the technician said, "it doesn't work that way here. You need an appointment, you have to schedule the tests in advance. We can't do this right now."

Mrs. Lubling wasn't moved. "I want my patient to have the tests," she said. "Dr. Cohen is ready to operate."

"But she's not on the schedule!" the technician protested.

"Okay," Mrs. Lubling said, leaning over the desk. "Give me a pencil, I'll put her on the schedule. You do the tests, okay?"

Once Mrs. Lubling got a call from a woman whose newly orphaned teenage nephew had developed severe pain after a routine dental procedure. Overnight his pain intensified to the point that he could not stop screaming from agony. His mother took him to a local Brooklyn hospital, where he was diagnosed with a serious hemorrhage. Knowing that this widow was very much alone, her sister-in-law got involved in the case.

"You must get him out of that hospital," she told the mother. "This is a very serious issue, and you need a top hospital."

"I hear you," the mother said, "but he's in critical condition. They'll never agree to release a patient in this state. What should we do?"

Her sister-in-law replied, "Don't worry, I know someone who will take care of it."

It was holiday season and most doctors were on vacation, but as soon as Mrs. Lubling got the call, she began to work the phones and reached an NYU doctor who was packing to leave on vacation.

"You can't leave until you see this child," she said. "He doesn't have a father; now imagine if G-d forbid something happens to him — how will the mother go on?"

"I hear you, Mrs. Lubling," the doctor said. "What do you want me to do?"

"I want you to go into NYU. I will have him transferred there. And I want you to treat him and make sure he will be okay."

The transfer was duly arranged. The doctor postponed his departure. And the boy received the treatment he needed.

Mrs. Lubling had long nurtured a close relationship with the Rebbes of Satmar, beginning with her initial meeting with Rebbetzin Alte Feiga Teitelbaum regarding the launch of Rivkah Laufer Bikur Cholim. She attended the family weddings, slipping a small hat over her *sheitel* as a sign of respect for the Satmar dress code.

But her relationship with the Satmar court became especially close when the Beirach Moshe's young daughter, Rebbetzin Chaiky Meisels, became gravely ill and was admitted to NYU. Mrs. Lubling spared no effort to attend to all her needs and make her as comfortable as humanly possible until she succumbed to her illness.

At that point, the Rebbe made a curious request of Mrs. Lubling. "There is a kabbalistic concept that the *neshamah* lingers in the lodgings of a deceased person for several days after their passing," he said. "We'd appreciate if the ICU room that was her final lodging could be kept empty for a few days, so the *neshamah* can rest there unhindered."

It seemed an impossibly ludicrous mission, but Mrs. Lubling was never afraid to try. "Worse comes to worst, they'll tell you no," she explained. "But why not try?"

She approached the hospital administration and explained the mystical meaning behind the request. "Mrs. Lubling, this is just too much," came the response. "To leave an ICU room empty in a high-traffic Manhattan hospital?"

"Listen," she said calmly. "If it's the last bed available and you have to place someone there, of course you should use it. But in the meantime, keep it empty if you can. This is a very big rabbi, one of the biggest in the world, and it will mean a lot to him."

When she put it like that, it sounded a lot less unreasonable. The room remained empty, and the Rebbe's appreciation for Mrs. Lubling only grew.

But sometimes she used a tougher approach to get what she needed. At one point, the hospital chaplain at NYU neared retirement and the board discussed a replacement. Mrs. Lubling, who served on the board as an official hospital trustee, didn't like what she was hearing about the proposed candidate. She knew her patients, and she wanted a rabbi who would be more *heimish*, more involved, more attuned to their traditional background and needs. At meeting after meeting, she voiced her concerns, but she realized they weren't being acknowledged.

During the next board meeting, she arrived with a list of Jewish patients. The chairman, finance committee, and board members were all there.

"Mr. Chairman," she said, "I want this rabbi working here in the hospital, my rabbi."

"Mrs. Lubling," the chairman said, "we have a rabbi we want to hire, and he's been highly recommended to the board."

"Yes, but I want *my* rabbi."

"We want to work with you," the chairman said tentatively, "but we have a hiring protocol for chaplains, you understand."

Mrs. Lubling nodded, and kept her voice pleasant but firm. "I understand. So I want to tell you. You don't bring my rabbi, I take all these patients I refer to NYU" — at this, she pulled out her list and showed him the names after names of Jewish patients — "and bring them all to another hospital."

Of course, she got her way, and the highly regarded Rabbi Yaakov Pollak of Boro Park's Congregation Shomrei Emunah was appointed to the post.

Mrs. Lubling once brought a mother and small child who'd just arrived from Cleveland, Ohio, to pediatric gastroenterologist Dr. Joseph Levy. They had hastened to New York without making an appointment, but she told them not to worry and promised to personally escort them through their medical journey.

"Come with me," she said, and took them through the warren of halls leading to his office. "We don't have an appointment, but we need to see the doctor," she told the secretary.

"Dr. Levy," the secretary called into the examining room, "we have a problem."

Dr. Levy walked into the reception area and blanched. "Mrs. Lubling, I can't stay late today!" he said. "I have an anniversary party for my in-laws, and if I come late my wife will kill me!"

"That's okay," Mrs. Lubling said serenely. She patted the seats where she had settled her visitors. "You go to your party. We'll spend the night here, and you can come forty-five minutes early tomorrow morning. We'll be your first appointment."

The doctor stood there for a moment, jaw tight. Mrs. Lubling didn't budge. Then he sighed. "Okay, Mrs. Lubling. I'll see your patient before I leave."

Just as he feared, Dr. Levy arrived late at the anniversary party, drawing a harsh glare from his wife. He took the microphone and addressed the crowd.

"You're probably wondering how I dared come late to such an important event," he said. "Let me tell you about a selfless patient advocate, a woman in her nineties. She's the reason."

He went on to describe the encounter, detailing Mrs. Lubling's stubborn insistence on putting her patient first, and her readiness to spend the night in his waiting room. When he concluded, the entire family — including his wife — stood up and applauded for the feisty nonagenarian who'd held him up in his office.

That wasn't the only time Mrs. Lubling put her patients between a doctor and his in-laws. Mrs. Lubling had a special relationship with pediatric neurologist Dr. Fred Epstein, a leading brain surgeon with a genuine Jewish heart.

Born in 1937 in Yonkers, New York, Fred Epstein was considered the least likely in his class to attend medical school, never mind become one of the world's most famous and successful neurosurgeons. He suffered from undiagnosed learning disabilities — likely a severe case of dyslexia — and failed miserably in most of his schoolwork.

Sympathetic teachers helped him catch up and he was able, against daunting odds, to fulfill his longtime dream of becoming a doctor. He trained as a resident under famed neurosurgeon Dr. Joseph Ransohoff at New York University Medical Center, where he took a special interest in treating pediatric neurosurgical patients, eventually opening a separate department for their treatment.

Pediatric neurologist Dr. Fred Epstein had a special relationship with Mrs. Lubling, whom he called "The Boss."

Dr. Epstein was never an aloof aristocrat. He wore his huge heart on his sleeve, allowed his patients to listen in on his telephone calls with his family — which he then used as icebreakers — and walked the halls of NYU in his trademark cowboy boots. He even encouraged his little patients, their parents, and his medical students to call him Fred.

But his medical prowess was unparalleled. As a young doctor, he performed the first surgical removal of a tumor in a child's spinal cord, using a specially modified version of a dental tool called the Cavitron. With exceptional skill and no small measure of guts, Dr. Epstein used the device to liquify the tumor and then deftly "suck" the invasive material up and out of the body. It was an epochal development that radically changed the medical outlook for children suffering from tumors previously considered inoperable.

Perhaps the most famous and quirky case of Dr. Epstein's celebrated career was his 1997 spinal surgery on a dog — in exchange for a pro bono surgery for a little boy. That story began when Dr. Nancy Brown, a Pennsylvania veterinarian and friend of Dr. Epstein, called him with a question.

"Would you be willing to take a look at some spinal scans of one of my patients?" she asked. "It's a dog named Tucket, an eight-year-old pug that's begun to lose his balance and is having trouble going up steps. The pattern of disease doesn't typify anything we know, but I thought you might have some insight."

Dr. Epstein examined the scans and spotted a spinal abnormality that he believed was the cause of the dog's deteriorating mobility. His medical colleagues were absolutely opposed to their esteemed department taking on the case, but he had an idea: The dog's owners were extremely wealthy. He proposed that they donate a sum sufficient to cover a needy child's brain surgery in exchange for his services. The owners agreed.

And that's how it happened that shortly before Thanksgiving, Dr. Fred Epstein, world-renowned pediatric neurosurgeon, entered an operating room in New York's Animal Medical Center and opened the spine of Tucket, the Pennsylvania pug. The spinal cord was about the same size as a human baby's, and he had lots of experience doing experimental procedures on cats, so he felt very comfortable doing a canine surgery. The only thing he found disturbing was the barking coming from the next room.

The next day, Dr. Epstein got a phone call from a desperate woman. Her nephew, five-year-old Jerry Martin, had just been diagnosed with a massive spinal tumor. The local doctors in his little Pennsylvania town gave his parents no hope — but his aunt had read an article about Dr. Epstein and she tracked him down in his Manhattan office.

"Get your nephew to New York immediately," Dr. Epstein said. "We'll see what we can do."

The Martins made the 5½-hour drive, hoping that Dr. Epstein could help Jerry while dreading the medical bills that would take a lifetime to repay. Imagine their shock when they learned that the wealthy owners of a dog named Tucket had already covered the costs of Jerry's surgery.

Both boy and dog recovered well from their procedures, in a testament to the astounding proficiency, bravery, and altruism of the doctor who saw new opportunities where others saw dead ends.

Of all the medical relationships nurtured by Mrs. Lubling, Dr. Fred Epstein was the doctor best suited to her personality. He, too, had experienced a childhood of adversity yet emerged a plucky pioneer convinced that with the right attitude and effort, new solutions could be found just around the next bend in the road. He was a risk-taker who wasn't afraid to try aggressive new procedures if they could possibly help his patients. And he was the perfect ally for Mrs. Lubling because he allowed his heart, rather than his bank account or status, to dictate the terms of his professional practice. He had deep-seated respect for her and deferred to her many requests with humility and admiration.

"Can I ask you something?" he once asked one of Mrs. Lubling's steady drivers. "Do you understand her? Because she speaks very fast, and often I don't. But she's the Boss, and we do whatever she wants."

Once, the "whatever she wants" seemed a bit too much, even for Dr. Epstein, who slipped in after-hours surgeries and waived fees regularly for Mrs. Lubling. A *frum* family traveling in the Catskills was involved in a horrific car accident. Two children died immediately. A third child lingered with catastrophic injuries in Westchester Hospital. The doctors assumed the child was brain dead, but then a staff member picked up some possible movement on a brain scan.

Mrs. Lubling decided that the scans had to be seen by Dr. Epstein — only he had the expertise and experience to make a definitive assessment. She called Dr. Epstein that evening in his Manhattan apartment. The doctor was dressing for a restaurant dinner with his in-laws.

"Dr. Epstein," Mrs. Lubling said, "you have to understand what this family is going through. We need you to come."

"Mrs. Lubling," Dr. Epstein said, "you heard what the doctors said. With these kinds of injuries, there's no chance the child will make it."

"I know this mother," Mrs. Lubling said fiercely, "and I know that the only way she will be able to live with herself is if she can say that she did everything she could — that she brought in the top doctor — to save her child. I will pick you up with a driver and take you to Westchester. You will check the scans and hurry back to the restaurant."

Dr. Epstein may have privately doubted her timetable, but he didn't even try to argue. For all that he was New York's elite pediatric neurosurgeon, Mrs. Lubling was the Boss.

Things went badly from the get-go. The driver got lost on the way to Westchester. Finally they reached the hospital and Dr. Epstein perused the scans. Sadly, he confirmed that there was no medical hope for the child. By the time he returned to the car, dinner was long over.

That Thursday, when Mrs. Lubling's volunteer driver picked her up for the usual trip to NYU, she said, "*Mammele*, today before we go to Manhattan, we're stopping at the bank." At the bank, the driver was instructed to withdraw one thousand dollars from Mrs. Lubling's account. They then proceeded to Manhattan.

The first stop in NYU that day was Dr. Epstein's office. Mrs. Lubling went into his room, put the pile of money on his desk, and said, "Dr. Epstein, I know your wife is upset. Here, take her out to eat."

CHAPTER 5

Guardian of the Soldiers

Back when the Lublings had consulted the Chazon Ish about Yaakov's brain clot, he told them to travel to America — but only *"al menas lachzor,"* with the intention of returning to Eretz Yisrael. So they maintained a distinct Eretz Yisrael flavor in their American home.

The children called their parents Abba and Ima, and Mrs. Lubling conversed with them in Hebrew. They hosted a steady retinue of Israeli guests and maintained a strong connection with the relatives and friends they had left in Tel Aviv. Mrs. Lubling kept up her fundraising activities for PAI, and the *Shearim* newspaper faithfully published mazel tov notices whenever the Lublings made a *simchah*.

Throughout those years in Crown Heights, Reb Yaakov yearned to return to Eretz Yisrael. He possessed a marked dislike for America and called it "the ghetto." Despite establishing a family, finding a shul, and working at a steady job, he never considered it home.

Miriam, in contrast, thrived in America, between her family, her circle of friends, and her expanding bikur cholim activities. All the Lubling children found spouses — Nechama married Avrohom Frankel, Chanoch married Rachel Rhein, and Peshi married Aharon Drillick — and Miriam delighted in the arrival of the grandchildren.

Mrs. Lubling and her *machateineste* Mrs. Rivka Rhein enjoying their shared *nachas*

The thought of leaving her vibrant community work and beloved children must have been wrenching for Miriam. She felt happy and fulfilled with her new life in America. But her husband, remembering the Chazon Ish's parting words, made his wishes clear; their place was in Eretz Yisrael.

In 1970, after the final *sheva berachos* of their youngest daughter Peshi, the Lublings packed up their possessions, said goodbye to their children, and returned to Tel Aviv. They purchased an apartment at 4 Rechov Oliphant. Yaakov was hired as a proofreader for PAI's *Shearim* periodical, and the couple settled back into life in the Holy Land.

Mrs. Bella Brodt assumed responsibility for Miriam's bikur cholim advocacy, helping patients find the resources they needed in NYU and the other top hospitals. The Rivkah Laufer organization continued raising and distributing funds to those in need. Volunteers kept up their visits, hosting, and driving — the system was strong and solid, even without its president on site.

But Miriam still burned with energy and drive. She utilized her new location to make many bikur cholim referrals for Israeli patients who needed treatment in America. She graciously hosted *yeshivah bachurim* and seminary students for Shabbos, plying them with copious quantities of homemade food. And she also resumed her PAI activities, traveling across the country and urging religious Jews to vote for a party that would represent their values in the halls of power.

In 1973, with the outbreak of the Yom Kippur War, she added visits to soldiers in hospitals and rehab centers to her schedule. She

With the outbreak of the Yom Kippur War in 1973, Mrs. Lubling found an important ally in Rabbi Yisrael Meir Lau — together they encouraged and supported soldiers who'd been injured at the battlefront.

found an important ally in Rabbi Yisrael Meir Lau, later to become Israel's Ashkenazic chief rabbi. Together they ran events providing encouragement and succor to injured soldiers and offered spiritual outreach and resources to Jews distant from Judaism.

On October 6, 1973 — right in the middle of Yom Kippur davening — warning sirens went off throughout Israel. A coalition of Arab nations led by Egypt and Syria had entered Israeli territory in a surprise offensive campaign, launching a horrific war. Still riding high after their commanding victory in the Six Day War of 1967, Israel's military and governmental top brass were woefully unprepared for the attack. They would pay very dearly for that hubris.

At 2 p.m., Yitzchak Drachsler, a 22-year-old Orthodox Jew from Tel Aviv who had studied as a *bachur* in the Erloi Yeshivah, was summoned from his shul and commanded to report to the outskirts of Bnei Brak. Still fasting, he boarded one of the buses that were waiting to transport soldiers to the front. Yitzchak had trained as a paratrooper but later joined a tank unit, the 679th Brigade. Now he was being called to battle, on the holiest day of the year.

Before he could process the events, he was on his way to the Ramat HaGolan region in Israel's north, which had been invaded by Syrian forces. Yitzchak was assigned to the gunner position of a Centurion tank. As the tank rolled along, the crew noticed a charred, smoking tank — then another, and then another. They grew very silent. No one dared voice what they were seeing.

Yitzchak and his fellow soldiers realized that the IDF was vastly outnumbered by the Syrian forces. The charred vehicles strewn across the area were IDF tanks that had been hit by Syrian shells. As the tanks exploded in flames, the soldiers trapped inside had met hideous deaths.

And their crew was heading directly into this valley of death and destruction.

Soon the driver drew to a halt. Near a blackened tank, Yitzchak saw a figure in IDF uniform. It was a Jewish soldier who must have escaped the burning tank. Now he was lying helpless, barely conscious. The crew pulled him into their tank and continued on their way.

Suddenly there was an ominous whistle. A Sagger missile hissed through the air and hit their tank. Before the soldiers could even process what had happened, their tank erupted in flames. The wounded soldier died instantly, and the tank commander went flying from the impact. His forced exit gave Yitzchak an escape hatch. Propelled by the flames and blinded by the smoke, he hauled himself out of the tank.

Yitzchak had been married for just seven months and his wife was expecting their first child. "Hashem," he davened silently, "do whatever You want, take me if You must. But one thing I ask: allow me to live long enough to hear my child call me Abba."

It took hours for Yitzchak to be rescued and administered morphine. He was transported by military helicopter to Rambam Medical Center in Haifa, unconscious, with burns covering close to ninety percent of his body.

When his parents came to visit two days later, they were allowed entry to the room only after suiting up in masks and gowns; the patients in the burn unit had lost so much skin that they were dangerously vulnerable to infection.

Yitzchak's mother walked among the beds, examining each face. She shrugged, left the room, and told the nurse, "*Yitzchak iz nisht du,* Yitzchak isn't here."

The nurse urged her to go check again, but none of the scorched, mutilated men remotely resembled her blue-eyed son. Finally, she began to call "Yitzchak, Yitzchak" as she circled the room.

One of the mummified bodies heard her voice. "It's me, Mamme," he said.

She wheeled around toward the source of the voice. All she could see were bandages — bandages covering the head, the blackened arms, the chest, the legs of what had once been a healthy man. She approached a little closer and studied the patient's teeth. It was her son.

Mrs. Drachsler spent most of the next six months at Yitzchak's bedside, returning home only to cook for Shabbos and tend to her apartment. During those six months, Yitzchak underwent close to seventy surgical procedures as the doctors tried to seal off his maimed body from infection and restore whatever skin they could. At one point, Mrs. Drachsler offered to donate her own skin for some of the skin grafts her son needed.

Yitzchak was in horrific pain, both internally and externally. And the emotional scars were even worse. The only bright spot was the thought of the child he would soon get to meet. Throughout the hospitalization, the surgeries, and the ensuing months of rehab, he remembered the prayer he'd sent up amid the Syrian bombardment.

At first, the family tried to shield Yitzchak's wife, Rivka Drachsler, from the reality of her husband's condition. But at some point she had to face the fact that her rosy newlywed existence was irrevocably shattered. The healthy, vibrant husband who'd hurried to his tank on Yom Kippur was never coming back.

The birth of a healthy baby girl gave Yitzchak a new boost of hope and energy. After months of grueling therapy, he was released from the Beit Kay military rehab center. The first time they went to Rivka's parents for Shabbos, her father looked at Yitzchak's grotesquely scarred face and started to cry.

"How will we make it through an entire Shabbos here?" Rivka asked. She took the baby and grabbed her suitcase. "That's it, Yitzchak," she said. "We're going home."

But there was one visitor who refused to give in to despair. Her name was Mrs. Miriam Lubling, and she knew the Drachslers as fellow members of PAI. Now that she was back in Tel Aviv, she had reconnected with them.

During those long months in the hospital and rehab center, she was one of the stalwart visitors who refused to be cowed by the demoralizing sights of disfigured soldiers, or the ear-piercing screams of men who literally had no skin.

She visited regularly, bringing comfort and hope to the patient and offering support and encouragement to the young woman who remained committed to a shared future with a very compromised husband.

Though he'd been horrifically burnt during the Yom Kippur War, Yitzchak Drachsler eventually regained his strength. Throughout his recovery, Mrs. Lubling was a steady source of support.

As time passed, Yitzchak regained his strength. He earned a college degree and was hired for the position of treasurer of the newly formed settlement of Emanuel. When that venture proved unsuccessful, he found employment at Israel's population registry. His body never completely healed — he endured pointing, stares, and whispers everywhere he went — but he was a successful, functional husband and father who took pride and pleasure in his six children.

Over the ensuing years, Mrs. Lubling maintained the connection with the Drachslers. She called and visited, inquired about the children's progress, and even attended their son's *bris*. Fifty years later, Rivka Drachsler remembers the words of admiration and encouragement that Mrs. Lubling shared during those dark months, when her husband was fully consumed by his searing pain, and a happy home and family were a far-off dream. "If someone would ask me to nominate the 'woman of the year,'" Mrs. Lubling told her, "you would be my pick."

CHAPTER 6
Hospital Rounds

After nearly a decade of sporadic visits by the Lublings to their married children and grandchildren in America, Peshi Drillick once told her children that Bobby would be arriving soon. "You mean Bobby from the pictures?" her little one asked.

When Mrs. Lubling heard about the comment, she made a decision. "I will not be 'Bobby from the pictures,'" she said. "I want to be a real-live Bobby, part of the children's lives."

"I will not be 'Bobby from the pictures' — I want to be part of the children's lives."
The Lublings at a Drillick family *simchah*

And so in 1980 the Lublings returned to America. Reb Yaakov, however, in keeping with the Chazon Ish's directive, still felt his place was in Eretz Yisrael. He refused to buy a property in *galus*. Instead, the Lublings rented an apartment on 51st Street in Boro Park, from Rabbi Yehuda and Mrs. Malky Weinberg. Rabbi Weinberg led the Slonimer *beis midrash* on the ground floor, and his family lived above the shul. Two flights up, the Lublings established their new home.

Reb Yaakov Lubling was very different from his lively, spontaneous wife, but they were true partners: she treated him like a king, and he encouraged her in her constant *chessed* work.

It was a good location: just two blocks away, on 49th Street, was the Gerrer *shtiebel* of Boro Park, where the Lublings found a waiting circle of friends. As for *parnassah*, Reb Yaakov took a job as a *mashgiach* for the Orthodox Union in the Lou G. Siegel restaurant in Manhattan. It was a good fit for his introverted personality and very organized work habits.

The workers at the restaurant knew that Rabbi Lubling trusted no one else with the keys to the refrigerator. "But my workers show up at 6 a.m. to start cutting vegetables," the chef protested when Reb Yaakov laid down the law.

"No problem, I'll be there at six to open up the fridge for them," Reb Yaakov said, and from that day on he woke up when it was still dark and headed to the train station so he could be in Manhattan before the kitchen staff arrived. That was his personality: responsible, steady, unwavering.

His wife, in contrast, was lively and spontaneous — the more activities she could cram into her day, the better. But as different as they were, she treasured him and treated him like a king, and he constantly encouraged her to continue her *chessed* work.

New York's demographics had shifted since the Lublings' initial arrival; most of Crown Heights' *frum* population had left, except for the Lubavitcher community, and Flatbush was now bursting with young families. Mrs. Lubling realized that those young families would need a kindergarten for their children, and so she partnered with Rebbetzin Pessel Teitelbaum to open a kindergarten on East 13th Street in Flatbush. The Teitelbaums had a shul in what formerly had housed an institute for the deaf. It was legally zoned for education and was therefore the perfect building to house the kindergarten.

Every morning, Mrs. Lubling would join her partner at work. They had very different personalities but became exceptionally close, working in sync to run what became a very popular kindergarten.

Both were survivors, both were strong women, and each brought different talents to the job. Rebbetzin Teitelbaum was the nurturer who cooked the children hot lunches in huge pots, then made sure they ate well and had their faces and noses wiped.

Mrs. Lubling posing with two of her young charges at a kindergarten graduation. Every creative detail was important to her.

Mrs. Lubling presiding over a grandchild's birthday party at the kindergarten

Mrs. Lubling was a creative dynamo with high standards. She planned the performances, led the circle time, and made sure each child's craft project turned out just right. Before the children climbed onto the buses heading home, she'd check that every face was clean and every shirt tucked in.

But even as she supervised the kindergarten, Mrs. Lubling had another pursuit. The *cholim* learned very quickly that their indefatigable advocate had returned to Brooklyn, and calls came in constantly from patients and families seeking help. So while the teachers sang and played with the children — and with the full support and encouragement of Rebbetzin Teitelbaum — she took bikur cholim phone calls in the kitchen. As the children painted and colored in the other rooms, she took down notes in a small composition notebook. One person needed an MRI. Another had just received a devastating diagnosis. Someone sought an expert doctor for an aging parent. Someone else had received conflicting information from different doctors and couldn't figure out which doctor to trust.

Mrs. Lubling had a reassuring word for each caller. More than that, she acted swiftly to address their questions.

Each weekday at 3:00, at the conclusion of the kindergarten hours, Mrs. Lubling began the next part of her day. A volunteer driver pulled up, she climbed into the car, and they headed toward Manhattan.

New York University Medical Center, currently known as NYU Langone, is an imposing complex spanning three city blocks on Manhattan's East Side. It includes a medical school, the Tisch Hospital for acute care, the Hospital for Joint Disease, the Hassenfeld Pediatric Center, and the Rusk Institute of Rehabilitation Medicine. It is a busy, bustling city with its own etiquette, bylaws, lexicon, and population, housing and treating hundreds of patients on any given day.

For the average patient or visitor, the hospital is an intimidating place to navigate. But Mrs. Miriam Lubling was not the average person, and even New York's elite medical citadels could not

New York University Medical Center, a busy, bustling hospital complex, was where Mrs. Lubling worked her unique brand of magic.

intimidate her. Every afternoon, she arrived at NYU, and with her fusion of charm, grit, and overflowing sincerity — spiced with a strong Polish accent and immigrant diction — she pulled strings, opened doors, and sliced through red tape for her patients.

During many of her years in action, the hospital provided her with a list of Jewish patients, and she did her best to check on each one. But her first stop was usually the windowless, airless admitting office. It may have looked like an aging bureaucratic headquarters, but this was where Mrs. Lubling often waged war.

First she waved at the security guard sitting in a glass enclosure and wished him a good day. Then she marched in her high heels to the tiny office where two women wielded control over the hospital's hundreds of beds. "*Mammele*, how are you?" she'd greet them with kisses and hugs. Then she'd get to business: battling to find an available bed for a patient desperately waiting to be admitted.

In the early days of Mrs. Lubling's advocacy, before a computer system was introduced, the admitting office used a felt board that hung on the wall behind them to track available beds. They could physically move the little pieces on and off the board, to denote empty or used beds. For Mrs. Lubling, that diagram was a very helpful device.

"I need a bed in cardiology," she said as she eyed the diagram.

"We don't have one," the women said.

"But I need one!" she insisted. "For my cousin!"

"Mrs. Lubling," the women repeated, "we don't have one."

At that point, Mrs. Lubling used one of three options.

The first involved the diagram. "Look," she pointed at the felt board. "I see there, you have a spot, right in cardiology, like I need. Right?"

It was hard to argue with the facts. And while the women could put up a good fight, they also respected this small woman with a heart of gold and spine of steel. "Okay, Mrs. Lubling, we can give your patient a bed in Room 805."

Anyone else might have puffed up with pride seeing their mission accomplished, but Mrs. Lubling would purse her lips as she scanned her mental database and visualized the room. "I don't like that room," she said. "It's dark, the air isn't good. Can you find something else for my patient?"

When the felt board was phased out, Mrs. Lubling used a different trick. "You don't have a room?" she asked. "Okay, I hear." Then she'd head to the elevator bank down the hall, hurry up to the ward, conduct a quick survey of the rooms, and return to the admitting office.

"How about 914?" she asked. "There's a bed in 914, I checked for you."

That usually did the job. But when it didn't, Mrs. Lubling used one last tactic. She sat down on the aged chair opposite the admitting desk, placed her bursting handbag on her lap, and crossed her ankles. "I can't continue," she said plaintively. "I can't go visit my patients. I need a bed."

There was another reason Mrs. Lubling visited the admitting office: so she could entreat the staff to switch an existing patient to a better spot.

A better spot usually meant a window; Mrs. Lubling was a big believer in the benefits of sunshine and a view. "Did that other patient get discharged?" she asked the admitting staff. "I want you should move my patient to his spot, the one near the window."

More often than not, the women acquiesced, earning a shower of effusive thanks and another round of hugs.

With that mission accomplished, Mrs. Lubling headed to her next stop: the NYU Emergency Room, a buzzing beehive marked by a curious mix of crisp efficiency for some patients and the misery of seemingly endless waiting for many others.

NYU's ER handles upward of eighty thousand patients per year. Many of the patients arrive at the behest of their doctors. Others are brought by ambulance. A large percentage come because they don't have health insurance, and hospitals are obligated by law to treat everyone who comes to an emergency room.

NYU's care was known to be superior — once a patient made it to a bed on a floor. But the ER experience could be dismal. Already nervous and tense, the patients filling the room were further humbled by the bureaucracy that forced them to wait, docile, as the staff tried to manage the never-ending stream of humanity that kept flowing through the facility.

When Mrs. Lubling entered the ER, it was as if the Malach Rafael had arrived. Eyes gleaming, back straight, her entire body exuding purpose and passion, she'd walk in and survey the scene. Something about the room — the helplessness of the waiting patients, the worry of their families, the atmosphere of uncertainty, and maybe also the power imbalance — seemed to infuse her with extra energy. This was a place where she could, and would, make a difference.

At the circular open office area, she spoke to the nurses and doctors. They knew her well. "I'm here to check on the Goldberg boy," she would say.

"Mrs. Lubling, I know he's your patient," the doctor answered. "Don't worry, we're taking care of him."

After procuring updates from the doctors and nurses about "her" patients, she headed past the rows of curtained-off cubicles for patients waiting to be admitted, to the open area lined with beds of waiting people. Often, family members of patients recognized her and came running. "How can I help you?" she asked. "What do you need?"

But even when no one approached, she had work to do. With zero formal medical education or ER training, she conducted her own rounds of the room and her own form of triage. "What's your name?" she said as she stopped at a bed. "What are you here for? How can I help you?"

Her keen eyes noticed when a non-Jewish patient followed the unusual scene of an Orthodox woman offering some sort of privileged treatment to her coreligionist, and she would turn to these patients and ask, "Can I help you too? What can I do for you?"

After hours of waiting, the sight of this little woman with her glittering jewelry and perfectly teased wig must have seemed like a mirage to many patients. But her concern was palpable and her expertise undeniable. From their hapless, helpless positions, the patients watched in awe as Mrs. Lubling got swift results. She knew which doctors to speak to and which levers to pull. With her input, wait times were cut, test results were interpreted, decisions were made, and patients were either released or admitted.

Now it was time to visit the patients on the floors. First, Mrs. Lubling went down to the bikur cholim room that was her personal brainchild and one of her proudest accomplishments as president of the Rivkah Laufer Bikur Cholim. She never had patience to wait — not at the bakery, the grocery, the wig stylist, or at the NYU elevator bank, where the elevators were notorious for their slow timing. She randomly pointed to an elevator, saying, "we're taking C," and then miraculously, Elevator C would appear.

In the bikur cholim room, Mrs. Lubling packed up some of the goodies that had been stowed in the refrigerator and cabinets. Then she once again summoned the elevator and ascended to the wards.

For the rest of the afternoon, she circled from floor to floor and from room to room, searching for the names on the list along with those she had penned on Post-it notes during the morning phone calls. She didn't always have the room number, but that didn't matter. Somehow, as she traversed the wards, floor after floor, she found everyone on her list.

When Mrs. Lubling came into a room, the patient always sat up straighter. "How are you feeling? Does anything hurt? You be good, I know, I know," she would reassure them in her heavily accented English. Then after hearing more details of their case she would ask, "Who's the doctor? I talk to him."

It was important to her to ensure her patients had nourishing kosher food, and she made sure they were included on the distribution list of the Satmar Bikur Cholim, which delivered hot, homemade food to patients' bedsides. And she spared no effort to make the patients comfortable. When she entered a room she fluffed up the patient's pillows, discarded any wrappers or used tissues, and cleaned off the windowsill.

She pressed the nursing staff to put "her" patients in rooms with a view of the Hudson River. And when she visited, she directed their attention to the river below: "Look out the window — see the boats, the sky, the work of the *Eibeshter*."

To each room she brought joy, light, and love. She pulled over a chair to the bedside, held the patient's hand, asked for her Jewish name and davened for her right there in the room.

Once she went into a room to visit a 90-year-old woman. "How are you feeling?" she asked.

"Hungry, hungry, hungry," the woman mumbled.

Mrs. Lubling took a spoon, pulled out some of the kosher food she'd packed up, and spoon-fed the woman. Nothing was beneath her. You do anything for family, after all — and Mrs. Lubling's patients were her family.

Mrs. Lubling didn't need much sleep. She spent most evenings at *simchos* — weddings, bar mitzvahs, or engagements of family, friends, and former patients — and retired at a very late hour. Every Friday morning, she woke up while it was still dark, cooking and baking all the Shabbos food: homemade challah, gefilte fish, fresh soup, trays of *galleh* (the men of the Gerrer *shtiebel* loved her *galleh*,

Mrs. Lubling's homemade *galleh* was famous — the men of Boro Park's Gerrer *shtiebel* looked forward to the trays she sent every Succos.

and as a special Succos treat, she dispatched Chanoch every Erev Succos to bring a few trays over to shul). Then, when she was done, she set out to Manhattan to check on her patients and make sure they had everything they needed for Shabbos.

On Friday afternoons, as the sun sank closer to the horizon, Yaakov Lubling would complete the final preparations for Shabbos. Then he stood on the porch waiting for his wife to return, reciting *Shir HaShirim*, his usual calm demeanor tinged by just a pinch of anxiety until she finally jumped out of the car service just as the Boro Park pre-Shabbos sirens would blast.

"Yankel, I'm home! *Es iz shpet,* I know it's late — I'm coming to light!" she reassured him as she hurried up the stairs and made one final phone call to the hospital admitting office to ensure all her patients had been placed in beds, as she'd requested.

Then, finally, she was ready to light the waiting Shabbos candles.

As the frenetic tempo of Mrs. Lubling's week finally slowed to the serene cadences of the Day of Rest, a line of neighbors, *mispallelim*, and local children would form before her. They weren't looking for candy or chocolate. "She was like a Rebbe," explains

Noach Schwartz, who davened in the Slonimer shul below their apartment, "and they all wanted to wish her a Gut Shabbos and receive her blessing in return."

"Mrs. Lubling," the children implored the angel of mercy who had just returned from the hospital wards, "give us a *berachah.*"

CHAPTER 7
Driving With Mrs. Lubling

Just about everyone in Boro Park and beyond knew that Mrs. Lubling worked miracles in the hospital wards. Many wanted to have a small share in her work, and over the years she attracted a cadre of special women who served as her personal drivers to and from NYU. Inevitably, they served as much, much more than chauffeurs — they became treasured friends and true partners in her bikur cholim work, encouraging, advocating, and sometimes even interpreting for patients and their families.

Some of these women were married, some single. Some had busy homes, some had demanding jobs. All remember those hours behind the wheel and the ensuing hospital rounds with warmth and longing — and a touch of disbelief.

Over the years, the drivers formed a rotation. Each woman took a different day of the week to drive Mrs. Lubling to NYU, accompany her on her rounds, and then drive her back home. On those weekly drives, each woman learned firsthand that the regular rules of traffic and nature bent and contorted to Mrs. Lubling's will.

One woman still remembers her first day driving Mrs. Lubling. Their destination was the Rusk Institute of Rehabilitation Medicine — part of the NYU complex — and as she pulled into the circular driveway, she paused for a moment so Mrs. Lubling could leave the car before she headed toward the parking lot.

The legendary trustee badge opened doors for Mrs. Lubling, allowing her to bypass bureaucracy and gain entrée to the hospital elites.

"Leave the car here," Mrs. Lubling said.

The driver looked at her questioningly. "I can't leave it here," she said. "I can't block the entrance of the hospital."

"Okay," Mrs. Lubling conceded. "So pull in on the side."

The woman shook her head. "I can't. It's illegal. I'll get towed!"

Mrs. Lubling refused to be cowed. "Leave it here," she said.

The woman wasn't quite sure why she let herself be convinced, but she tentatively pulled her car up at the side of the entrance. A uniformed hospital guard approached. Mrs. Lubling rummaged in her pocketbook and pulled out a badge. "You see, I am a trustee of the hospital here," she explained to the new driver as she affixed it to her black suit.

The guard jumped to attention when he saw her exit the car. "Hello, Mrs. Lubling!" he greeted her warmly.

"How are you, Scott?" Mrs. Lubling said. "Okay, the car here, you see it? That's my car."

"That's fine, Mrs. Lubling," the guard said. "Just leave your bikur cholim card in the window, so we'll all know this car is yours."

And that became their steady parking spot.

Mrs. Eva Stern was a longtime friend of Mrs. Lubling. Her one-family home on 49th Street off 14th Avenue in Boro Park was a hub of *chessed* and a constant address for fundraising events. Like Mrs. Lubling, she integrated *chessed* into the fabric of her life, and they became close allies in the bikur cholim enterprise.

A confident and experienced driver, Mrs. Stern was one of Mrs.

Lubling's first chauffeurs. She spent hours behind the wheel, driving Mrs. Lubling to the hospital. It even became a family affair. For the Stern children, it was the most natural thing to help Mrs. Lubling get to NYU; they absorbed a culture of *chessed* as Mrs. Stern guided her car up the FDR Drive.

The extra mileage from those trips translated into a firm friendship between the families. Mrs. Lubling got to know the Stern children very well and even came up with endearing nicknames for each one. She attended all their *simchos*, bringing appropriate gifts, and the Stern children loved her right back.

One winter Friday, Mrs. Lubling called her friend. "Eva," she said, "I need you to drive me to Maimonides for a quick trip — there's someone I need to check on."

As a rule, Mrs. Stern was very accommodating. On this short Friday, however, she simply couldn't spare the time. Her daughter Tova, a twelfth-grader, had just gotten her driver's license, so Mrs. Stern suggested that Tova take Mrs. Lubling instead.

Tova (Stern) Salb still remembers easing the large Oldsmobile Ninety-Eight through the traffic-snarled streets of Boro Park that Friday afternoon. Mrs. Lubling surely sensed how nervous she was, because she complimented her young driver on every successful turn.

Kranie (Stern) Liebhard will never forget the time Mrs. Lubling called the house — only this time, instead of asking for a ride, she asked to speak to Zofia, the Polish cleaning woman. A quick conversation in fluent Polish ensued, after which Mrs. Lubling instructed Kranie, "Zofia will give you eight hundred dollars — quickly bring it to me; I need it for a patient."

Later she learned the full story: Just a few moments earlier, Mrs. Lubling had prevailed upon a doctor to take an emergency case. The doctor agreed on one condition — that he receive immediate payment, in cash.

At that hour, all the local banks were closed. But Mrs. Lubling was a quick thinker. She realized that a Polish cleaning woman was likely to have a ready stash of cash. That very night, the doctor had his payment.

After the Stern children married, Mrs. Lubling remained a part of their lives and they remained part of her bikur cholim. It wasn't unusual for Kranie, who lives in Brooklyn, to receive a phone call from Mrs. Lubling asking for a ride ("Mommy can't drive me today, can you come instead?"), and all the children pitched in to raise money for the Rivkah Laufer Bikur Cholim annual luncheons.

Some of the Stern grandchildren attended Mrs. Lubling's kindergarten too. That, too, was channeled toward bikur cholim. One day Mrs. Stern's phone rang. "Eva? I want you to know, your grandson here in the kindergarten, he didn't make it to the bathroom in time. I cleaned him up, and now you owe me! What time can you pick me up and drive me to the hospital?"

Those who drove Mrs. Lubling on a regular basis — and with whom she developed close personal friendships — include Mrs. Shifra (Shiftchu) Scharf, who headed the Pesha Elias Bikur Cholim of Bobov and who often partnered with Mrs. Lubling in raising funds to help pay medical bills for the needy, along with her sister-in-law Mrs. Esther Scharf of Flatbush.

Other long-term drivers who not only accompanied Mrs. Lubling to NYU, but also hosted and cared for families who came to NYU from abroad, include Mrs. Esther Paskesz, Mrs. Bella Weinreb, Mrs. Dina Feldman, Mrs. Miri Kauftheil, and Mrs. Chana Malka (Lowy) Heller. Many of these women were honored by the Rivkah Laufer Bikur Cholim with *hachnasas orchim* awards — but no award could even begin to encapsulate their full dedication.

Mrs. Miriam "Pupsie" (Scharf) Beer became a driver almost by accident. She had known Mrs. Lubling even as a teenager, through a family connection. When she married and moved to Flatbush, she sent her little ones to the kindergarten. It happened more than once that during pickup time, Mrs. Lubling grabbed her and commanded, "Come, Pupsie, I need you should drive me to NYU."

Pupsie had no choice: she buckled her kids into the backseat and headed to Manhattan.

Leibish Kamenetsky was another inadvertent driver. When his

newborn daughter was hospitalized in NYU, he got to know Mrs. Lubling, who visited every day and was constantly in action — nurturing, encouraging, and helping out the patients.

"Leibish, I see you're getting ready to leave. Can you give me a ride back to Boro Park?" she asked one afternoon.

Somehow, he can't figure out how, the trip back to Brooklyn — which usually took from forty-five minutes to a full hour — took just twenty minutes. And this was during rush hour, via the heavily-traveled FDR Drive and Brooklyn Battery Tunnel. It made no sense, and it never repeated itself — but with Mrs. Lubling in his car, the newly designated chauffeur merited a biblical sort of *kefitzas haderech*.

Esther Chaviva (Zucker) Svei took a different route to the driver's seat. She had always felt a tug toward *chessed*; she often volunteered in local organizations and drove cancer patients to Manhattan for treatment. On one such trip to Memorial Sloan-Kettering Cancer Center, she noticed Mrs. Lubling — a familiar figure to most Boro Parkers — jumping out of a taxi and striding into the hospital. Where was her driver, Esther Chaviva wondered.

That night she saw Mrs. Lubling at a wedding and approached her. "You don't have a driver?" she asked.

Because it was the summer, Mrs. Lubling explained, many of her usual drivers were away.

"I have a car," Esther Chaviva offered. She knew this was an opportunity to form a relationship with a woman at the helm of a *chessed* empire — but she didn't quite realize the adventure she'd signed up for.

The next day at 3 p.m. the phone rang. "You ready to take me?" a heavily accented voice asked. "Pick me up in half an hour at the Boro Park Y." Somehow Mrs. Lubling had tracked down her phone number.

During that summer, Esther Chaviva drove Mrs. Lubling every afternoon from Sunday through Thursday. Pickup was at 3 p.m., and the adventures continued until at least 9 or 10 p.m. She kept a steady post at the wheel for more than two decades, until Mrs. Lubling's passing.

"Mrs. Lubling was the original Waze," Esther Chaviva remembers. "She directed me which lane to drive in, which route to take. She'd sometimes say, 'Don't go that way, there will be traffic.' And she had unusual *siyata d'Shmaya* — she was always right!"

Esther Chaviva quickly learned that despite her years, Mrs. Lubling was extremely vivacious and contemporary. She knew the latest trends and songs; she collected information about the younger generation's likes and dislikes. And she possessed a subtle sense of mischief that ran through her interactions with the hospital staff.

Driving Mrs. Lubling required flexibility; the itinerary was fluid, based on whatever she needed that day. Often, Mrs. Lubling would direct her driver to the Whispers 'n Whimsies gift shop on 16th Avenue in Boro Park, so she could stock up on gifts for the patients and hospital staff.

The store was usually crowded with people of all ages seeking that perfect gift or treat. But as soon as Mrs. Lubling said, "Barbara, I need a few nice things," Barbara Bookson, the proprietor, was at her service. She pulled out item after item, showing her the newest offerings. When it came time to ring up Mrs. Lubling's selections, she often threw in some items for free.

Mrs. Lubling wasn't content to take Barbara's recommendations; she tried out each item. She was especially delighted by one gift, a sunflower in a pot that played "You Are My Sunshine." "Let's buy twenty of these!" she said. That afternoon, she distributed an extra dose of her usual sunshine on the floors of NYU.

Miriam Turk remembers the first cryptic instructions she was given after offering to take a day along with her friend Chevy Kramer: "Be at the preschool at 3." Then there was a dial tone.

Puzzled, Miriam called back. "I'm sorry, I didn't understand," she said.

Mrs. Lubling gave her the address of the playgroup on East 13th Street and explained that she would be waiting there. After that first Tuesday drive, she asked, "Do you have more time? How about Thursdays?" For the next nineteen years, Thursday was their day.

Over those nineteen years of Thursdays with Mrs. Lubling, Chevy and Miriam never conducted that initial "getting to know you" shmooze. They never learned Mrs. Lubling's maiden name or how her *chessed* ventures had started. There was no time for social niceties; there was too much work to be done.

When Chevy and Miriam picked up Mrs. Lubling, she was simultaneously handling two phones — the preschool phone and her cellphone — along with her beeper. She'd bring her cellphone into the car and keep talking while Miriam pulled out, Chevy settled in next to her, and the pair asked, "Where are we going today?"

Often she commanded them to head directly to NYU, but sometimes she had them stop at a store to pick up a gift, or at a doctor's office to make a delivery. Once they reached NYU, they avoided the visitors' parking lot entirely, and parked in the emergency parking area. Not once did a guard object. The guards even learned — thanks to Mrs. Lubling — that they should not request hospital IDs from Orthodox Jews visiting on Shabbos, since Jews are prohibited from carrying on their holy day.

The guards considered Mrs. Lubling, who addressed each one by name and who delivered generous gifts to them, an honored member of the board, someone exempt from the regular rules.

For years, Mrs. Judy Klein of Boro Park picked up Mrs. Lubling every Tuesday and drove her to the hospital. Then they visited the wards together, dispensing encouragement and noting which patients needed assistance. Mrs. Lubling always thanked Mrs. Klein, then found something to compliment — her clothing, her bag, her *sheitel*. Though her aims were lofty, she was grounded and perceptive and noticed small details.

Mrs. Klein knew she would not be home until much later that evening, so during the commute to Manhattan she called her teenage daughter Sarala. "Sarala," she said, "the chicken is waiting in a pan in the fridge. Please heat it up. And sauté some onions to spread on top, and prepare some potatoes."

Mrs. Lubling then took the phone. "Sarala," she said, "it's so wonderful that you're helping us out! Because of you, your mother is able to do so many mitzvos. You should know, Sarala, the *zechus* of your mother's mitzvah belongs to you!"

Mrs. Lubling used to work from the car; it was an office of sorts for her. She was one of the first women of her generation to own a beeper and later, a cellphone — a gift from then-Agudah activist (and currently chairman) and Gerrer patron Mr. Shlomo Werdiger, a family friend and staunch admirer who realized how much more she could accomplish with this groundbreaking device. Mrs. Lubling embraced the new technology enthusiastically. As they headed out of Brooklyn, she took calls, scheduled appointments, and arranged for Israeli patients to be picked up at the airport and transported to the hospital.

Mrs. Gita Muller is a resident of Boro Park who often volunteered in New York hospitals, driving patients for treatment or visiting *cholim* on the wards. One afternoon in the late 1980s, she encountered Mrs. Lubling in the hospital. "Why don't we work together?" Mrs. Lubling suggested.

From that moment, they became a team. Mrs. Muller drove and accompanied her new friend on bikur cholim rounds for years. And she watched with bemusement, and sometimes amazement, as Mrs. Lubling's sheer will overpowered the laws of nature.

At around 11:30 a.m. one Friday, after Mrs. Muller had returned from an Erev Shabbos visit to the Manhattan hospitals, she got a phone call from Mrs. Lubling.

"*Gita'she, mein otzar*, Gita, my treasure," Mrs. Lubling said with her usual warmth, "I need your help. Chedva Silverfarb was recently moved from Mt. Sinai Medical Center to Westchester. [Chedva was an incredibly strong and inspirational woman from Eretz Yisrael who, despite suffering from a serious illness, was a renowned public speaker who encouraged people to improve their knowledge of the laws of *shemiras halashon* and to increase their recitation of *Tehillim*.] I'm sure she is very lonely there. We have to go visit her."

"How can we leave now?" Mrs. Muller asked. "It's Erev Shabbos!"

"It will be fine, we have time," Mrs. Lubling insisted. "She's there all alone; we have to go wish her a good Shabbos."

Mrs. Muller sighed and picked up her car keys, all too aware that it was pointless to protest. She headed toward Mrs. Lubling's apartment and then out of Brooklyn. Maybe it was because of her vague sense of nervousness that she missed their usual exit.

"That's it," she said regretfully. "The next exit is at least ten minutes away. Then we'll have to get off, turn around, and travel another ten minutes just to get to the right exit. There's no way we can visit Chedva and still make it home in time for Shabbos."

"We're going to Chedva!" Mrs. Lubling said. "Stop the car."

Mrs. Muller looked at her in disbelief. "We're on the highway," she said. "I can't just stop!"

"Listen to me," Mrs. Lubling said breezily. "You stop the car and let me out. And then you will drive in reverse back to the exit we missed."

Before Mrs. Muller could protest, Mrs. Lubling had already opened the car door and slipped out. She began walking along the highway, signaling to the oncoming traffic to stay clear of the lane while directing Mrs. Muller to keep driving in reverse.

Mrs. Muller clenched the steering wheel. She realized she had no choice, and followed Mrs. Lubling's bizarre instructions until they reached the missed exit. Then Mrs. Lubling hopped back into the car, not a *sheitel* hair out of place.

"Okay, so now we found our exit, let's go to the hospital!" she said brightly to a shaken Mrs. Muller.

Sure enough, they made it to the hospital, and Chedva was thrilled to see them. When Mrs. Muller arrived home just moments before *licht-bentchen*, her husband was standing next to her candlesticks, matches outstretched. She took the matches, hands trembling, wondering if anyone would ever believe the wild adventure she had experienced that day.

That's how it was when you drove Mrs. Lubling: she was a woman who could defy traffic laws, time constraints, and driving conventions in her burning ambition to help a Jew in need. And when you agreed to drive her, you agreed to abide by her unique take on the rules — namely, that rules were for other people with less important things to do.

Once, though, Mrs. Lubling asked Mrs. Muller to make a U-turn on the FDR Drive in Lower Manhattan. Even in the suspended reality that came with chauffeuring the Queen of NYU, this was just too much.

"I can do anything you want," Mrs. Muller said, "but not a U-turn on the FDR."

CHAPTER 8
Building Trust

When she was in her early eighties, Mrs. Lubling underwent several spinal surgeries. "You'll have to wear comfortable shoes," the doctor told her afterward. "High heels aren't good for the spine."

Mrs. Lubling nodded. The next time the doctor saw her, she was back in her high heels, marching along the floors of NYU.

"You have to understand," she said, "I'm not a tall person. I need the doctors to respect me."

It's debatable whether she really needed those high heels; the respect she had won was much deeper and more substantial than the prestige created by any surface impression. What is undeniable is that the medical staff looked up to this petite woman and obeyed her commands, no matter how unconventional they were.

On one of her visits to check on a patient after emergency surgery, Mrs. Lubling took in the woman's weakness and pallor and pronounced, "You need a blood transfusion." When Dr. Clarel Antoine came to the room on his daily rounds, the woman told him, "Miriam Lubling was here and she thinks I need a transfusion."

"Well, tell me, dear," Dr. Antoine said, "who are you going to be listening to, Dr. Lubling or me?"

But the funny thing was that the doctors did in fact listen to her

— against their instincts, against hospital protocol, and sometimes against their own better judgment.

She nurtured her relationships with the medical staff — doctors, secretaries, nurses, even hospital guards — through holiday gifts. And not just any gifts: her motto was "*di shenster un di bester* — the nicest and the best," and she aimed for that standard in everything she did.

Using her connections in the *frum* community, she approached store owners and importers, and collected donations of crystals, electronics, perfumes, and gadgets. In fact, the owner of 47th Street Photo told his staff, "Whenever Mrs. Lubling comes into the store, fill up bags with whatever merchandise she chooses, and don't take a penny." They all knew the gifts had a higher purpose.

Mrs. Lubling's dear friends and neighbors Rabbi Yehuda and Mrs. Malky Weinberg, who lived in an apartment on the floor beneath hers, still remember the tractor-trailers that used to pull up outside their home every year before the December holiday season. Long before Amazon delivery trucks became part of the landscape, Mrs. Lubling's neighbors gaped as the drivers unloaded boxes and boxes of expensive electronics, cobalt tableware, perfumes, crystal dishes — thousands of dollars' worth of gifts — all for Mrs. Lubling to gift to others as an expression of *hakaras hatov*.

Along with the cadre of volunteers Mrs. Lubling had drafted for this project, the Weinberg children carried the boxes upstairs. Then they helped Mrs. Lubling quickly and efficiently sort them into piles. "These are for the secretaries," she said as she directed her youthful helpers, "and these are for the doormen. We gave the nurses crystal last year, so let's give them perfume this time. And here, I want this doctor to get the camcorder, he likes electronics — put it here."

When the children wondered why she had to give out so many gifts, she told them, "*Dus zennen de shlisalach*, these are the keys, that will open the doors for people who need help."

Mrs. Lubling's daughter Peshi once questioned why she was bringing a camcorder — then a new and trendy device — to a wealthy doctor. "You think he can't afford it?" she asked. "Does he really need you to buy it for him?"

To which Mrs. Lubling answered pragmatically, "Of course he can afford it. But if I buy it for him, he'll remember me."

Before Pesach, she distributed shemurah matzah and wine to all the Jewish doctors, some of whom looked forward all year to those crunchy round matzos that tasted like tradition.

The gifts weren't just a once-yearly token, and they weren't a mere formality or bribe. They were a tangible expression of the genuine gratitude that Mrs. Lubling felt toward the doctors. It was a real relationship, with the giving going both ways.

One of her drivers remembers delivering a gift to the mother of a doctor — this mother helped Mrs. Lubling connect to her son whenever she needed a quick appointment, and Mrs. Lubling wanted to show her appreciation.

Once she escorted an elderly man to the doctor's appointment she had arranged, carrying an envelope of cash and a box of pizza. "This is for your services," she told the doctor, handing him the envelope, "and this" — she put the box down on the desk — "is your lunch."

She knew which nurses liked chocolate, which appreciated a creamy cheesecake, and which couldn't turn down a caramel log from Seigelman's specialty bakery. She even discovered that one doctor had a hankering for duck.

The unusual discovery had a backstory: Mrs. Lubling had just established a relationship with Dr. Patrick O'Leary, a prestigious spinal surgeon whose patients included celebrity sports stars from the Mets and the Knicks. For years, he'd been considered "untouchable" by *frum* medical advocates. Somehow she breached the barriers and found a path to his heart — and surgery calendar.

As Mrs. Lubling steadily thawed the ice encasing the celebrity physician, she encouraged him to shmooze about his mother. "My mother made a great duck," he said.

Mrs. Lubling didn't waste a moment. That very day, she called Hudi Silber, who managed Boro Park's Khal Chassidim catering hall. "Hudi, I'm sending you *drei katchkes* — three ducks — from the butcher on 13th Avenue. Roast them and pack them up, and send them to the hospital. And make sure they are delicious!" she cautioned.

When Mrs. Lubling brought the fragrant offering to the sophisticated surgeon, he wept from emotion. "Just like my mother's," he said.

Sometimes the gifts Mrs. Lubling provided were intangible but just as powerful: a listening ear and empathetic heart. She connected with the nurses on an intimate level, and knew which nurse was going through a divorce and which needed money. She offered effusive compliments to the orderly who'd just gotten a haircut, along with empathy and advice for the secretary going through a hard time with a troubled teenager.

In September 2001, pediatric neurosurgeon Dr. Fred Epstein suffered a traumatic head injury during a bike accident. He spent the next twenty-six days in a coma. Mrs. Lubling kicked into high gear, appealing to family and friends to daven for "Fred ben Leah." "He helped so many people, he did so much for us, it's our responsibility to daven for him!" she said.

(Dr. Epstein fought hard for many months to recover from the injury. While he never returned to the operating theater, he did resume teaching, and helped colleagues around the world by providing guidance and consultations.)

Gifts and compliments never hurt, but doctors quickly learned that it was worthwhile to accommodate Mrs. Lubling for a more practical reason: she was, in the most literal sense, good for business. When she saw that a doctor achieved the desired results, she brought other patients. Not only that, she made sure that every patient she brought had insurance, or some other means of payment. So doctors understood that Mrs. Lubling was a woman who could bring them work — and work that paid.

The hospital administration realized this as well, and in both 1992 and 2002, they hosted official hospital receptions honoring Mrs. Lubling for her devoted service. Then, in 2002 they decided that a person of Mrs. Lubling's stature would be a valuable addition to the Board, which was lacking a member solely focused on patient care. Shortly thereafter, she was nominated as a trustee of the NYU Medical Center.

When the secretary noted that it was standard practice for new members to donate or raise a quarter of a million dollars, several members responded that with all the patients she brought NYU, Mrs. Lubling netted the hospital more than that. And so she was elected by a unanimous vote as a hospital trustee, and an associate trustee on the Patient Quality Assurance Operations Committee.

For the rest of her life, Mrs. Lubling proudly wore her board ID badge on a chain around her neck as she made her daily rounds. She knew the badge would ensure her the respect and cooperation of the staff, to better service her patients.

During the years that she served on the Board, she developed close relationships with several influential board members, especially with famed philanthropist Mr. Thomas Tisch. Mr. Tisch recognized Mrs. Lubling as a treasured asset of the hospital — a trusted ally who looked out for her people and brought NYU valuable business as she did so. In a sign of that respect, whenever she was invited to attend board meetings, he made sure that trays of special kosher food were brought in.

As a hospital trustee, Mrs. Lubling was also invited to attend the yearly graduation ceremonies of NYU's medical school. The first time she was invited, she was awarded an honorary degree of her own and was bedecked with a cap and gown. Every year after that — even when her advanced age made it difficult for her to get around — she showed up at those graduations, sitting proudly on the dais with the requisite cap and gown. Her children couldn't quite hide their embarrassment at the yearly charade. "Ima, why do you have to wear that silly hat?" they asked her.

"I wear it," she explained, "because I want all those new doctors to remember this face when I show up in their offices next year and ask them to help my cousins!"

Along with the steady flow of patients, the doctors also valued Mrs. Lubling's respect for their hard-won expertise. They quickly

After she was awarded an honorary degree by NYU's medical school, Mrs. Lubling showed up at every graduation bedecked in a cap and gown. "This way all the new doctors will remember me when I ask them to help my cousins."

grasped that she was a discerning woman who valued quality care, that she followed up after appointments and surgeries to ascertain the results.

Dr. Leon Pachter, chairman of the Department of Surgery at NYU, worked with Mrs. Lubling for decades. Of all the professionals and organizations who referred patients to him, she was the only one who consistently followed up on each procedure. "Sometimes it was that afternoon, sometimes the next day — and sometimes she was standing there outside the operating room, waiting for a report."

In the busy world of hospital care, with constant pressure and turnover, professional excellence and personal attention aren't always noticed. But Mrs. Lubling noticed — and rewarded — the truly superior doctors, and it made them all stand a little taller.

Dr. Pachter cannot remember a single time that she questioned his medical judgment. "In the thirty-five years that I had the *zechus* to work with her, she never once asked me why I was doing operation X over Y," he says.

She held "her doctors" to high standards, but if they met her expectations, she would extend them abiding respect. That respect became a two-way dynamic. Douglas Jablon, the longtime vice president of Patient Relations at Maimonides Medical Center, watched Mrs. Lubling in action for decades. She sniffed out the good doctors not just by bedside manner, but by results. "You loved her," he says. "But when she walked in, you knew you had to produce. She demanded that."

Dr. Patrick J. Lamparello originally trained to become a cardiac surgeon. Then he discovered the transformative power of vascular surgery, a new specialty that used minimally invasive procedures to treat a range of problems inside the narrow byways of the blood vessels. Dr. Lamparello switched tracks, gaining proficiency in the fine art of repairing and refining the crucial network of arteries and veins that transport blood throughout the human body. He soon became a renowned vascular surgeon in NYU.

"I remember the first day I met Mrs. Lubling," he says. "I was a very young doctor, and my senior doctor was in the OR. She walked right into the OR and sat down to talk to him right there — that was my introduction to her."

He learned very quickly that she wouldn't take no for an answer. If he was ever skeptical about treatment, doubting whether a patient could really hope for a good outcome, Mrs. Lubling urged him onward. "Give him a chance," she beseeched. "If it doesn't work, you'll send him on, but at least you'll know that you tried."

"She believed in life," he says simply. "That's what was most important to her."

One memorable day, Mrs. Lubling asked Dr. Lamparello to accompany her to the chassidic village of New Square, to make a rare house call. "The Grand Rabbi of the Skverer chassidim, a very holy man, needs an expert vascular surgeon," she said. "You are my choice — not only because of your expertise, but also because you care so much about each patient."

Needless to say, Dr. Lamparello was honored to make the trip, and he became the personal physician of the Skverer Rebbe.

Famed oncologist Dr. Yashar Hirshaut, the Torah-observant physician known as an indefatigable champion of even the sickest patients, saw Mrs. Lubling as the representative of the greater *frum* community. Over the course of several decades, he partnered with her to get the best care for their people.

Her first step, he observed, was to identify her allies. He noticed the way Mrs. Lubling kept her ear tuned to the frequencies of the medical world, and how she homed in on those doctors who practiced more aggressive, successful approaches.

Once she learned which doctors didn't give up easily, she channeled that knowledge into referrals and unspoken expectations. She set in motion a trend, Dr. Hirshaut says, in which the medical and Orthodox communities became more connected and more attuned to one another.

"The medical world appreciated that here was a therapeutic community striving for the best outcome," he says. "There was this attitude of mutual appreciation — Mrs. Lubling for the doctors who kept exploring new ways to help patients, and the doctors for Mrs. Lubling who never gave up."

One of those doctors is OB-GYN Dr. Clarel Antoine, born in Haiti, educated in Columbia University, and revered in *frum* homes in Williamsburg, Boro Park, and Lakewood for his skillful and compassionate handling of high-risk pregnancies. For thousands of *frum* women, Dr. Antoine was the Divine emissary who brought their new babies safely into the world. And it was Mrs. Lubling who made the connection.

Dr. Antoine came from a deeply religious background and had studied for the priesthood. Then his mother encouraged him to consider medicine. He traveled to the United States in 1966 and attended Columbia University's medical school, specializing in maternal-fetal medicine and completing a fellowship in high-risk pregnancies. He steadily acquired a new identity as a promising clinician — but still held on to his firm religious principles.

Dr. Antoine began working in NYU in 1979, but Mrs. Lubling

Dr. Clarel Antoine considered it an honor and privilege to see patients referred by Mrs. Lubling.

"discovered" him in the '90s. For decades, conventional medical wisdom dictated that women who had undergone two or three Caesarean sections could not safely deliver another baby. But Mrs. Lubling learned that Dr. Antoine had the surgical skills to help these women safely have the large families they dreamed of — and the religious sensitivity to value every new life brought to the world.

Mrs. Lubling also connected the soft-spoken doctor with his trademark bowtie and Creole lilt to several leading *poskim*, notably the Tosher Dayan, Rav Binyomin Landau. Like his patients, these *poskim* quickly learned to appreciate Dr. Antoine's medical perspective, and to view him as a trusted professional and partner who lived and acted in concert with their values.

"You will never have children," several leading doctors told Debby, a young *frum* woman. Debby had been exposed to a potent hormonal drug in utero, resulting in a medical condition that caused severe structural damage to her reproductive system.

Debby finally found a fertility specialist who agreed to take on her case. She was thrilled to discover that her dream of becoming a mother looked like it might come true. Then, in the early months, the specialist told her to find another doctor. "I'm a fertility doctor; I don't deal with advanced pregnancy," he said. "You'll have to find someone else to take you to the finish line."

Debby didn't know where to turn. She knew her situation would be extremely complicated, and that she would need a very supportive, skilled doctor who was willing to think out of the box. But all the conventional doctors she had approached previously had discouraged outright her desire for a family.

Then a family friend remembered a certain doctor that Mrs. Lubling was recommending — a very sympathetic obstetrician who took on the most difficult cases with great skill and confidence. "Go see Dr. Antoine," she urged Debby. "If anyone can help you, he can."

Dr. Antoine took on Debby's case. He tried his best to stabilize her damaged reproductive system so she could carry the fetus until viability. Unfortunately, she had found him too late. At twenty-four weeks, she delivered a stillborn.

Debby didn't give up. When she was next expecting, she visited Dr. Antoine right at the outset. He performed several innovative and daring interventions that empowered her compromised body to carry through to thirty-five weeks, after which she delivered a healthy child.

Dr. Antoine later accompanied Debby through another gestation, even more complicated than the previous one. Thanks to his devoted care, the woman once written off as a hopeless case is now the mother of a beautiful family.

All the doctors who worked with Mrs. Lubling appreciated the way she followed up after appointments and surgeries to ascertain the outcome of their care. When it came to Dr. Antoine, the results were obvious: healthy mothers, healthy babies, large and happy families. Soon Dr. Antoine became one of Mrs. Lubling's most-referred doctors — she spoke weekly if not daily to him — and he willingly gave up lunch breaks, dinnertime, or precious hours of sleep, making the drive from his home in Englewood, New Jersey, back to the hospital whenever she asked him to help a patient in need.

In the end, though, what motivated the staff to expedite appointments, rush a surgery, or find a better room for Mrs. Lubling's patients wasn't the gifts. It wasn't the financial payoff. It wasn't even the acknowledgment of their expertise. It was their realization that here was a woman dedicating much of her life to a single pursuit with zero self-interest.

For all the idealism that goes into the medical field, a hospital is a moneymaking venture. Yet Mrs. Lubling gained nothing and took no kickbacks for her referrals. Her hours in the hospital yielded her neither money nor career advancement. This was a woman whose only goal was to help people in need. The doctors, secretaries, and nurses couldn't help but be awed and moved by the most altruistic person they had ever met. How can you say no to such a woman?

"You have to understand how the doctors viewed her," Douglas Jablon says. "Yes, she brought them business. Yes, she got things done. But more than anything, they saw her as a partner with G-d in healing."

"G-d put her in a league of her own," Dr. Antoine says. "She helped many thousands of women and their families. She was a G-d-given gift to the community and world, who just wanted to help make people healthier and their families happier.

"It was an honor and a privilege that she chose my consultation and chose me as one of the messengers she associated with, because she trusted that I would provide quality, compassionate care for the people she brought.

"And," he marvels, "she got nothing out of it — except making sure her people's needs for good care were met."

Vascular surgeon Dr. Lamparello easily pinpoints the reason he respected Mrs. Lubling: "She never advocated for herself, only for someone else."

As Dr. Lamparello gained experience and seniority, he became a "favorite" of Mrs. Lubling, who knew she could rely on him to expedite appointments and procedures for her patients. His secretaries learned to put through her calls and to reshuffle the doctor's schedule at her command.

But the younger, newer doctors were puzzled by Dr. Lamparello's esteem for her. He was an elite physician at one of the world's top medical centers, and here he was taking instructions from an elderly religious woman whose English was barely intelligible.

"Who is this woman — some donor? Why does everyone listen to her?" they asked him.

"I'll tell you why," he replied. "Because all she wants is to help people."

CHAPTER 9
No Is Not an Option

Mrs. Lubling lived in the United States for decades, but she was never able to shed her accent. Not that she didn't try. In addition to attending night classes at the Bank Street College of Education, she also took private lessons in proper pronunciation. She then practiced her English in front of a mirror, positioning her mouth as she'd been directed so that it

Mrs. Lubling spoke rapidly, with a strong European accent — but somehow all the doctors obeyed her every command.

would produce a proper American "apple" instead of "eppel." But when it came to real life, her brain worked very quickly, and the words tended to pour out before she could bother focusing on pronunciation. "Apple" remained "eppel."

Still, for some reason no one could understand, the doctors obeyed her rapid-fire, accented commands. When she finished her phone conversations — she moved on so quickly to her next task that she often left them with a dial tone — they invariably adjusted their schedules to accommodate her latest request.

A doctor once confided in Ohel president Moishe Hellman, a close friend and supporter of Mrs. Lubling, "I say yes to everything she asks for two reasons. One, I know she's looking out for others, not herself. And second, I don't quite understand what she's asking for — so I have no choice but to agree."

Dr. Clarel Antoine quickly learned that it was pointless to say no, because Mrs. Lubling called his private number whenever she had an urgent case. "Dr. Antoine, are you in the hospital?" she asked. "I have a lady here whose baby is in a breech position, and I need you to deliver her. She's on her way to the hospital now and her name is Berkowitz. So you will meet her in the labor room, yes?"

Mrs. Lubling rarely gave Dr. Antoine a chance to respond — once she relayed the essential points of a case, she hung up and turned to her next task.

If Dr. Antoine attempted, ever so delicately, to explain that he was too busy to fit in another patient, she plowed on with a "thank you-thank you-thank you, Doctor," then there was a dial tone — and before he knew it, Mrs. Lubling would appear in his office, patient in tow.

Dr. Martin Kahn, a top cardiologist at NYU, once ruefully told Chanoch, "Tell your mother that she messes up my day! I have all these appointments scheduled, and then she calls and I have to shuffle everything to get in her patients." But his respect, even awe, for Mrs. Lubling was clear — he spoke to her in the third person and if ever a secretary kept her waiting, he'd admonish her, "The 'G-d' is here, how can you make her wait?"

Once, after receiving yet another pre-Pesach gift, Dr. Pachter told Mrs. Lubling, "You always bring me these round matzos and never ask for anything in return. What can I give you?"

Mrs. Lubling jumped on the opportunity. "Give me your personal cellphone number," she said.

"I came to regret it," Dr. Pachter confesses with a smile. "Only my family and close staff have that number — but once Mrs. Lubling had it, she would call me on a Saturday night and ask me to do a standard hernia operation when there were eight other doctors on my team all perfectly capable of doing it instead."

There's an NYU legend about a doctor who jumped into his closet when he heard Mrs. Lubling was headed his way. He simply couldn't fit in another patient — but he couldn't say no to Mrs. Lubling.

But Mrs. Lubling had her ways to approach even recalcitrant doctors. When she wanted a favor from renowned gastroenterologist Dr. Charles Friedlander, she'd enter his office through the back door and seat herself in his chair, waiting patiently if pointedly for him to finish in the examining room. Dr. Friedlander only startled slightly when he returned to his office to find this woman in a neat suit and pearls seated in his chair — they had a warm, respectful relationship that could accommodate some quirks.

She even went so far as to discuss a complex case with a doctor she trusted, and then asked him bluntly, "So tell me, Doctor, are you the right one for this surgery, or should we try the other surgeon down the hall?"

No one else could do that.

Mrs. Perie Hirshaut, the wife of prominent oncologist Dr. Yashar Hirshaut, was one of those trusted contacts who could never say no to this diminutive woman she privately termed "The Cannon." Although Dr. Hirshaut employs an office staff in Manhattan, Mrs. Hirshaut runs the back end from her home — dealing with purchasing agents, bookkeeping, payroll, and the financials. She does not handle appointments; the doctor employs a very efficient secretary who deals with that on site, in the Manhattan office.

"Back then our secretary was not a gentle woman," Mrs. Hirshaut acknowledges. "Some people even called her 'The Dictator' — although she wasn't mean, just very firm about not allowing a busy practice to descend into chaos."

When Mrs. Lubling wanted Dr. Hirshaut to see a patient, she circumvented the unyielding secretary and instead called Mrs. Hirshaut at home. "Hello-dahlink-how-are-you-today?" she asked, all in one breath. Then came a stream of words, so fast as to be almost unintelligible, concluding with, "Where is the doctor? My patient needs an appointment."

Mrs. Hirshaut then dropped her usual duties and got to work scheduling an appointment for the next day or two. There was no way she could turn down Mrs. Lubling.

Over the years, the business relationship blossomed into a true friendship. Mrs. Lubling, already an ardent admirer of Dr. Hirshaut's medical prowess and strong moral backbone, became a close friend of his wife and an honorary member of the family who attended all their *simchos* and danced in the inner circle with true joy.

While she couldn't always understand Mrs. Lubling's accented English, Mrs. Hirshaut marveled at her youthful attitude. Here was a great-grandmother at ease with a cellphone long before it became widespread, a woman of the older generation who embraced technological advances to her advantage. A woman who, after losing her husband, refused to retreat inward but instead increased her activism to ever larger circles of beneficiaries. And she had absolutely no fear — she could talk to doctors of every caliber, and knew what to say and how to say it in order to get results.

As she escorted her patients through their consultations and treatments, Mrs. Lubling realized that many families encountered real difficulty navigating the stairs of the eighteen-story hospital on Shabbos. To her, the solution was simple: ask the hospital administration to convert one elevator to a Shabbos elevator.

The senior vice president in charge of NYU's facilities received the request incredulously. "We're running a hospital!" he said. "We need to make this place as accessible as possible to as many people as we can. How can we effectively paralyze an elevator for twenty-five hours of the busiest visiting day of the week?"

The same response greeted Mrs. Lubling's request for a dedicated room to serve as her bikur cholim headquarters. How and why would a busy hospital devote a precious room to storing and distributing kosher goodies?

But both the Shabbos elevator and bikur cholim room came to be. Mrs. Lubling simply wouldn't take no for a response; she took the matter up the executive ladder until she got the answer she wanted. And once NYU set the example, most of the major New York hospitals followed.

Mrs. Lubling used the same insistence to establish "bikur cholim apartments" — apartments near the hospital where families of patients could stay over Shabbos. The Rivkah Laufer Bikur Cholim pioneered this innovation by renting two nearby apartments for relatives: one for men, and one for women. The apartments provided clean, comfortable linens and full Shabbos meals. And they set a standard that many other organizations have followed, in hospitals across the country.

Today, thanks to the precedent she set, thousands of Shabbos-observant families know there will be comfortable accommodations for family nearby, and a fully-stocked bikur cholim room with *kiddush*, challah, hot meals and fresh snacks awaiting them when they spend Shabbos in the hospital.

Late one Chanukah night, on a dark Boro Park street, an elderly Reb Nechemia Werdiger was hit by a car. His son Reb Shlomo Werdiger was immediately summoned to the scene.

"The first call I made was to Mrs. Lubling," he remembers. Their families had always enjoyed a close relationship, and he knew that "Tante Miriam" would ensure his father got the best care — even if it was close to midnight.

"Tante Miriam, it's Shloime. My father was just in a car accident," he explained. "Hatzolah came right away, and they think that everything is okay, but just in case, we should have a medical professional rule out any trauma to his head."

"I will make sure he gets checked by the best doctor!" Mrs. Lubling said. "Go to NYU right now, and I will take care."

Then she grabbed the other phone and Mr. Werdiger listened raptly as a conversation unfolded on speakerphone.

"Hello, Doctor, this is Miriam Lubling," Mrs. Lubling said. "I need you to help me with something very important. My cousin was in an accident, and we need you to come to the hospital right away to examine him."

"But Mrs. Lubling, I'm already in bed!" Mr. Werdiger heard the doctor protest. "Let someone else check him; whoever's on call will do a fine job."

"I don't care if you're in bed," Mrs. Lubling pushed back. "I don't even care if you're in pajamas. You're coming to the hospital right now to examine my cousin!"

When the Werdigers pulled up at the hospital entrance, the esteemed doctor was there waiting for them — along with the small, determined woman who saw every task through to completion.

(More than a decade after Mrs. Lubling's passing, Mr. Werdiger — much like that doctor — is still obeying her personal request. He serves as the long-term benefactor of a car service that transports patients to doctor's appointments or hospital treatments when volunteer drivers are not available.)

When Leah Horowitz, the daughter of Mrs. Lubling's kindergarten partner Rebbetzin Teitelbaum, was a young newlywed, she suffered from a paralyzed vocal cord. An initial scan revealed a shadow that suggested a possible mass, and a second, more sophisticated scan was recommended. At the time, CT scans and MRIs were very new technology, and appointments weren't easily available. What to do?

Simple: call Mrs. Lubling. It took almost no time before Mrs. Lubling called back, saying, "No problem; tomorrow morning you have an appointment with Dr. Mark Persky, the famous Head and Neck surgeon at NYU."

The next afternoon, Leah got a call from her doctor's secretary, with a strange request. "Hi, this is Betty from Dr. Persky's office. Can you please tell Mrs. Lubling to stop calling us? She's been calling every ten minutes to find out the results of your CT scan."

But soon enough Leah got another phone call — this one from Mrs. Lubling. "Everything's okay, Lai'ah," she said. "The doctor said he'll call you later, but I want you should know."

That night, Dr. Persky called Leah and told her the full story. "I had just finished a surgery, and came out of the OR to scrub up for the next one. And who was standing there in the scrubbing room? Mrs. Lubling, that's who."

Mrs. Lubling pulled out a CT image and shoved it at the doctor. "This is my daughter's scan," she said. "I need you should look at it."

"Mrs. Lubling, I'm between surgeries," the doctor protested.

"So?" she countered.

He put down his gloves. "Okay, show me the scans."

When Shani Grossman started complaining of headaches in the 1980s, her mother took her to their local pediatrician in Boro Park. The pediatrician — a very responsible practitioner — examined the nine-year-old gently but thoroughly.

"Everything looks fine," he said. "I'm going to do some bloodwork, but I don't think there's anything to worry about."

The bloodwork came in just about normal, so the pediatrician wasn't alarmed. Shani went off to summer camp. The headaches, however, came along with her. Even in the fresh mountain air, they persisted and came more frequently.

"You really should check this out," the camp nurse told the Grossmans. "Something's not right."

The Grossmans were familiar with Mrs. Lubling's extraordinary network of medical referrals, so they immediately turned to her for help.

"I will make you an appointment with Dr. Irving Fish at NYU," she told them. "He's a top pediatric neurologist — if something is wrong with Shani, he'll find it."

When Dr. Fish examined the little girl, he saw no reason for alarm. As a precaution, however, he sent her for an MRI. That's how the Grossmans learned the terrifying news: their beautiful daughter had a growth in her brain.

Mrs. Lubling swung into action, referring them to a renowned pediatric neurosurgeon, Dr. Jeffrey Wissof, for an immediate appointment. Dr. Wissof — a student and later colleague of the famed Dr. Fred Epstein — was pretty confident the tumor was benign. "Really, it shouldn't be any more threatening than a green pea," he told the Grossmans, "but it's in a bad place and must come out, because of the damage it can cause to Shani's brain."

The Grossmans suddenly found themselves in a strange new reality. All mundane concerns — home, work, and the other children — faded in comparison to their fear as they prepared their daughter for an extremely delicate surgery in the most sensitive organ of the body. Throughout that period, Mrs. Lubling stayed on top of the case, involving herself in all aspects of the upcoming surgery.

The surgery went well, and Shani spent the next few days in the pediatric ICU under careful supervision. Brain surgery can affect function, mobility, and sensation throughout the entire body, and the post-op period is a very critical time.

Eventually, Shani received the all-clear to leave the ICU for a regular bed in the pediatric ward.

The Grossmans followed along as Shani was transferred down the long corridor to her new room far beyond the nurse's station. "Here you go," the orderly said, nudging open a door and wheeling the bed into a cramped open space nearby, right near the bathroom.

The Grossmans took a quick look at Shani's new surroundings, and they were horrified. The other patient in the room — whose bed was near the window — was, unfortunately, in the final stages of a battle with terminal cancer. The bathroom was covered with the sad signs of her condition. It wasn't just unappealing; it was terribly demoralizing.

Mr. Grossman went straight to the nurses' station to plead for

Shani. "Our daughter was transferred to a room here on the ward, after brain surgery. But the room... I know my daughter. She's been through a lot, she's been so brave — but she's not going to be able to recover her strength and optimism in this kind of environment. Can you please try to find her a different room?"

"Sorry," the nurse said bluntly. "There's nothing we can do. You'll have to make the best of it."

Mr. Grossman returned to his wife and daughter. "We'll wait for the next shift and try again," he promised.

Less than thirty minutes later, the familiar figure of Mrs. Miriam Lubling swept into the room. "How are you, how's Shani?"

In muted voices, the Grossmans explained the situation. "We're hoping the nurses on the next shift will be more flexible," they said.

"No, we're not waiting for the next shift," Mrs. Lubling proclaimed. "Come with me; we're going to check all the rooms on the floor and find a better place for Shani."

Mr. Grossman followed Mrs. Lubling's orders. They set out together and surveyed the ward, peeking into each room and seeking a possible better space for Shani. Soon enough they found a room with an empty spot. It was the kind of spot Mrs. Lubling liked — adjacent to the window, overlooking the river, with lots of sunshine streaming through.

"Come," she said. As Mr. Grossman followed Mrs. Lubling back to Shanis' room, he wondered how she would convince the nurses to agree to the transfer. But she had a different plan.

She grabbed one end of Shani's bed. "Here," she gestured, "you take one side, I'm taking the other. We are going to move her right now."

"But Mrs. Lubling," Mrs. Grossman said in shock, "we didn't get any clearance from the nurses!"

"Don't worry, I'll deal with them," Mrs. Lubling answered with complete confidence. "Right now, let's get Shani to a better place."

And with that, they began rolling the bed out the door, into the hall, walking with brisk determination toward the room she had selected. Shani was now in a room more suited for her recovery.

The next day while on her "rounds," Mrs. Lubling came to visit

Shani, presenting her with a jumbo-sized doll. The Grossmans dubbed the doll "Boobah Miriam," in tribute to the indomitable woman who wouldn't allow hospital staff or protocol to keep her from easing her patients' recovery.

As a proud student of Sarah Schenirer, Mrs. Lubling maintained uncompromising religious standards in every environment. She spent thirty years on the floor with doctors and never shook hands with any men, no matter what. When she ate, she sat down, made a *berachah*, and then when she finished, she *bentched* slowly and deliberately. If a phone call came in during *bentching*, she kept her slow, deliberate pace — she knew her priorities. She davened three times a day. And whenever she had a free moment, she opened a *Tehillim*.

Yet the same woman who slowly and carefully pronounced every word of *bentching* was quick-thinking and gutsy when it came to her patients. After the secretary of a famous neurosurgeon refused to expedite an appointment for one of Mrs. Lubling's patients, she took the elevator to the twelfth floor and waited until the surgeon appeared. She straightened her necklace, pulled herself up to her full height, approached the famous doctor, and asked why his staff refused to accommodate her.

He tried to brush her off with some vague answer, but Mrs. Lubling didn't do vague. She pressed on unapologetically. "You know, Doctor, this is so urgent!" she insisted. "My patient can't wait! He needs the appointment tomorrow."

The doctor tried again to shift Mrs. Lubling back to his secretary, but she remained very politely but very firmly immovable. There was no way out and nowhere to escape — Mrs. Lubling was blocking the elevator door.

The doctor had no choice but to accede. "Tell your patient to come to my office tomorrow at 8:30 in the morning," he said.

A wide-eyed volunteer who'd seen the entire exchange asked her, "Are you going to buy something for him, some sort of gift, to make up for nudging him so much?"

Mrs. Lubling snapped back, "Absolutely not!" she said. "He should be buying *me* something!"

In the early years of the twenty-first century, Rabbi Boruch Ber Bender began to dream of a new umbrella organization that would be a one-stop address for the religious community of New York's Five Towns, where he lives. Too many Jews were drowning when crisis hit, unsure of whom to call and how to access the right resources and solutions. His dream organization would help people navigate every sort of crisis, be it medical, emotional, financial, or logistical.

He realized early on that a significant part of his work would involve medical referrals, and so he began to research the field. As he heard story after story about *frum* medical advocates, the name Mrs. Miriam Lubling stood out. No one else seemed to be quite as fearless and persistent as this elderly woman who could get New York's elite doctors to postpone dinner or even vacation when she deemed it necessary.

Shortly after Rabbi Bender launched his organization, a friend of his hosted a fundraising event in the Five Towns, and Mrs. Lubling was slated to attend. Rabbi Bender could barely contain his excitement when he finally met the woman he privately considered one of the *frum* world's top celebrities. He folded his 6'2" frame into a chair, sat down next to the petite Mrs. Lubling, and introduced himself.

"I heard a story," he said, "about the time that you barged into an operating room during surgery to check on a patient. Did that really happen?"

Mrs. Lubling smiled and gave a chuckle. She didn't confirm the story, but she didn't deny it either. "We do whatever it takes," she said.

Rabbi Bender then asked her to describe her methodology. He had just launched an organization to help people, he explained, and he wanted to know how Mrs. Lubling got all those doctors to bend their schedules. Her response was simple and very modest: "Just do for people, and everything will work out."

About two weeks later, Rabbi Bender got a call: a local woman had recently been diagnosed with a hernia. Hernia surgery is usually quite standard, but this case would necessitate a complex procedure, because there was a suspicious mass alongside the hernia. The best doctor for this particular procedure worked at NYU. Could Rabbi Bender arrange for him to perform the surgery?

Rabbi Bender called Mrs. Lubling and described the situation.

"Okay," she said. "What's the problem?"

"I don't have a relationship with the doctor," Rabbi Bender said.

"What day is it today?" Mrs. Lubling thought aloud. "Tuesday, right? He's operating today."

"Okay, so what do we do?" he asked, waiting for the *frum* doyenne of medical advocacy to share her sophisticated strategy.

"You go down to NYU," she said simply, "wait outside the OR, and when the doctor comes out, tell him he has to do the procedure for your patient."

It sounded like a dubious plan at best to Rabbi Bender, but this was the expert speaking. He looked up the doctor's photo online, drove to NYU, and waited in the lobby until he saw the familiar face. Then he introduced himself, described the woman's case, and mentioned Mrs. Lubling.

A flash of deference and respect crossed the doctor's face. Apparently "Lubling" was the magic word. The doctor instructed Rabbi Bender to have the woman report to the ER the next day, and he would perform her surgery.

Today Rabbi Bender is widely known as the president of Achiezer, the dream organization that has become a most impressive reality. He has helped tens of thousands of people since its official launch in 2008. Specialists and surgeons recognize his number and often accede to his requests at once. But when they don't, he remembers the short woman with no medical training who never took no for an answer, and as he makes the trip to Manhattan to corner a doctor in the hallway, he thinks, "Mrs. Lubling did this — you can, too."

Rabbi Dovid Mendlowitz is a longtime Boro Park resident with a warm heart and open home. For decades, he has hosted fellow Jews who travel from Eretz Yisrael to New York to benefit from the advanced medical treatments available in Manhattan, and he often worked closely with Mrs. Lubling to arrange the details of their care.

Rabbi Mendlowitz was once asked to host a child from Eretz Yisrael who required treatment for a brain tumor. The family situation was complex, and there was no money to cover the treatment. Rabbi Mendlowitz called Mrs. Lubling. "Send me the X-rays," she commanded.

Within hours, she called him back. "I sent the scans to Dr. Epstein," she said, "and he will do the surgery. How soon can you get the child here?"

The night before the little patient's arrival, Mrs. Lubling called Rabbi Mendlowitz. "I want you to come to the airport with me at 5 o'clock tomorrow morning," she said. "Take along your *tallis* and *tefillin*, because we're going straight to the hospital."

And that's exactly what happened. Mrs. Lubling whisked the new arrival into a car and by 8:30 a.m., she had already directed their little group to Dr. Epstein's secretary. "Good morning, dahlink!" she greeted the secretary like an old friend.

"Good morning, Mrs. Lubling," the woman said warmly — she was, in fact, a good friend at this point. "I'm so sorry, but the doctor's in a conference right now."

Mrs. Lubling loved a challenge. "Where's the conference?" she asked.

The secretary shrugged. "Why does it matter?" she asked, casually motioning down the hall.

"Come with me!" Mrs. Lubling commanded Rabbi Mendlowitz, as she tapped along the hall in her heels. Without missing a beat, she opened a door and entered the conference room.

Inside, doctors and residents were assembled around a table, notepads open, listening intently to Dr. Epstein, who was describing a complex case he was working on while pointing to MRI images projected onto the wall. Undeterred, Mrs. Lubling tapped to the front of the room.

"Dr. Epstein?" she said brightly.

The tall, lanky doctor stopped talking. He looked at her, then at the group of medical professionals who'd been hanging on to his every word. "I'm sorry," he told them. "You'll have to excuse me for a moment. This is The Angel. I have to talk to her."

In 1998, Dr. Epstein proved just how highly he regarded the commands of the "Angel." The story began on an autumn night in Jerusalem, when a twelve-year-old *cheder* boy woke up, moaning in pain.

"What's wrong, Binyamin?" his mother asked.

"My stomach," he said. "My stomach is hurting me so much!"

Chavi sat next to him and rubbed his stomach gently until the pain receded. She stumbled back to bed and figured she would let him sleep late the next morning. After a cup of tea, he would probably be ready to go to *cheder* as usual.

But the next night, the episode was repeated. Chavi made an appointment with their pediatrician, who gently examined Binyamin's stomach.

"He seems just fine," the pediatrician said. "Maybe he ate something he shouldn't have. Or maybe he's worried about an upcoming test in school? Lots of kids feel stomach pain when they're anxious." He patted the boy on the head and sent him home.

But the pain kept recurring — and getting worse. Chavi took Binyamin to a different doctor. This doctor, too, couldn't pinpoint any cause for the pain.

Chavi began to dread the nights. Binyamin's stomachaches became so severe that he couldn't lie on his back. He rolled himself up into a wretched ball and clenched his fists tight, trying not to wake the other children as the pain ripped through his body. Chavi piled pillows beneath and around him, hoping to cushion her son from the invisible monster that was torturing him.

After a few months of shattered sleep and one night of pain so intense that Binyamin almost ripped his sheet in desperation, she bundled him into a taxi and took him to the emergency room. The staff poked and prodded Binyamin, drawing blood, tracking his pulse, checking his appendix. At this point, Chavi was frantic that they find something, some cause for her son's suffering. But the doctor on call was skeptical.

"Kids complain about stomach pain all the time," he said. "And more often than not, the cause is emotional — they think they're feeling physical pain in the stomach but it's really because they're anxious or upset about something. We're going to order an MRI, but I'm warning you: if I don't see anything on the MRI, your son needs to see a psychologist."

MRI, short for Magnetic Resonance Imaging, is a sophisticated scan that utilizes magnetic fields and radio waves to "photograph" the inside of the body without any invasive or painful means. But it does require the patient to lie perfectly still inside a large tube for long periods of time while a technician operates the scan apparatus from outside the room.

Binyamin's pain was so intense that he simply could not lie in place for the duration of the MRI. "We'll schedule him for Wednesday in Hadassah-Ein Kerem," the doctor said. "On Wednesday we conduct MRIs for children — we anesthetize them before the scan, so they'll stay immobile."

That Wednesday, Chavi and her husband brought Binyamin in for the scan. For one blessed hour, he was anesthetized and free of pain. The staff remained poker-faced throughout the procedure, and Chavi wondered if she should, in fact, start researching child psychologists.

Late that afternoon, the family got a call. "Our radiologist read the MRI, and we want you to come down to discuss the results," they were commanded.

Binyamin wasn't suffering from an overabundance of nerves, or from emotional issues. He had an extremely rare and aggressive tumor growing inside his spinal cord. His prognosis was very bleak: without surgery to remove the tumor, it would steadily overtake the nerves in the spinal cord, causing paralysis and eventual death. But surgical excision of the tumor was not an option, they were told: the tumor extended up into the brainstem, which controls the body's vital functions — including respiration and cardiac function

— and it was impossible to operate in such a sensitive area.

The family immediately called Rabbi Elimelech Firer, the renowned Israeli medical advocate. "The doctors are telling us there is no way to operate on this tumor," they said, utterly broken. "The brainstem controls the body's breathing and heartbeat, and no doctor will dare open it up to operate."

"Actually, there is one doctor who will dare," Rabbi Firer said. "His name is Fred Epstein. He practices in NYU. For the past ten years, he's been perfecting an experimental technique with a device called the Cavitron that is able to access tumors inside the spinal cord without harming the essential nerves around them. You must get to New York as quickly as you can. Every hour is crucial."

The medical *askanim* reached out to Dr. Epstein's secretary, in an attempt to schedule an emergency surgery for Binyamin. "I'm so sorry," she said, "but the doctor is in Florida, on vacation. There's no way to reach him right now. You can try again in a week or two."

By Thursday morning, the entire extended family had gotten involved. Phone wires buzzed as they shared a desperate volley of updates and information. There had to be some way to get the doctor to see Binyamin! What could they do?

"Wait," one of Chavi's sisters-in-law said. "My mother has a friend who used to live in Tel Aviv. Now she lives in America, and she's very involved in bikur cholim. Her name is Miriam Lubling. Maybe she can help."

Mrs. Lubling was duly contacted, and she sprang into action.

First, she called Dr. Epstein's private phone. "Dr. Epstein," she said forcefully, "I know you are on vacation. But if you don't operate on this little boy, he will *never* be able to go on vacation. You must get on a plane and come right back to the hospital!"

Dr. Epstein couldn't refute her elegant logic. "Okay, Mrs. Lubling," he said. "You get the boy to New York, and I'll get on the plane."

Mrs. Lubling instructed the family to get on the next available flight, and she set to work. On Sunday morning, when the young patient landed in John F. Kennedy International Airport, an ambulance was waiting on the runway to transport him to a host family in Brooklyn. (Berachya Binik or Beinish Mandel, both devoted Hatzolah EMTs, were often contacted by Mrs. Lubling to transport patients from the airport directly to the hospital.)

The EMTs who gently transferred the little patient to a stretcher took note of his off-the-charts pain as they made the short trip: Binyamin could barely hold still as his father clutched him tightly, and with every rough turn or bump, a cry of agony burst through his tightly pressed lips.

"Mrs. Lubling," the driver reported to her, "we need a different way to get him to NYU tomorrow morning."

Early the next morning, while the Brooklyn sky was still dark, a Cadillac with tinted windows pulled up for Chavi, her husband, and Binyamin. They bundled Binyamin into the car and held their breath. Miraculously, the drive to Manhattan felt like one smooth, extended glide on a glass surface. Mrs. Lubling had thought of every detail.

Binyamin was directed to pre-op, but he refused the wheelchair he'd been offered — sitting was too painful. He could only stand, and the tumor was pressing so fiercely on his nerves that he tried to shift all his weight onto one foot. In the end, his father had to carry him through the endless hospital halls until they met the surgery team.

Reluctantly, Binyamin agreed to put on a hospital gown. "We're going to put this needle in your vein," the anesthesiologist explained, "and a medicine inside will drip slowly into your body. It will make you relax and fall asleep."

Chavi and her husband watched as Binyamin's muscles finally relaxed from the terrible, protracted pain of the last few months. Within a few minutes, he went under and was wheeled into the OR.

They watched as multiple nurses, orderlies, and doctors swarmed into the room where their son's spinal cord was to be opened and the monstrous invader to be excised. The staff seemed kind, but also very busy and official. "Where is Dr. Epstein?" Chavi begged. "They told us Dr. Epstein would do the surgery."

"Dr. Epstein isn't here," one of the nurses said. "Two of the doctors on his team are going to start the surgery."

"But they told us Dr. Epstein is the doctor we need!"

The nurse nodded sympathetically, clucked something reassuring, and then headed to the scrubbing station to wash up before entering the OR.

Chavi and her husband sank into the couch in the waiting area, bristling with tension and fear. They tried to focus on their *Tehillim*, but it was hard. What was happening to their son? Where was the promised doctor? How long would they have to wait for answers?

About an hour later, they heard brisk steps coming down the hall. A tall, lanky man with twinkling eyes and green clogs appeared.

"Are you Binyamin's parents?" he asked.

They nodded.

"Nice to meet you. I'm Dr. Epstein. You can call me Fred. Your son's spinal cord is open, and my team is reporting that the tumor is exposed. It looks just like it did in those scans that Mrs. Lubling sent, so we're going to proceed with our operating plan. The team is just about ready for me to come in and get rid of the nasty thing. I'm sorry I didn't get to meet you before your son went into the OR, but what could I do? I was still on the plane. As soon as it landed I came straight here, just as I promised Mrs. Lubling."

When Binyamin emerged from surgery, many hours later, he was completely immobilized. "Your son won't be able to move for the next while, but we got it," Dr. Epstein said confidently. "We got the whole thing out. We're sending it to the lab for testing, but from the looks of it, it's benign. This means that your son will need rehab and some physical therapy, but you have every reason to hope that he'll make a good recovery."

Three weeks later, Binyamin was on a plane back home. He worked very hard at his daily rehab sessions, and with the resilience and optimism of the young, he progressed from paralysis to a wheelchair to walking on his own. Today he is a healthy husband and father. If you look carefully, you might notice a slight limp when he walks, the result of minor nerve damage left by the tumor. That's the only evidence of the ultimatum Mrs. Lubling boldly delivered to Dr. Epstein, jolting him from his Florida vacation to the operating room so he could save a young boy.

CHAPTER 10
You Have to Help My Cousins

Each of Mrs. Lubling's grandchildren has experienced a variation of the same story. A child needed some sort of medical assessment, so Bobby Lubling was enlisted to make the appointment. The grandchild showed up, approached the secretary, and proudly introduced herself with what she thought was a surefire formula: "Hi, I have an appointment for two o'clock today — I'm Mrs. Lubling's grandchild."

The secretary inevitably grimaced.

"They all say that," came the answer.

Each of Mrs. Lubling's patients was hustled into his or her appointments by dint of being "my cousin" or "my grandchild" or "a very important rabbi." At first, the secretaries used to wonder how many cousins this one immigrant woman could possibly have. Then they understood that her use of the word wasn't quite in keeping with the dictionary definition. But with time, as they saw how much effort she devoted to these people she'd never met, they realized that she just had a very different concept of family. And so they goodheartedly accommodated her requests for her sisters, brothers, cousins — and the biggest rabbis in the world.

In a sort of self-fulfilling prophecy, some of the beneficiaries of her advocacy actually became true friends, pseudo-family. Though the circumstances that brought them together were the technicalities of appointments or surgeries, the ensuing bonds left them soul sisters or extended family with emotional ties that lasted long past the hospitalization.

Once, during her rounds, Mrs. Lubling met a young woman whose husband had been diagnosed with cancer two days earlier. He had just been admitted to a room, and they were trying to digest the news — what it would mean for their children, their finances, their future. Mrs. Lubling introduced herself and asked how she could help.

The woman shrugged. It was all so surreal, so overwhelming.

"Food, kosher food, that you for sure need," Mrs. Lubling said. "I will arrange food for you, I take care."

From that moment on, they never had to worry about kosher food. But that wasn't all. As the days went on and Mrs. Lubling became a steady, trusted presence, the young woman began to open up to this unanticipated confidante with her Yiddish-accented English.

"You know, my husband was admitted on Shabbos," she said. "We started out in the emergency room, and they realized pretty quickly that we were dealing with something big. But a few days earlier — on Wednesday — I had just found out that I'm expecting a baby. How — what — when…" she couldn't quite finish the question.

Mrs. Lubling patted her on the shoulder. "I take care," she said. "Here in NYU is the best obstetrician, Dr. Antoine. I will arrange for you to see him, right here in the same hospital as your husband. You won't have to leave him too long, even when you have appointments. You'll see, it will all work out."

During every round of treatment — throughout all six weeks of the hospital stays — Mrs. Lubling was there, with daily visits and constant encouragement. When the ICU doors were locked, she used her walker to bang on the door and get the nurses' attention. She had to check on "her patient," and nothing would stop her.

It got to the point that the young woman was almost embarrassed by the constant visits. "I know she said she's my aunt," she told the doctor, "but she's not related."

"That's fine," the doctor said knowingly. "We all know about Mrs. Lubling's cousins."

Like any doting aunt, Mrs. Lubling likewise kept tabs on the patient's spouse. When the baby was born in NYU, she offered to arrange a private room for the new mother.

Even when a patient's hospital story was over — be it a happy ending or a tragic one — Mrs. Lubling usually managed to write an epilogue. In this case, she maintained the connection long past the three and a half years of this man's illness, becoming an honorary grandmother of the baby who'd been born while his father was in the oncology ward. She even joined the extended family at a hotel for his bar mitzvah.

And later, when she got a phone call about a Yerushalmi father and grandfather who needed delicate spinal surgery to save his mobility, she enlisted this young mother, who'd been blessed with financial means, to move from the taking to the giving end of her bikur cholim enterprise, and help finance the surgery.

"Ima," says Rabbi Mordche Gefner, a pedigreed Yerushalmi who grew up as one of seventeen children in a one-bedroom Meah Shearim apartment and watched the city expand over the decades. "That's what Mrs. Lubling was to us — an Ima."

Rabbi Gefner had long suffered from serious spinal issues that compromised his mobility and caused almost unbearable pain. He underwent three complex surgeries to repair his spine. After the third surgery, he battled recurring infections. The doctors in Israel did what they could, but the infections kept returning, causing more damage each time. At some point, the doctors grew concerned that Rabbi Gefner might suffer permanent paralysis if a solution could not be found.

"You have to come to America," a cousin in Monsey urged him. "The world's top neurosurgeons are here. Get on a plane, and we'll work out all the details."

Rabbi Gefner had been in the United States before, for a previous surgery. But the trip seemed more daunting this time. It was just a week before Pesach. The house was filled with trays of eggs and bags of potatoes for the upcoming Yom Tov. He had a newly married couple relying on him for the Yom Tov meals. And he had no American medical insurance. How could he leave?

Shabbos HaGadol was excruciating. The pain was so staggering that he couldn't even make it to the Shabbos table. The most he could do was hop on one leg while his children supported him.

As a faithful chassid, he asked his Rebbe, the Yeshuos Moshe of Vizhnitz, whether this was the proper time to leave his family. The Rebbe told him to go.

Rabbi Gefner did not have an up-to-date passport or visa. Since it was Sunday, all the American government offices were closed. What to do? He contacted Rabbi Menachem Porush, who exercised his connections with Israel's Internal Ministry and the American ambassador. As the hours ticked on, a passport and visa were arranged.

Next, a generous friend made the travel arrangements for Rabbi Gefner, whose condition necessitated four adjacent seats, as well as seats for his wife, daughter, and son-in-law.

Twenty-four hours later, they were on a plane to New York.

During their journey, Rabbi Gefner's cousin put in a call to Mrs. Lubling. By the time the plane touched down on *bedikas chametz* morning, everything had been arranged. A Hatzolah ambulance greeted the Gefners at the airport, and the practiced medics gently maneuvered him onto a stretcher. Then they proceeded to NYU, where an angel in heels and pearls was waiting for them.

Mrs. Lubling greeted the new arrivals and brought them to meet the doctor she had handpicked for Rabbi Gefner's complex surgery. His name was Dr. Vallo Benjamin, and even today, Rabbi Gefner thinks of him as "Professor High Class."

Dr. Benjamin was a world-renowned neurosurgeon and chairman of the Department of Neurosurgery at NYU. He was an elegant man who performed some of the most daring and delicate procedures of his era. On any given week, he conducted from three to five surgeries, each of which could last ten hours or longer. Doctors across the world admired and studied his work.

Dr. Benjamin loved culture and the arts. He had studied professional acting, enjoyed a thorough grounding in the nuances of classical music, literature, and fine wine, and planned every detail of his Midtown East Manhattan duplex along with a celebrated architect. But when he stood before Mrs. Lubling, he was completely submissive, like a little boy before a schoolmarm.

Though he had climbed to the top of his field, Dr. Benjamin actually began his life as a member of a persecuted minority, the Assyrians of Iran. Unlike the Persian majority, Assyrians speak a language derived from Aramaic, and they worship in the Eastern Christian church. Dr. Benjamin was born in Hamadan, where Mordechai and Esther are buried. He studied medicine in Teheran and then immigrated to the United States, where he completed his medical training and specialized in neurosurgery.

After the Islamic Revolution of 1979, the Assyrians faced increasingly severe persecution and danger. As Dr. Benjamin tracked the deteriorating situation in Iran from afar, he pulled every string he could to bring his mother Maro to the United States — all to no avail. One day during hospital rounds, he lost his typical reserve and shared his frustrations and fear with the immigrant woman with the bulging handbag and compassionate eyes.

"That's the problem?" Mrs. Lubling asked. "I take care."

No one is quite sure which of her extensive connections Mrs. Lubling tapped, but within a week, Dr. Benjamin's mother had received the necessary permits to immigrate to America. After that incident, he did whatever she asked.

And so she introduced him to Rabbi Gefner, the bearded chassid from Yerushalayim lying immobile on a stretcher — yet still managing to crack a joke in his very basic English.

"Rabbi Gefner," the doctor asked, "how are you smiling and joking?"

"I have two options," Rabbi Gefner said simply. "I can cry, or I can smile. What do I gain by crying?"

"But you know that this is a very long and difficult surgery," the doctor pressed on. "Aren't you frightened? Why don't you seem tense?"

In response, Rabbi Gefner related the famous story of the Frierdiker Rebbe of Lubavitch, Rebbe Yosef Yitzchak Schneersohn. During the early days of the Soviet regime, the authorities imprisoned and tortured the Rebbe for what they termed his "counter-revolutionary activities" — spreading Yiddishkeit and teaching Torah.

During one interrogation, the interrogators pointed a revolver at the Rebbe and said, smirking, "You know, this toy has a way of making people cooperate."

"That toy," the Rebbe replied calmly, "only holds power for a person with many gods and one world. I, however, have One G-d and two worlds."

"I, too, have One G-d and two worlds," Rabbi Gefner told the polished physician. "My G-d will look after me, and if He determines that my time has come, I know there is a better world waiting for me. Why should I be frightened?"

And with that, he went into surgery.

Twelve long hours later, when Rabbi Gefner came to in the recovery room, the newly familiar face of Mrs. Lubling was there. She knew that he would feel more secure seeing his advocate right there in the room. Never mind that it was Erev Pesach, the busiest day of the year. She was going to be there for the Gefners no matter what.

When Rabbi Gefner was deemed ready to leave the recovery room, Mrs. Lubling accompanied the family to the floor. Then she began puttering around the room, almost as if she were hosting personal guests there in the hospital. She made sure the bed was set up properly, and that there was light and air. She made sleeping arrangements in the nearby bikur cholim apartments for Rebbetzin Gefner and the daughter and son-in-law who'd made the long trip from Israel. Then she hurried out of the room, down to a storage room in NYU's basement, and came back wheeling a mini-fridge, one of a dozen donated by the Rivkah Laufer Bikur Cholim.

Until today, the Gefners still marvel at the way this woman made herself available on Erev Pesach. The whirlwind that had deposited them in this big, strange building had left them lost and confused, the language and mannerisms were so foreign, and

Rabbi Gefner's medical situation was difficult to witness. But Mrs. Lubling's presence conveyed optimism and confidence. They knew they weren't alone.

That evening, Rabbi Gefner could barely move. It was Leil HaSeder, and there were so many precious mitzvos he couldn't fulfill. For the first time the entire journey, he wept.

Rebbetzin Gefner collected two tray tables from an adjoining room. She put the tray tables together and covered them with a white sheet. Then she set their improvised Seder table with the Pesach food her relatives had brought. And somehow, Rabbi Gefner was imbued with the strength to conduct a proper Seder, lasting until one in the morning. He drank all four cups and ate the requisite amounts of matzah. It was a Pesach miracle.

On Chol HaMoed morning, the Gefners had a visitor: Mrs. Lubling. The entire Yom Tov, she'd been thinking of them. Now she had come to check on them in person.

Throughout the duration of their stay, not a day went by without a visit from Mrs. Lubling. When Rabbi Gefner no longer needed formal hospitalization, she arranged for him to continue recovering while receiving intravenous antibiotics in the Seagate convalescent home.

She was there with the Gefners at every doctor's meeting and made sure they understood the recommendations. "When you're in such a vulnerable position, when you literally can't move," Rabbi Gefner says, "even the tiniest things feel insurmountable. I couldn't get out of bed without pain. But knowing she was our champion meant we weren't powerless.

"I can't think of anyone I ever met — even a man — with that degree of confidence and control. She was never aggressive, but she was very firm. If the bed linen wasn't fresh, she would go bring fresh sheets herself. She could be as soft as butter; I saw tears fill her eyes sometimes when she saw a patient suffering. But if she wanted something to happen, there was this steel inside of her. It would happen."

Eventually Mrs. Lubling bid the Gefners goodbye and they returned to their apartment in Jerusalem. But they had become family. Every time she flew to Israel, she visited them. Every year, on Reb Yaakov Lubling's *yahrtzeit*, Rabbi Gefner joined the group of people reciting *Tehillim* at his graveside on Har HaZeisim.

And every Erev Shabbos, the Gefners made an overseas call to wish Mrs. Lubling *gut Shabbos*. "Long-distance calls were expensive back then," Rabbi Gefner says. "But before Shabbos, you call your mother. So we called Mrs. Lubling. That's what she was to us, an Ima."

Toward the end of 1983, Rabbi Avraham Yitzchak Neria, a prominent member of Israel's Religious-Zionist rabbinic elite and leader of the Haifa community, began to suffer from debilitating headaches. His wife, Rabbanit Temima, still remembers the stunning speed with which events unfolded. At first his doctor thought he was suffering from some sort of virus, but when the headaches didn't let up, they began to suspect something more sinister. On the first day of Chanukah, he had his first scan. By the eighth day of Chanukah, they were in New York, seeking treatment for an aggressive brain cancer.

The Israeli *askan* who advised them to travel to NYU said the name "Mrs. Lubling" with such conviction that they embarked on their journey with full faith that she'd be waiting at the airport and continue to remain at their side throughout the ordeal. And in fact, a Hatzolah ambulance was waiting when they landed, arranged by Mrs. Lubling, who met them in NYU.

"It was amazing to see how every door opened for her," Rabbanit Neria remembers. "The small things she requested — like long-sleeved pajamas because 'he's a rabbi, he needs dignified sleepwear' — were delivered immediately. Of course, the hospital gave us a private room, because Mrs. Lubling explained that this was 'a very important rabbi from Israel.' And more important things like tests, insurance arrangements, payment details — she was the address for every issue we faced."

Rabbi Neria underwent a difficult surgery soon after his arrival, and Mrs. Lubling spent those fraught hours in the waiting room along with Rabbanit Neria. She arranged Shabbos food for the Nerias, and even brought a mini fridge into their room. She attended all the doctors' meetings with them, making sure they understood the reports and instructions.

Then, when Rav Neria started to regain his strength, she expanded her advocacy beyond the walls of the hospital. "I want the rav to give a *shiur*," she told Rabbanit Neria one day. "He is a *talmid chacham*, he should have a formal position." She knew that this would be an invaluable part of his recovery.

The right venue for Rav Neria's *shiur*, Mrs. Lubling intuited, would be the Gruss Kollel of Yeshiva University. And so she picked up the phone and got to work scheduling a lecture by the visiting scholar. On the appointed day, Rav Neria dressed in his rabbinic garb and a driver arrived at NYU to transport him and the rabbanit to the Yeshiva University campus in Washington Heights.

Decades later, Rabbanit Neria still remembers the topic of the *shiur* that her husband — his face slightly pale, but his voice steady and clear, nurtured by something more eternal than his medical infusions — delivered before the students and their brilliant rosh kollel, the young Rav Hershel Schachter, who had been appointed a rosh yeshivah in his twenties.

During Rav Neria's eleven-week stay in NYU, his room was graced by many distinguished visitors. As the son of Rav Moshe Tzvi Neria, rosh yeshivah of Bnei Akiva, he was a very prominent patient. Mrs. Lubling had a keen understanding of his status and made sure to be present when visitors like Israel's Consul General in New York City, Naftali Lau-Lavie, or Rav She'ar Yashuv Cohen, chief rabbi of Haifa, came to visit. She sensed that these people had the ability to open doors for her patients in the future, and she made sure to establish a connection.

After Rav Neria returned to Israel, Mrs. Lubling maintained the bond with her new friend. She called often and sent gifts. Rabbanit Neria remembers beautiful dresses that Mrs. Lubling sent for her daughters, and Erev Yom Tov calls wishing the entire family well. She also remembers the soft spot that Mrs. Lubling had for her youngest son Chanoch — perhaps because her own son has the same name.

The months passed by, filled with gratitude and optimism — until later that summer, when the headaches returned. A scan revealed that the cancer was back. Once again, the Nerias traveled to NYU. This time, the doctors offered less hope, less confidence. But Mrs. Lubling did her best to soften every blow. At one meeting, she turned to a doctor and plaintively asked, "Do you need to say everything so strong?"

Rabbanit Neria knew English well enough to understand the subtext.

A second surgery gave Rav Neria another year with his family and community in Haifa. By the end of the summer, the cancer had overpowered all his resources. There was nothing left to do — not even for Mrs. Lubling.

But Mrs. Lubling kept up the friendship even after Rav Neria's passing. She personally attended the *vort* of the Nerias' oldest daughter half a year later, and continued to send gifts and to call regularly.

While they were not related, in the colorless rooms of a Manhattan hospital overlooking the Hudson River, these two women connected profoundly. They were both European immigrants who'd come to Israel as youngsters and who helped build the religious character of the new country. They both came from chassidic stock (the rabbanit is a granddaughter of the Koidenover Rebbe) yet mastered Ivrit and Israeli culture. And they both knew what it meant to have a strong, capable husband suddenly become weak and vulnerable.

When Reb Yaakov Lubling experienced his final illness, Rabbanit Neria was able to pick up the notes of worry over the phone lines. Mrs. Lubling — usually so crisp and efficient, so optimistic and buoyant — sounded worried. Diminished.

"I realized what was happening," Rabbanit Neria says. "All that 'lokshen' — that nonsense — she used to sell to everyone else, the assurances that everything would be okay, that it would all work out fine, she couldn't sell to herself.

"Back when my husband had been sick, she used to give everything a positive spin. If he was sleeping a lot, she told me, 'It's wonderful that he's sleeping — resting is the best thing! Nothing better for a sick person!' If he was awake, she'd say, 'Such a good sign! It means he's getting stronger!'

"But when her own husband was sick, she knew all too well what it really meant. All those stories she told the patients, she couldn't tell herself. She knew the truth. She knew he wasn't going to get better."

That was the connection a soul sister could feel over the phone line.

One snowy winter night, Leah Horowitz's son — a grandson of Mrs. Lubling's dear friend and kindergarten partner Rebbetzin Teitelbaum — started exhibiting the classic signs of appendicitis. Leah called her pediatrician, who directed her to the NYU emergency room. She bundled the little boy into a car and set out in the raging snowstorm for Manhattan.

Soon a call came in from her brother. "Call Mrs. Lubling!" he advised her.

"I don't need her," Leah countered, thinking of Mrs. Lubling's advanced age — she was already in her nineties and surely could use her sleep. "I'm here in NYU already, and I have a doctor assigned to the case."

"No, you have to call her," he said. "She'll be very upset to hear that you were there and didn't get her involved."

He was right, Leah realized. So she called Mrs. Lubling and apprised her of the situation. Then she hung up and focused on her son, who was in considerable pain. The ER staff examined him and determined that he needed an emergency appendectomy. They took him into the waiting area outside the operating rooms and began to prep him for surgery.

Suddenly the door swung open. First Leah saw the metal legs of a walker — then the familiar figure of Mrs. Lubling, every *sheitel* hair in place.

"Mrs. Lubling," she said in shock. "It's snowing outside! Why did you come?"

"Why?" Mrs. Lubling asked. "This is my *einikel* lying here, that's why."

Despite the fear, despite the wild weather, the room felt warmer.

Finally the surgeon came out to examine the little patient. "Are you the mother?" he asked. "We're almost ready."

Leah nodded. But Mrs. Lubling looked appraisingly at the surgeon. "I don't know you," she said.

His body language screaming *who cares?* he answered, "I don't know you either."

She straightened her shoulders, pulled out her trustee badge, and said, "I'm the oldest trustee of this hospital. I've been here for thirty years. How long have you been here?"

"I'm here for three months," the surgeon said, with more respect this time. "I used to work in Columbia-Presbyterian."

"Well, my name is Miriam Lubling," she went on. "I'm the oldest trustee in the hospital. And *this* is my grandson" — with a nod to the gurney — "and you'd better take good care of him."

"I will most definitely try my best," he answered with newfound humility and respect.

Later in life, Rebbetzin Teitelbaum, Mrs. Lubling's kindergarten partner, needed emergency cardiac surgery to replace an aging valve. Mrs. Lubling was in Eretz Yisrael at the time, but she worked the phones from abroad. Even though it was Martin Luther King Day, a legal holiday, she tracked down senior cardiothoracic surgeon Dr. Stephen Colvin. "This time, Dr. Colvin," she promised, "this is really my sister. I need you to open the operating room and do the surgery."

The surgery was complex and protracted, and the family hovered anxiously for at least ten hours, waiting for the surgeon to phone the desk with an all-clear.

Finally the phone rang. "We're done," Dr. Colvin said wearily, "and it looks like your mother will be okay."

"Thank you!" the children said.

"Wait!" Dr. Colvin said. "I need something from you. Give me

Mrs. Lubling's number in Israel. She's waiting for an update. I can't leave without calling her first.

"And," he asked, "you have to tell me, is this *really* her sister?"

"Dr. Colvin," Rebbetzin Teitelbaum's daughter said, "these are the two closest sisters you ever met."

CHAPTER 11
The Money Will Come

Mrs. Lubling was never a woman of great means, but she took on immense financial commitments without a speck of anxiety. Her fundraising techniques were a far cry from the sophisticated methods utilized today, but the returns were just as impressive. Money didn't worry her in the slightest; if a patient needed money, she innately trusted the Divine Banker to provide it.

"The doctor wants payment for the surgery in advance?" she'd say. "Okay, we'll have it ready for him tomorrow."

Then, as her drivers shuttled her from the hospital to a wedding in Williamsburg or bar mitzvah in Boro Park, she conducted impromptu fundraising campaigns from her cellphone, tapping a proven network of donors who readily pledged thousands of dollars to this angel of mercy.

On one trip to the hospital, Mrs. Lubling was very concerned about a patient who'd just arrived from Israel in critically ill condition. He was hovering between this world and the next, and had no insurance or funds to cover the thirty-thousand-dollar treatment that could potentially save his life.

Mrs. Lubling somehow managed to get the doctor on the phone. "Listen, Doctor," she said, "I need you to do this surgery for my cousin right away. You do it now, and tomorrow I will get you the money."

She then punched the number of a well-known Brooklyn philanthropist into her phone and began fundraising. "*Tattele*," she said — she called all her donors "*tattele*" — "I need ten thousand dollars. Really I need thirty, I'm only asking you for ten."

A pause.

"Can I pick up a check tonight?"

Another pause.

"Thank you, *Tattele*, we'll be there this evening."

Then she dialed another donor. "*Tattele*, I need ten thousand dollars," she launched into her fundraising pitch again.

Another phone call, another pitch... By the time the hospital loomed into view, Mrs. Lubling had raised the entire sum.

Even as a newly arrived immigrant in Crown Heights, she had no hesitation in reaching out to donors to raise money. In the late 1960s, Reb Hershel Weber inaugurated the first Hatzolah emergency medical responder unit, after watching a fellow Jew die while waiting for an ambulance to arrive with desperately-needed oxygen. Instead of waiting for an ambulance, he thought, why not train volunteers right here in the neighborhood to provide emergency care?

After a similarly tragic incident occurred in Crown Heights, Mrs. Lubling met Rabbi Josh Silbermintz in 1968 and urged him, "We must do something to help!"

They arranged to meet with Reb Hershel Weber, and invited Mrs. Lubling's son Chanoch along with his friend Yonah Blumenfrucht — both young, energetic "doers" — to train in CPR and form the kernel of the new emergency response team in Crown Heights.

Chanoch and Yonah enlisted eight additional volunteers to the new Hatzolah unit for a total of ten: five were local storekeepers who could be available to answer calls during the daytime hours; that left five *yeshivah bachurim* committed to taking calls on nights and weekends.

It quickly grew clear that the volunteers would need oxygen

tanks. But Hatzolah was a new organization with no overhead and no coffers; where would they get money for ten tanks? Mrs. Lubling stepped in and tapped the coffers of the Rivkah Laufer Bikur Cholim to cover the expense (and she also devoted the newly installed private telephone line of her daughter Peshi to incoming Hatzolah calls).

Hatzoloh — EMERGENCY HELP הצלה — ערשטע הילף

171 Taylor Street, Brooklyn, N. Y. 11211

Emergency Phone: EV 7-1750

•

Branches in: Williamsburgh, Crown Heights, Boro Park

בס"ד

ה צ ל ה   ר ע פ א ר ט

כל המציל נפש אחת מישראל , כאילו קיים עולם מלא !

דער בריעף איז דיא ערשטער רעפארט וואס ווערט געשיקט צו עסקנים און מעמבערס
פון ה צ ל ה !

ז ע ה ר   ו ו י כ ט י ג ,   ז ע ה ר   ו ו י כ ט י ג !

(1) אלע עסקנים מוזען געדענקען צו וואשען די "אקסיזשען מאסק" מיט "אלקאהאל"
פון צייט צו צייט און שטענדיק האלטען דיא מאסק איבגעדעקט אין א ריינע פלעסטיק בעג

(2) גיט אכטונג אז דיא "טענק" זאל גוט ארבעטען און זיין פול מיט אקסיזשען ,
אויב איר ווייסט נישט וויא אזוי דאס צו טאן רופט 387-7630 .

וויליאמסבורג !

12 אזייגער באנאכט האט ר' שנעפצלער פון 131 הייווארד סטריט פארלוירען 45%
פון זיין בלוט דורעך אן "אלסער" מען האט עם געדארפט נעמען זייער שנעל אין
שפיטאל צו ראטעווען זיין לעבען .

ר' אברהם סלו' עפשטיין און ר' צבי וועבער האט גענומען א "סטעשאן וועגאן"
און געמאכט פון דעם אן אמבולאנס און אריינגעפירט און מיימאנידעס האספיטאל וויא
ער איז אנגעקומען 15 מינוט נאך 12 , און געקראגען פרישע בלוט .

היינט איז ער ב"ה און דער היים און איז שטארק מכיר טובה די חסד פון די
הצלה עסקנים וועלכע האבין געהאלפין ראטעווען זיין לעבען .

קרוין הייטס

מיט די הילף פון השי"ת האט אונז געלונגען צו פארשפרייטען די ארבייט פון הצלה
אויך פאר קרוין הייטס .

די איבערגעגעבענע אייוויגער פון קרוין הייטס , הרב יהושע זילבערמינץ ,
ר' חנוך לובלינג און ר' יונה בלומנפרוכט וועלכע האבין מיטן גאנצען הארץ געוואלט
האבין א חלק אין די מצוה פון פיקוח נפשות האבין געארבייט צו קריגען וואלאנטירען
(עסקנים) צו טאן די "הצלה" ארבייט און אויך גענומען אויף זיך צו שאפען דיא
גאנצע הוצאה פאר קרוין – הייטס .

דיא רבקה לויפער "ביקור חולים" פון קרוין הייטס וועמענ'ס אנפירער איז די
חשובע מרס לובלינג האט געגעבען פאר דער צוועק די סומע פון $500

אין חודש אייר האבין מיר געהאט 30.. הצלה קאלס .

אויב איר האט וואס צו באריכטען פאר די קומענדיגע הצלה רעפארטס אדער איר ווייס
פון אידען און בארא פארק וועלכע וואלטען געקענט אנטייל נעמען אין די ארבייט פון
"הצלה" שרייבט צו אונז אדער רופט 387-7630.

צו מפרסם זיין די טעלעפאן נאמבער "הצלה" 171 טעילאר סטריט ברוקלין נ"י 11211

A Hatzolah report from the Crown Heights branch's early days, delineating the five-hundred-dollar donation arranged by Mrs. Miriam Lubling

Gita Muller remembers a call that came in to the Rivkah Laufer Bikur Cholim from a distraught family in Israel. A mother of four children was steadily losing her mental function and muscle control. The local doctors determined that the cause was the presence of a pneumocephalus — a buildup of air that usually takes place after trauma — inside her brain. They could not pinpoint any obvious cause, and needless to say, they were not equipped to treat it. She urgently needed treatment in the United States — but how to get there? The pressurized air in the airplane cabin would likely be fatal for a brain under so much stress. And a transatlantic boat journey would squander too much valuable time.

Mrs. Lubling started calling her Israeli contacts, and she learned that the IDF had planes that could fly at lower altitudes, without the usual high-pressure oxygen. Years before, she had helped an army commander with a medical issue. She called him now, and without any hesitation or apprehension, asked him to make the invaluable army plane available to her patient.

"If you cover the costs, I can make the arrangements," he said.

"Good, good," Mrs. Lubling said.

"But it will cost fifty-one thousand dollars," the commander said.

Mrs. Lubling thought quickly. The Rivka Laufer reservoirs were not deep enough just then for that kind of donation. But she knew someone who could help. She made a personal visit to one of her faithful donors, who wrote out a check on the spot. The flight took off, and the woman was brought directly to the hospital, where she underwent lifesaving surgery that restored her functioning.

Mrs. Lubling always maintained an open attitude to innovations, gadgets, and gimmicks. As noted, she was one of the first laymen to possess a beeper at a time when only doctors or EMTs owned the device. For at least two decades, her beeper constantly buzzed and vibrated with updates and alerts, but Mrs. Lubling managed it with aplomb.

Her openness to innovation was evident much earlier: as a newly arrived immigrant, she embraced the American concept of fundraising luncheons. As mentioned, the first such event was held in the Freschl home in Crown Heights. It was so successful that it became the social event of the year — and the precursor to the annual Rivkah Laufer luncheons that were held for decades in Queens, Boro Park, and Flatbush.

When it came to the luncheons, Mrs. Lubling employed a keen understanding of management and delegation. She rarely delegated in the hospital, preferring to talk to the doctors and secretaries herself, but she trusted a team of volunteers to arrange and run the yearly fundraising events. They may have been young mothers without much of a track record, but Mrs. Lubling got her volunteers to take on responsibility at a young age. The empowering message they got from her was, "This is your job and you can do it."

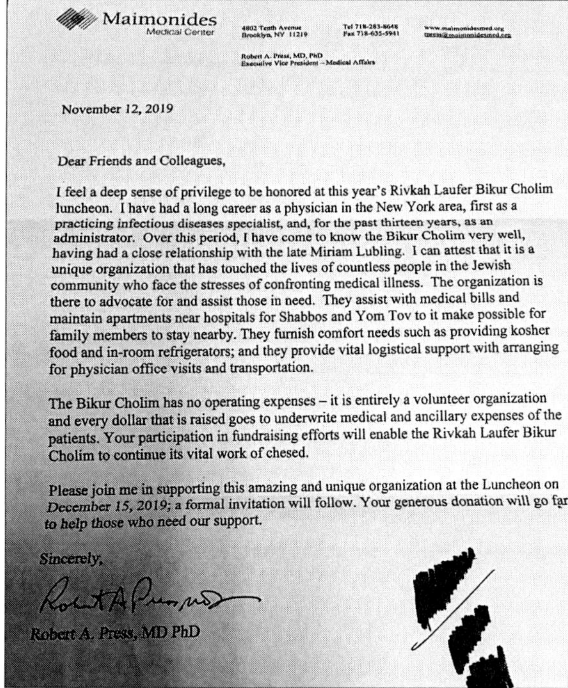

Maimonides
Medical Center

4802 Tenth Avenue
Brooklyn, NY 11219

Tel 718-283-8648
Fax 718-635-5941

www.maimonidesmed.org
[illegible]

Robert A. Press, MD, PhD
Executive Vice President – Medical Affairs

November 12, 2019

Dear Friends and Colleagues,

I feel a deep sense of privilege to be honored at this year's Rivkah Laufer Bikur Cholim luncheon. I have had a long career as a physician in the New York area, first as a practicing infectious diseases specialist, and, for the past thirteen years, as an administrator. Over this period, I have come to know the Bikur Cholim very well, having had a close relationship with the late Miriam Lubling. I can attest that it is a unique organization that has touched the lives of countless people in the Jewish community who face the stresses of confronting medical illness. The organization is there to advocate for and assist those in need. They assist with medical bills and maintain apartments near hospitals for Shabbos and Yom Tov to it make possible for family members to stay nearby. They furnish comfort needs such as providing kosher food and in-room refrigerators; and they provide vital logistical support with arranging for physician office visits and transportation.

The Bikur Cholim has no operating expenses – it is entirely a volunteer organization and every dollar that is raised goes to underwrite medical and ancillary expenses of the patients. Your participation in fundraising efforts will enable the Rivkah Laufer Bikur Cholim to continue its vital work of chesed.

Please join me in supporting this amazing and unique organization at the Luncheon on *December 15, 2019*; a formal invitation will follow. Your generous donation will go far *to help* those who need our support.

Sincerely,

Robert A. Press, MD PhD

A fundraising request from Dr. Robert A. Press of NYU, one of Mrs. Lubling's "favored doctors" whom she prevailed upon to serve as Guest of Honor at a Rivkah Laufer Bikur Cholim luncheon

At the yearly fundraising luncheons, Mrs. Lubling led the crowds in *Tehillim* before handing over the mic to the emcee.

Still, like a good manager, she never left them entirely on their own. Mrs. Ruthie Braunstein of the Flatbush branch remembers how Mrs. Lubling selected (and persuaded) guests of honor to grace each event, often one of her favored doctors. She checked on her teams to make sure their invitations had gone out, the preparations were proceeding apace, and that they had managed to amass sufficient prizes from local businesses for the raffle drawings. And on the morning of the luncheon, she showed up in her suit, rolled up her sleeves, and got to work.

Mrs. Miriam "Pupsie" Beer, who chaired and emceed the Flatbush luncheons (Mrs. Lubling led the crowd in *Tehillim*, but then passed along the microphone), remembers Mrs. Lubling pulling on her skirt as she introduced each speaker. "Pupsie!" Mrs. Lubling interjected in her mixture of English and Yiddish. "Don't forget to say this! And don't forget to mention that!"

Back in the '70s and '80s, the women didn't use computerized lists or slick brochures. They appointed "chairladies" who compiled lists of friends, relatives, and potential donors. Then each chairlady sent out personalized invitations and followed up by phone, urging the women in her social circle to attend the event and pledge donations.

When it came to the food, the organizers didn't use professional catering services or party planners. They created their own centerpieces and found tablecloths to match. Schick's Bakery donated trays of cake. The women organized a Cheesecake Committee and a Quiche Committee, distributing instructions and recipes so

Mrs. Lubling didn't need or appreciate public acclaim, but she accepted a Guest of Honor designation at one of the annual luncheons, knowing it would help the *cholim*.

volunteers could prepare the delicacies in their own homes (one mushroom quiche recipe was so popular that sixty women were enlisted to make it!).

The organizers ordered massive quantities of vegetables, tuna, salmon, and eggs. A few hours before the luncheon, the young women were joined by Mrs. Lubling and her friends, and together the two generations of volunteers assembled vegetable platters, scooped tuna onto plates, prepared coffee in huge urns, and set the tables in the rented hall.

When the guests arrived in their suits and heels, the atmosphere was warm and welcoming. There was light chatter with good company, a few inspiring speeches, fresh food, and raffle prizes — and most importantly, a cause they all believed in. Everyone knew someone who'd been helped by the bikur cholim, and those who could not donate large sums were happy to donate what they could.

Even the yearly mailings — done the low-tech way, with hand-stuffed envelopes and handwritten labels assembled by a volunteer team of women and teenage girls, usually on Tishah B'Av afternoon — yielded an impressive return. In the days before computerized databases, the teams kept stacks of index cards with names and addresses of donors. They would carefully check for doubles, reluctant to waste even a few cents on an extra stamp.

But the lack of glamor didn't translate into a lack of effectiveness; even during their initial years, the bikur cholim branches were bringing in at least half a million dollars a year.

Mrs. Lubling didn't only raise money for bikur cholim. Step inside the dormitory of Yeshivas Sfas Emes on Rechov Yosef Ben Mattisyahu in Yerushalayim — the flagship institution built by the Beis Yisrael of Gur — and if you look carefully, you might find a plaque. The plaque declares that the building was constructed with the help of funds raised by the Gur sisterhood, under the leadership of Miriam Lubling.

Another plaque, in Yeshivah Chiddushei HaRim of Tel Aviv, acknowledges the same help. (In fact, after her *petirah* the Gerrer

Mrs. Lubling retained a lifelong connection to Gur, raising money for the yeshivos and consulting with the Rebbes for advice and *berachos*.

rosh yeshivah in New York reviewed the proposed text for her *matzeivah* and specifically requested that the family add a line noting her support of yeshivos and *limud Torah*; when the current Gerrer Rebbe reviewed the final text, he was pleased to see that addition.)

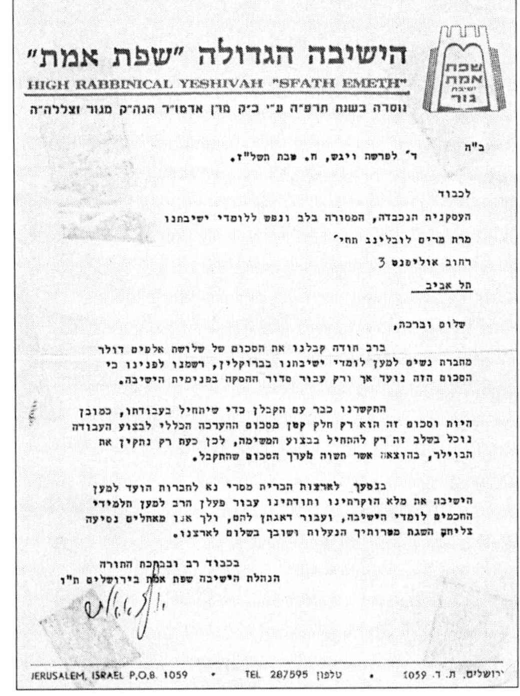

הישיבה הגדולה "שפת אמת"
HIGH RABBINICAL YESHIVAH "SFATH EMETH"
נוסדה בשנת תרפ"ה ע"י כ"ק מרן אדמו"ר הגה"ק מגור זצללה"ה

ב"ה

ד' לפרשה ויגש, ח. טבת השל"ז.

לכבוד

העסקנית הנכבדה, המסורה בלב ונפש ללומדי ישיבתנו

מרת מרים לובלינג תחי'

רחוב אוליפנט 3

תל אביב

שלום וברכה,

ברב תודה קבלנו את הסכום של שלושה אלפים דולר מחברת נשים למען לומדי ישיבתנו בברוקלין, רשמנו לפנינו כי הסכום הזה נועד אך ורק עבור סדור ההסקה בפנימית הישיבה.

התקשרנו כבר עם הקבלן כדי שיתחיל בעבודתו, כמובן היות וסכום זה הוא רק חלק קטן מסכום ההערכה הכללי לבצוע העבודה נוכל בשלב זה רק להתחיל בבצוע המשימה, לכן כעת רק נתקין את הבוילר, בהוצאה אשר תשוה לערך הסכום שהתקבל.

בנספך לארצות הברית מסרי נא לחברות הועד למען הישיבה את מלא הוקרתינו ותודתינו עבור פעלן הרב למען תלמידי החכמים לומדי הישיבה, ועבור דאגתן להם, ולך אנו מאחלים נסיעה צליחה השגת מטרותיך הנעלות ושובך בשלום לארצנו.

בכבוד רב ובברכת התורה
הנהלת הישיבה שפת אמת בירושלים ת"ו

JERUSALEM, ISRAEL P.O.B. 1059 • TEL. 287595 טלפון • ירושלים, ת. ד. 1059

A thank-you letter from Yeshivas Sfas Emes, dated 1977, thanks Mrs. Lubling for raising money to install heating in the dormitory building.

During her years in the United States, the Gerrer yeshivos in Eretz Yisrael always remained an honored cause, and she raised significant funds to modernize the kitchens and outfit the buildings with air conditioning.

The same Mrs. Lubling who served as president of Nshei Gur once attended a fundraising dinner for Lakewood's Beth Medrash Govoha. She didn't have any family connections to the yeshivah at that point, but she had helped the family navigate the illness of Rav Meir Kotler, the oldest son of Rav Shneur. Ever since that trying time, she and Rav Shneur's wife, Rebbetzin Rishel, had exceptional respect for one another, and would bow graciously when they met.

At the dinner, the emcee announced the writing of a *Sefer Torah*. Donors and patrons could sponsor letters or *parshiyos*, thus benefiting the yeshivah. "We're looking for a volunteer to be in charge of *Sefer Devarim*," the emcee announced. "That's the only *sefer* left. Who wants the *zechus*?"

The room was silent. Then, from the women's section, came an accented voice. "*Ich nem*, I'll take it," said Mrs. Miriam Lubling, the Polish immigrant, PAI activist, and Gerrer chassidiste with zero connection to Beth Medrash Govoha.

Sure enough, she took on the commitment and tapped her network of connections to bring in the money for the yeshivah.

In 1991, during a trip to Israel, Mrs. Lubling's good friend from her PAI days, Mrs. Nechama Lifschitz, introduced her to a group of prominent rebbetzins and *baalos chessed*. These women had recently formed Avnei Noam, the sisterhood organization of the Agudas Yisroel movement.

Rebbetzin Tziporah Faiga Alter of Gur and Rebbetzin Leah Esther Hager of Vizhnitz served as chairwomen, and Mrs. Masha Burzhekovsky and Mrs. Sarah Halpert (the wife of Vizhnitz MK Rabbi Shmuel Halpert) worked under them to run a large and effective *chessed* network. One of their main areas of focus was hospital volunteerism, and Mrs. Lifschitz thought Mrs. Lubling could be a valuable ally and mentor to this new generation of activists.

Mrs. Lubling thrilled at the idea of a new cadre of chassidishe women learning the ropes of medical advocacy and support, and she developed a warm friendship with Mrs. Halpert. Mrs. Halpert coordinated the bikur cholim activities in Tel Hashomer Medical Center (now called Sheba), which was in close proximity to her Bnei Brak home. She set up a network of volunteers to make medical referrals, expedite the waiting process, accompany patients to appointments, and help them navigate the emergency room.

Mrs. Halpert quickly learned that Mrs. Lubling would drop everything the moment she called, and marshal all her connections and medical knowledge to help the women of Avnei Noam.

At some point it grew clear that the bikur cholim needed its own dedicated driver and vehicle — ideally an ambulance, since it would have the necessary medical equipment for patients on their way to and from treatments. But where could the women obtain that kind of funding? Mrs. Halpert had phoned Mrs. Lubling in the past to get her advice regarding medical referrals. Now she picked up the phone again.

"I will get the money," Mrs. Lubling promised. She immediately phoned a philanthropist who had benefited from her medical advocacy, and enthusiastically described the new cause.

The philanthropist was eager to hear the details, but he couldn't quite decipher Mrs. Lubling's accented words.

"I don't understand, can you explain it again?" he asked.

She repeated her pitch again, with the same enthusiasm — and the same rapid-fire presentation. He made out the words "Bnei Brak" and "bikur cholim" and "ambulance," but the rest wasn't clear.

"I'm sorry, Mrs. Lubling, can you repeat that?" he asked.

Mrs. Lubling explained once again.

Finally the philanthropist gave up. "Yes, yes, of course, Mrs. Lubling, whatever you say. Of course I want to help," he said. "Tell me how much money you need."

Within weeks, the Avnei Noam organization possessed its own dedicated ambulance, complete with a driver who worked close to eighteen hours a day, transporting volunteers and patients to and from Tel Hashomer.

Sometimes, even Mrs. Lubling was surprised and moved by the way funds materialized. In the early '90s, she was alerted to a truly wrenching case. The story had begun years earlier in Israel, when Rav Shlomo Zalman Auerbach was introduced to a man who was blind and refused to marry.

"You may not be able to see," Rav Shlomo Zalman told him, "but you still have a mitzvah to bring children into the world. You should get married, and you will see, you will merit tremendous *berachos* and a beautiful family."

The man followed the *gadol's* instructions and was blessed with a large family of seven children. Then disaster struck: one of the children was diagnosed with cancer.

Mrs. Lubling sprang into action and arranged for the sightless father and his son to travel to New York at once, where she arranged for an immediate appointment at NYU, to be followed by a delicate surgery.

Before his surgery, the little patient was placed in a hospital room with another cancer patient, a non-Jewish child. This child's father was sitting at his bedside when Mrs. Lubling entered the room to visit.

After some small talk and introductions, he cleared his throat. "I hope it's okay if I ask you an honest question. What is your connection to this little boy from Israel? And why do you look so terribly worried?"

Mrs. Lubling hurriedly explained the story, and told the man that she still had to raise a considerable sum of money to pay the hospital fees.

"You have nothing to worry about," the man said. "I'll get you the money."

Even for Mrs. Lubling, this was an almost fantastical promise. "How?" she asked.

"I'm the editor of a newspaper. This story has all the elements to tug at readers' hearts — a father who overcame blindness to build a family, a sick child whose only hope is a risky, delicate surgery, a journey across the world to a top hospital, an altruistic doctor waiving his fee... It's perfect! I'm going to publish it in my paper and you'll see, my readers will respond with donations."

Mrs. Lubling shrugged. It was certainly worth a try.

The editor published his story, and just as he'd promised, he was flooded with checks totaling tens of thousands of dollars. Mrs. Lubling had arranged the surgery, confident that the money would come — and the Divine Provider had done His part to justify her absolute, unquestioning trust.

One of Mrs. Lubling's less glamorous methods for covering medical costs was Middle-Eastern style haggling with the providers for "deals" on surgeries and treatments. She knew just how to appeal to these professionals, and many slashed their fees for her.

Rabbi Asher Labin traveled from Jerusalem to America so his wife could undergo a complex double surgery in NYU. He watched in disbelief as Mrs. Lubling negotiated with two world-class surgeons — Dr. Ransohoff and Dr. Persky — over their fees. The bewildered Rabbi Labin felt almost as if he were in the Machaneh Yehudah *shuk* as he watched her in action.

To one surgeon, she said, "How can it be that the other doctor wants five thousand and you want eight thousand? Your surgery is much less complex than his!"

Rabbi Labin was shocked when the surgeon acceded. He was even more shocked when Mrs. Lubling met a wealthy relative of his. She summarily informed this philanthropist that he would of course be paying for Mrs. Labin's medical treatment.

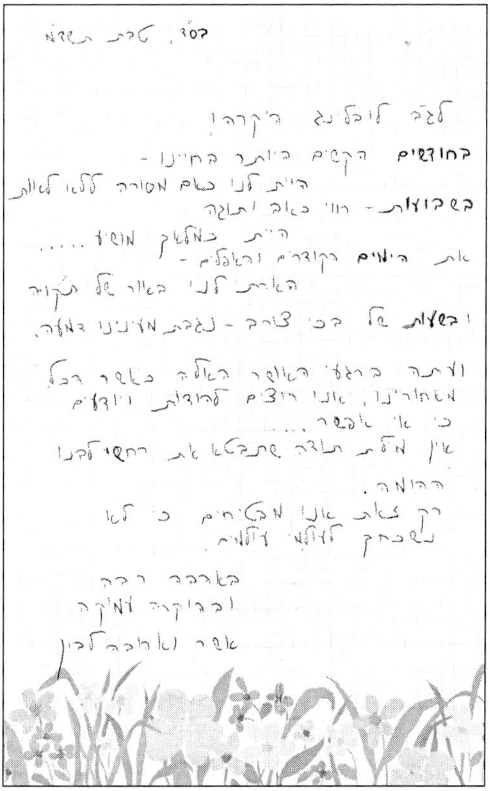
בס"ד, טבת תשמ"א

לגב' לובלינג היקרה!
בחודשים הקשים ביותר בחיינו -
היית לנו כאם מסורה ללוות
בשבועות - רווי כאב ותוגה
היית כמלאך מושיע......
את הימים הקודרים והאפלים -
האירת לנו באור של תקוה
ובשעות של בכי צורב - נגבת מעינינו דמעה.

ועתה ברגעי האושר הגדולה כאשר הכל
מאחורינו, אנו רוצים להודות ויודעים
כי אי אפשר......
אין מלות תודה שתבטא את רחשי לבנו
ההומה.
רק זאת אנו מבטיחים כי לא
נשכחך לעולמי עולמים.

באהבה רבה
ובהוקרה עמוקה
אשר ואהובה לבין

A thank-you note from the Labins to Mrs. Lubling: "You wiped our tears during the hard times; now that it's all behind us, we want to thank you." Rabbi Labin went on to host generations of Lubling grandchildren in Yerushalayim.

Throughout the months of their stay, Mrs. Lubling maintained contact with the wealthy relative, collected his pledges, and dealt directly with the hospital administration to transfer the money. Rabbi Labin did not have to deal even once with the financial aspects of his wife's illness.

When her treatment stretched on longer than they'd initially planned, he realized he would have to extend their plane tickets. "It will cost a lot of money," he said ruefully to Mrs. Lubling.

"Why should it cost you any money?" she shot back. "I want you to go to the main El Al office in Manhattan and ask for the manager. Tell him, 'Mrs. Lubling said you should change my ticket.'"

Rabbi Labin quashed his nerves — and his doubts — and followed Mrs. Lubling's instructions. The manager raised his eyebrows when the bearded *chareidi* man entered his room, insisting on speaking to him and only him. But when he heard Mrs. Lubling's name, his demeanor was transformed.

"Whatever she says, I will do," he said.

Four minutes later, the Labins had been issued new tickets — without having to pay a dollar more.

For all her skill at bargaining, Mrs. Lubling could intuit when a tough approach was ineffective, and then she used other tools. At one point, she gathered a few community activists to arrange a meeting with the president of a major Manhattan hospital which, she felt, could be offering better accommodations to religious Jews.

"This fellow has no great liking for the chassidic community," the activists told her. "There's nothing to be gained by meeting with him."

"But it will be good for his bottom line!" she insisted. "If he agrees to give us better prices, imagine what kind of business he'll get. The hospital has some specialists who can really help us. I can bring him so many patients who would benefit from the doctors and care here."

The activists were unconvinced, but they agreed to attend the meeting. They filed into the room and shook the hand of the hospital president, who greeted them coldly.

One of the younger activists, who had a gift for language, gestured toward Mrs. Lubling. "The 'Mother Teresa' of our community is this woman, Mrs. Miriam Lubling," he said. "I'm not sure how good her English is, but she will speak for us."

Mrs. Lubling began to speak, but it did not go well. In her accented English, she described the knotty bureaucratic processes that were so difficult for her patients to navigate.

"Okay, but we don't need your referrals," the polished gentleman said.

Mrs. Lubling pressed back. "Tell me," she said, "why are you running this hospital? What's your mission? Is it just a business?"

The man shrugged.

"You're a human being, a healer," she said. "You took this job because you care about sick people. How can you be so tough, so hard, with people who look and dress differently?" Now she was openly emotional, and her eyes were wet. "Is it really your job to make it so hard for sick people, just because they need religious accommodation?"

The president was shaken. "I hear you," he murmured.

In the months that followed, there was a marked change in the hospital's atmosphere, and Mrs. Lubling and her fellow medical activists began referring patients there for treatment. Eventually, the hospital even allowed a dedicated bikur cholim room off its main lobby.

Once again, she had found the right key to access a crucial portal.

Reb Shloime (Solomon) Mayer, famed medical advocate and a founding member of Chai Lifeline's presidium, never consciously chose to become an *askan*; it was the previous Rebbe of Sanz-Klausenberg, the Shefa Chaim, who intuited his talents for advocacy and assigned him his very first case.

The Rebbe, a Holocaust survivor whose revenge against the Nazi slaughter of his entire family included rebuilding his chassidus, ambitiously initiated institutions and Torah projects, and even the construction of Laniado Hospital. He became acquainted with Shloime during the 1970s, when the Williamsburg-born *bachur* learned for a period in the Rebbe's yeshivah in Kiryat Sanz.

When Shloime bid the Rebbe goodbye before his return to America, the Rebbe cryptically told him, "I know you have to go back to your family, but make sure to keep in touch with your friends here in Eretz Yisrael. If they need you, they'll have someone to call, and if you need them, you'll know how to reach them."

Just a few months later, Shlomo was learning in the Klausenberg yeshivah in Union City, New Jersey, when he received a telephone call from the Rebbe himself. "I have a job for you, Shloime," the Rebbe said. "There is a Yid here in Eretz Yisrael suffering from a bad case of diabetes. His leg has become gangrenous and the doctors here determined that the only way to stop the gangrene from spreading is to amputate it. I want you to find a doctor in America who can save his life — and keep his leg intact."

Shloime wanted to protest. He was just a *bachur*, and he had zero knowledge of diabetes, let alone of specialists in the field. But the Rebbe had given him his marching orders. So he began working the phones and soon found a doctor in the Bronx willing to accept the case.

The sick Jew flew in to New York, and for the next six months, Shloime arranged for him to be treated daily by the doctor. When Shloime finally sent a healthy, healed patient back to Israel, he realized he had found a calling.

Over the next few years, as he married and began to build a family, he also built up a network of doctors and a roster of leading hospitals for various procedures. Naturally, as he navigated his way through the medical world, he built a relationship with Mrs. Miriam Lubling. She was one of the few "superpowers" in the field at the time, and every new *askan* acknowledged and valued her unusual success.

Countless times, he joined her on her daily trips to NYU, and then accompanied her through the floors, watching her in action and taking mental notes on the self-assured yet very polite way she interacted with the staff. Most of all, he was taken by the esteem that doctors, nurses, administrators, and even board members accorded this persistent woman with heavily accented English and no medical degrees. It was her consistency and sincerity, he believes, that won her that respect.

But Mrs. Lubling's utter sincerity also led her to become frustrated and disillusioned when several new organizations were formed to help Jews navigate the hospitals — and, instead of utilizing volunteers, as per the policy of the Rivkah Laufer Bikur Cholim, they offered their staff members a proper salary.

"Since when is bikur cholim a paid job?" she protested to Reb Shloime, who was part of the founding team of Chai Lifeline and several other medical advocacy initiatives. "*Chessed* should never be paid. It should come from the heart and stay far from the wallet!"

Reb Shloime was not sure how to deal with this passionate argument. Then he had an idea. "The Gerrer Rosh Yeshivah [later to become the Rebbe known as the Pnei Menachem] will be visiting New York soon," he said. "Let's go see him then. We will raise the issue and follow whatever he says."

As a faithful Gerrer chassidiste, Mrs. Lubling warmed to the idea. When Rav Pinchos Menachem Alter arrived in New York, Reb Shloime and Mrs. Lubling went in to see him, and Reb Shloime gave voice to this issue that so pained Mrs. Lubling.

"What does the Rosh Yeshivah say? Is it proper to pay salaries to people who work in *chessed* organizations?" he asked.

"The Chiddushei HaRim actually related to this issue," the Rosh Yeshivah told them. "In *Tehillim* 106, *passuk gimmel*, Dovid HaMelech writes, *'oseh tzedakah b'chol eis*, he performs charity at all times.' Whom does this refer to? Chazal tell us it is a person who sustains and supports his wife and children.

"Yet we might ask: why is someone who supports his family described as performing '*tzedakah*'? Isn't this a basic obligation? No, that is not the way to understand it. The *pshat* is like this," Rav Alter said, and he began to describe a scene familiar to the two seasoned *askanim* in the room. "Sometimes you see a renowned *askan* going around the hospital, helping this person today, another person the next day, and you are amazed at all that he accomplishes. Then, six months later, you visit the hospital and he isn't there anymore. This Jew who did so much is no longer helping anyone.

"What happened? Why did he stop? I'll tell you why." The Rosh Yeshivah smiled. "Yes, he was helping so many Yidden. But he didn't have *parnassah* to feed his wife and children — so he had to stop his *chessed*. If you want someone to do '*tzedakah b'chol eis,*' then first you have to make sure, as Chazal say, that he can support his family — that he has a proper *parnassah*.

"Mrs. Lubling," he said warmly, "has a business. She has a

playgroup that gives her *parnassah*. So she can afford to be a volunteer. But these new organizations are hiring people who will spend all their time helping the *cholim*, and they have to be able to support their families. If we want them to be constantly immersed in *tzedakah* and *chessed*, we must make sure that they have *parnassah*."

Mrs. Lubling nodded — and she accepted the Rosh Yeshivah's words. The concept of paid volunteers may have gone against her grain, but in all the years that Reb Shloime interacted with her, he never again heard her say a word against the practice. As strong-minded as she was, the *daas Torah* had ruled — and her *emunas chachamim* was infinitely more powerful than any personal feeling or preferences.

One of Mrs. Lubling's dreams — likely inspired from those early days when she recruited the women of Crown Heights to cook meals for the patients of Chronic Disease Hospital — was a dedicated bikur cholim room, where families of patients would have easy access to kosher meals and snacks to nourish them through their stay, to supplement the hot meals delivered daily by the Satmar Bikur Cholim.

In Tammy Klein, she found the perfect partner. Tammy was a young wife and mother who grew up in Los Angeles and settled in Boro Park after her marriage. She knew of Mrs. Lubling — everyone knew of the indefatigable *chessed* icon — and one day she introduced herself. "My name is Tammy Klein," she said. "I heard you help people in the hospitals, and I want to help you."

Mrs. Lubling sized up the hopeful volunteer. "I have a job for you," she said. "I want you to take on the bikur cholim room."

The room, at that time, was still a dream. But Mrs. Lubling was confident the hospital would allow her to actualize it. And she was fully confident, too, that the necessary funding would present itself.

The moment NYU agreed to allot a room to Mrs. Lubling, Tammy got a call. "We got the room!" Mrs. Lubling exulted. "Now we have to set it up."

Tammy drove to Manhattan and Mrs. Lubling showed her

around the empty space, off the lobby of the Rusk Institute, which was part of NYU. She pointed and gestured, articulating her vision: "Here we will have tables and chairs. Here we will put two recliners. The hospital will give us cabinets and a refrigerator. We will make sure they are always filled with snacks, coffee, and good, nourishing food."

Tammy took mental notes. "Okay," she said. "I'm going to reach out to an organization I know, maybe they can help."

"But the recliners — we need them now."

"Now?" Tammy asked. "Don't we have to plan everything first, get the funding in place?"

"Now," Mrs. Lubling answered. Foremost on her mind was a Boro Park family whose son had been hospitalized in serious condition. The family had nowhere to stay, nowhere to sit — except at their son's bedside — and Mrs. Lubling was determined to help them immediately.

Tammy understood a command when she got it. Soon the recliners were prominently placed in the bikur cholim room, a welcome refuge for the parents taking turns at their son's bedside.

Then Tammy arranged a meeting with an organization that had expressed interest in the assignment. When Mrs. Lubling asked about their plans, the volunteer was decidedly lukewarm. "We'll try our best," he said. "I think it would be realistic for us to bring some tuna sandwiches every two days or so. How does that sound?"

Mrs. Lubling looked at Tammy. Tammy looked back at her. "We have a different vision for this room," Mrs. Lubling said grandly.

And so she did.

Tammy began stocking the room as generously as she could, with the help of the Satmar Bikur Cholim. Then she connected with Mr. Yossi Lamet, a Brooklyn businessman whose mother Sally had been a good friend of Mrs. Lubling.

Mr. Lamet and his business partner Mr. Yanky Schwartz already had experience in this "line of work" — they initiated a 24-hour kosher food station in Lutheran Hospital, which had an oncologist on staff who treated many *frum* Jews. When Tammy heard about the generous, fresh, and *heimishe* meals they provided at Lutheran,

The bikur cholim room was one of those dreams Mrs. Lubling was determined to actualize. Thanks to her vision and dedication, *frum* patients and their families now enjoy fresh, *heimishe* food in hospitals across the country.

she got in touch with them. "Would you want to help out Mrs. Lubling in NYU?" she asked.

Mr. Lamet was honored to help his mother's friend — he had seen her in action and harbored significant respect for her dedication to Jews in need. Twice a week, he filled a truck with individually packed snacks and meals and dispatched it to NYU.

Tammy's family became faithful partners of the initiative, helping to provide the bountiful and delicious spread for hungry patients and their visitors — a true tribute and merit to her grandparents, Rabbi and Rebbetzin Avram Shea Rubin.

Perhaps Mrs. Lubling's proudest moment was the *hachnasas Sefer Torah* she organized in the spring of 2008. Food and accommodations weren't enough for *frum* Jews to truly feel at home in the hospital, she realized. Jews need to daven, and three days a week, that means they need a *Sefer Torah.*

First she approached the board of NYU. "The Jews in this hospital need a Torah scroll to read from during their prayers," she said. "I want to arrange it."

The board members were a bit apprehensive. "What will you need from us?" they asked.

"Nothing," she said blithely. "I take care of everything. Only one thing you need to give me — a safe, so we can lock up the Torah scroll when it's not in use."

The board agreed.

Mrs. Lubling then asked Rav Shmiel Dovid Friedman of Boro Park, whose wife often helped her out, to donate the *Sefer Torah*. Rabbi Friedman seized the opportunity.

Hachnasas Sefer Torah at N.Y.U. Langone Medical Center

By Shimon Golding

An historic celebration was held at NYU Hospital recently that brought tears of joy to hundreds. A premier hospital renowned for its excellent medical care, in the Jewish world, NYU is also known as the home of the "Mrs. Lubling Hospitality - Bikur Cholim Room." The room is named for the Rubin family from Los Angeles. Here, family members can find respite from the medical crises they must confront. Foods for nutrition, reading materials for the mind, and a place to sit and breathe are generously offered. Now, the room has something else — its own *sefer Torah*!

On the day of the *hachnasah*, excitement built as over a hundred doctors, Bikur Cholim volunteers and friends, as well as executive members of the hospital, filled the auditorium for the expected introduction of the new Torah. Rav Yakov Pollack, Senior Chaplain, thanked the hospital administration, especially Dr. Robert Grossman, Dean and CEO of the hospital. He described Dr. Grossman as a true friend of the community and an individual who has dedicated his life to helping others.

The smile on Dr. Grossman's face was ample proof of how much he relished this moment and how proud he was to be participating in this most beautiful affair, where both medicine and

(L) Dr. Robert Grossman, Dean and CEO, NYU Hospital;
(R) Dr. Andrew Litt, Vice Dean, holding the new *sefer Torah*.

HAMODIA PHOTOS/GEDALIA STUDIOS

Mr. Thomas Tisch, Trustee of the hospital, lovingly dancing with the new *sefer Torah*.

Torah values converged. Dr. Grossman promised to continue working towards making NYU a friendly environment for all. He acknowledged that his staff is happy to do all it can to maintain its close relationship and sensitivity to the Orthodox Jewish community.

As a *chuppah* was being set up to bring in the beautiful *sefer Torah*, the assembled were privileged to hear from the Ridnicker Rav, Harav Baruch Shamshon Halberstam. Harav Halberstam told the audience, "I am not here only as a Rav in the community but as a veteran user of the NYU facilities for my congregants and even my immediate family over the past 18 years."

He added, "It clearly states in the Torah, *V'rapoy Y'rapeh*. This alludes to the fact that not only should one go to a doctor, but one should seek out the best in medical care when necessary. In utilizing the NYU Medical Center and its wonderful, professional staff for one's medical needs, we are fulfilling, to the fullest, the Torah's *mitzvah* of utilizing the best facilities to care for our bodies!"

The volume of Orthodox Jews from Williamsburg, Borough Park, Monsey, and other neighboring communities that utilize NYU's services has dramatically increased. The need to serve these communities with

Please turn to page C42 ▶

Mrs. Lubling's proudest moment, as documented in the June 25, 2008 edition of *Hamodia*, was the *hachnasas Sefer Torah* at NYU — now *frum* patients and their families truly had everything they needed at the hospital.

They discussed the unique circumstances with the *sofer* — this *Sefer Torah* would not have the luxury of being housed in a large, spacious *aron kodesh* — and the *sofer* agreed to create a very small, albeit perfectly kosher, Torah scroll.

On Sunday afternoon, June 20, 2008, more than one hundred NYU board members, executives, and hospital staff converged on the NYU lobby, along with the extended Lubling family and a cadre of volunteers. A strain of lively accordion music broke through the sterile hospital setting and the completed *Sefer Torah* (the final letters had been written in the Friedman residence in Boro Park) was escorted under a canopy through the halls of NYU.

Mr. Thomas Tisch, chairman of the board, and Dr. Robert Grossman, CEO and dean of the hospital, were honored with the privilege of carrying the *Sefer Torah*, and Reb Itche Laufer, the very first patron of the Rivkah Laufer Bikur Cholim, watched his initial donation to the nascent organization come full circle.

The board members looked on, fascinated, as a crowd of *frum* men in dark suits and black hats danced through the hospital corridors, singing "*Toras Hashem Temimah*" and "*Se'u Shearim Rasheichem.*" An entourage of patients who'd emerged from their hospital rooms clapped along to the lively rhythm. At the end of the procession marched Mrs. Lubling, glowing with pride and satisfaction.

Finally, the *Sefer Torah* reached its new home — a locked cabinet in the bikur cholim room. It was gently stowed there, and then various board members addressed the crowd. The last speaker was Mrs. Lubling. Despite the high emotion of the day, she retained her diplomatic savvy, and thanked the hospital management for its sensitivity toward the Orthodox patient body, naming every board member and administrator who'd helped her transform the bikur cholim room into the haven of her dreams.

Just as Mrs. Lubling had hoped, the bikur cholim room became a magnet, a meeting point, and even an improvised shul. Patients in wheelchairs, warm-hearted visitors, and weary family members formed minyanim in the conference room next door — an arrangement made at Mrs. Lubling's request. They reverently brought the *Sefer Torah* along for *Krias HaTorah*, and doctors joined the davening in their white coats or scrubs.

On Erev Shabbos, the aroma of chicken soup and cholent wafted out to the corridor, beckoning to Jews with the fragrance of home. Families of patients caught their breath and regained their composure as they treated themselves to the fresh coffee, cake, and soup and exchanged notes and encouragement.

And whenever Mrs. Lubling visited, she inspected the refrigerator and cabinets, making sure they were clean and fully stocked. Then she presided over the room like the visionary hostess she truly was — offering cookies, drinks, and reassurance to anyone in need. The hospital could be an impersonal and daunting place, but here in this room, she made sure there was nourishment for body and soul.

CHAPTER 12
Party Time

One winter afternoon in the 1980s, David Nachman Golding's phone rang.

David Nachman — known to everyone simply as "Ding" — had established a solid reputation as one of the *frum* world's top music producers. Along with his musical partner Rabbi Suki Berry, he nurtured many singers and musicians, produced numerous recordings and performances, masterminded the prestigious and groundbreaking HASC concert to benefit special-needs children, and even released a new concept in *frum* music: the iconic Uncle Moishy, a singer who taught Jewish children about Torah and mitzvos through lively songs and concerts.

But the phone call that day launched a side pursuit that he still treasures. Mrs. Miriam Lubling was on the phone, and while her hurried diction was hard to decipher, Ding understood the gist of her request. "I am making a Chanukah party in NYU for the patients," she said, "and my singer canceled. I need you should help find a new one."

Oh, and the party was scheduled for the next day.

"When it came to Mrs. Lubling, her words came out so quickly that we often weren't clear on what she said," Ding confesses. "But

Mordechai ben David at the mic, bringing the sounds of Yom Tov
to patients and families confined to the hospital

we always knew what she meant. And this time I knew it meant that I had to drop everything and produce a musical performance for the very next night."

Thankfully, Mordechai ben David was available. Ding's next phone call was to a keyboardist. Then he made sure he had speakers and microphones — this was before the days of digital sound systems — and the performance was ready to roll.

The next evening, he and his small team showed up at NYU and tentatively made their way to the large room the hospital had granted Mrs. Lubling for her party. They weren't sure what would be waiting for them.

In the room, they found a small contingent of patients and families, with a smattering of staff and a cadre of volunteers. Unlike the usual concerts Ding produces, most of the attendees at this event were clad in hospital gowns and accompanied by nurses. Several were in wheelchairs or connected to oxygen. Many had that pallor that comes with too many weeks spent indoors, with no exposure to the sun and sky, but it couldn't mask the hunger in their eyes.

The party began with menorah-lighting, and then Mordechai

Music producer Ding shares the mic and spreads the joy.
Mrs. Lubling's wish was his command.

ben David took the microphone. With warmth and vigor, he filled the sterile room with the celebratory sounds of Chanukah. "*Yevanim, Yevanim.*" "*Al HaNissim.*" The songs of *Hallel.*

The volunteers clapped and danced around the room, sweeping the families into their circles. Some of the patients hummed along, some tapped their feet to the beat. The nurses clapped appreciatively as the singer and dancers infused the room with the festive Chanukah spirit.

Ding realized that something special was happening. When Mrs. Lubling called again before Purim, he didn't just book a singer and musician. This time he brought his children, nieces, and nephews — all in costume — to be part of one of the most draining yet fulfilling performances he'd ever produced.

The tradition endured for twenty-eight years, and the parties got bigger and more ambitious as the years went on. The Purim parties always began with a proper *Megillah*-reading and the Chanukah parties with menorah lighting. The program escalated each year, as one-time participants felt drawn back, as more religious patients were admitted to the hospital, and as Mrs. Lubling developed her little party into a full celebration complete with costumes

Srully Williger singing and Yossi Rosenberg playing for the patients at one of Mrs. Lubling's famous parties

and *mishloach manos* for Purim, gifts for Chanukah, and an explosion of enthusiastic music for every season.

After the party concluded, the patients went back to their rooms and the volunteers headed home — but the performance wasn't over. Mrs. Lubling graciously albeit firmly directed Ding's team to the floors, so they could share the gift of music with those patients who weren't well enough to attend the performance.

One year, after the Purim party concluded, Mrs. Lubling approached Ding. "There's a woman in the ICU I want you to visit," she told him. "She wasn't able to come to the party, but you can bring her the music."

It was getting late and there was a busy Purim day awaiting them, but Ding and singer Srully Williger followed Mrs. Lubling's command. In the ICU, they found a woman suffering from a terrible debilitating disease: her mind had developed normally, but her body was withered and stunted, with her internal organs struggling to function.

After Srully sang for her, Ding sat down to talk.

"Are you really Ding?" the woman asked, eyes shining. "The one who produces the HASC concerts? I'm a massive fan — I can't believe I'm really talking to you!"

Then she turned wistful. "I really wish I could go," she said. "It would be a dream come true, to be there in the concert hall, with the lights all dimmed and the curtain going up on stage..."

"We're going to make it happen," Ding promised. "This year, you're going to be at the concert."

The day before the HASC concert, Ding got a phone call. It was Mrs. Lubling, and she was very agitated. "Remember the woman from the ICU?"

"Sure I remember her," Ding said. "She's coming to the concert, right? I have her ticket waiting."

"No," Mrs. Lubling said. "The doctors said she's in no condition to go anywhere. Isn't there anything you can do?"

There was so much Ding had to attend to that day — consolidating some of the musical numbers, adding last-minute narration, speaking to the arranger about some confusion regarding the order of songs, and soothing the performers' nerves — but the plight of that woman just wouldn't leave his thoughts.

The next day, D-Day, he arrived bright and early at the Metropolitan Opera House and set up the team for final rehearsals. Maybe it was last-minute jitters, maybe it was some tension among the musicians, maybe it was something else — but for some reason, he lost his patience as he watched yet another argument erupt over some petty detail.

Ding turned to Mordechai ben David, who was surveying the scene with an air of detachment.

"Do you want to get out of here?" he asked.

"Sure, how did you know?" Mordechai ben David said.

"I have an idea," Ding told him.

The two slipped out of the concert hall and headed to NYU. There they made their way to the ICU and conducted a private pre-concert performance for the patient who had dreamed of going to HASC.

Mrs. Lubling's intuition was right on target, he thought that night as the storied curtain rose and the HASC concert began. There *was* something he could do.

Mrs. Lubling's Chanukah and Purim parties became legendary events, where volunteer musicians and singers brought cheer to patients and their families.

Rabbi Zelig Prag met Mrs. Lubling when he accompanied his uncle, the victim of a terror attack, through surgery and a hospital stay. Even after his uncle returned to Israel, Mrs. Lubling remained a fixture in his life.

"Rabbi Prag," Mrs. Lubling telephoned him, "I am making a Purim party at NYU, and I need someone to *lein* the *Megillah*."

Rabbi Prag was happy to be there for the woman who'd been there for his uncle, and so he made the trek from his Boro Park home to Manhattan on Purim night. There in a room, he found an assortment of patients, family members, and volunteers, all waiting for the promised party.

He unrolled his *Megillah* and began to *lein*, not realizing that he'd just taken on a yearly commitment. Over the years, he discovered many other "regulars" — people who'd once been patients, or whose family members had been hospitalized, and who kept coming back to the party that had delivered an infusion of joy and hope.

Once, a man wearing a Rutgers University sweatshirt entered the room. He looked around quizzically, trying to make sense of the scene. Rabbi Prag approached, explained that this was a Jewish holiday celebration, and asked him if he'd like a yarmulke. The man accepted.

"Tell me something," he said. "How much do these people get paid to conduct this party?"

"Nothing," Rabbi Prag answered.

"So why do they do it?"

"Because they care about people."

Every year, before the Purim party, Mrs. Lubling urged her children to join her. Every year, they declined. As much as they admired their mother's activism, they had young children of their own and were reluctant to trek to Manhattan.

One year, however, Mrs. Lubling prevailed upon her son Chanoch to drive her to the party. For some reason, none of her other drivers were available. Chanoch sighed and got behind the wheel. He picked up his mother and began heading out of Boro Park.

"Wait," Mrs. Lubling said. "First we stop at the bakery, to pick up the hamantaschen."

Chanoch obliged.

"Now to Manhattan?" he asked.

"Soon," Mrs. Lubling said. "First we stop at a different bakery, to pick up the sugar-free hamantaschen."

Chanoch realized it would be a long night.

Mrs. Lubling in her element at a hospital party. Today there are many organizations and initiatives bringing music to hospital patients — back then it was a novel idea.

Eventually they pulled up at the hospital, and entered the room. Chanoch looked around at the patients, the staff, the volunteers — and he began to sob with emotion.

A prominent New York *mechanech* approached him. "What your mother does, no one can do," he said. "My daughter was here in the hospital on Purim eighteen years ago, recovering from a car accident. Your mother found us and took care of us, and she brought us down to her party. Since then, I keep coming back every year. To me, it's not Purim unless I attend Mrs. Lubling's party in NYU."

Mrs. Ella Adler was a wife and mother at the helm of a lively, bustling Brooklyn household. She has always been a creative, exuberant woman who exerts a magnetic pull on children of all ages, and her home was the place where kids of every stage would gather to play, chat, and hold choir rehearsals.

In the early 1990s, she started hearing about Mrs. Lubling from a close family friend, Miriam Turk, who volunteered along with Chevy Kramer as a weekly driver. Miriam regaled Ella with tales of Mrs. Lubling's *chessed*, her medical advocacy, and her golden heart.

One dark winter day in 1995, Ella's teenage son Michoel collapsed. The emergency crew that sped to their house tried mightily to revive him — to no avail.

The perpetually sunny Adler home was abruptly thrust into mourning.

After the *shivah* concluded shortly before Purim, Ella found herself groping, trying to navigate the new reality. Nothing was the same. She had her own grief and loss to process, in addition to the shock and sorrow plaguing all her children. She pasted a smile on her face for the children's sake, but she knew they could see right through her hollow facade.

How could they possibly recover? Would her home ever be happy again?

Then, one day while Miriam Turk was speaking with Ella, she mentioned casually, "By the way, Mrs. Lubling said you're coming to her party."

Ella swallowed hard. "I know she's very sweet and very nice and I appreciate it," she told Miriam, "but I'm not up to partying."

The days passed. Taanis Esther drew to a close, and Ella braced herself. She knew she had to go to shul to hear the *Megillah*, but she couldn't reconcile the bleakness of her tragedy with the Purim cheer.

Suddenly the doorbell rang. A petite woman with an elegant *sheitel* and black coat was standing there expectantly. It was Mrs. Lubling.

"Come," she said, "we go."

"Where — where are we going?" Ella stammered.

"To the party!" Mrs. Lubling answered emphatically. "To give *shalach manos* to the patients!"

"What are you talking about?"

"We go," Mrs. Lubling repeated. "I have a car waiting outside. The patients are waiting for us. We have no time. Get your family, put on your coats, and come."

The next thing Ella knew, her entire family was on their way to NYU along with Mrs. Lubling. When they arrived, they found a room suffused in warmth. First there was *Megillah*-reading, then entertainment arranged by Ding, with Mordechai ben David sweeping everyone into his music. Then volunteer girls wove among the patients carrying boxes of brightly packaged *shalach manos*, including masks and *groggers*.

"Come, you help!" Mrs. Lubling directed Ella and her children. The kids didn't know quite what had hit them, but they followed the directions of the European grandmother who was clearly captain of this bizarre ship.

Soon enough, the children had been swept into the music. Ella's husband Yanky was dancing with an elderly man. Ella was holding the hands of a patient, gently rocking to the rhythm of the singing.

Even today, Ella shakes her head in disbelief as she envisions the scene. Her husband — always more introverted — had just lost a beloved son. Her children's world had been overturned. Her own days and nights had fused into one cold, numb existence. And there they were, singing and dancing and spreading joy.

For years after that experience, the Adlers joined Mrs. Lubling's Purim and Chanukah parties at NYU. Both dates held special significance for them — Chanukah had been Michoel's birthday, and Purim would always be a reminder of the close of *shivah*. Now they'd found a way to fill those vulnerable days with meaning and giving.

The hole would always remain, but with time the Adler house filled with laughter and song once again. And their small living room became Mrs. Lubling's *mishloach manos* headquarters, where hundreds of packages were packed for the patients.

"I never dreamed I'd be able to have a Purim that year," Ella says. "Mrs. Lubling saved us. We were floundering — until an angel named Mrs. Lubling came into my life.

"'You see,' Mrs. Lubling told me during that first Purim party, 'I told you this is good. You will be happy now because you are helping sick people. When you bring them *simchah*, you bring it to yourself too.'"

CHAPTER 13
Bobby Lubling

Mrs. Lubling's grandchildren knew she was famous. They understood that she was well connected and powerful, that she had a unique ability to schedule medical appointments, scans, and surgeries, and that virtually everyone in the *frum* community of Brooklyn and beyond nodded with respect when they heard the name "Lubling."

Her grandson Mendy Drillick remembers that even the car service drivers who drove his *chevrah* around Boro Park for their Purim collections puffed up with importance when he asked them about her. "Of course we know Mrs. Lubling," they said.

And it was a point of pride for the *einiklach* that every Agudah Convention session opened with the same announcement: "Will everyone please turn off your cellphones — except Mrs. Lubling."

But to them, she was Bobby Lubling, the grandmother whose entire living room was decked out with their framed faces, the matriarch who hosted a monthly birthday party for her grandchildren, the nurturer who supplied them with fragrant *halupches* every Succos, the endlessly patient Bobby who sat with them and played Rummikub after a Friday night *seudah*.

Even as she filled the typical grandmotherly role of gift-giver and nurturer, though, they sensed that there was something supernatural about her abilities. As her grandson Menashe Frankel puts it, "There was nothing she couldn't do."

As children they all heard the story of the time, back in the Crown Heights days, when Zeidy Lubling had received the honor of *chassan Bereishis* on Simchas Torah. After davening, he announced to all his fellow *mispallelim*, "Everyone's invited to my house for *kiddush*!"

Chanoch, who was then a little boy, panicked and ran home. "They're coming, they're coming!" he told his mother.

"Who's coming?" she asked.

"The whole shul! They're all coming for *kiddush* and we don't have anything prepared!"

Mrs. Lubling didn't panic and she didn't falter. She pulled this and that out of the fridge, arranged fruits on platters, put out drinks, and when the parade of men arrived in her home, a full *kiddush* was waiting for them. There was nothing she couldn't do, nothing that could make her lose her equanimity.

The grandchildren also learned early on that Bobby Lubling was not the type of grandmother who sat and crocheted booties. She had a fire perpetually burning within her, a simmering drive to get things done.

With her *machateineste*
Mrs. Chani Feigenbaum

Ruchi (Drillick) Klein remembers her daughter Rivky's bas mitzvah. She merited to have two great-grandmothers present at the event, and both were asked to share a personal message with the bas mitzvah girl. Bobby Feigenbaum got up to speak and said in her composed way, "Rivky, remember, you should be *mevater*, stay calm. Even when people make you angry, never answer them back."

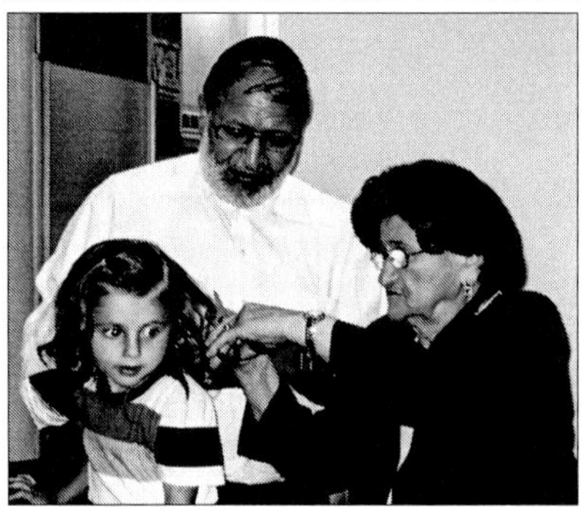

את

Then Bobby Lubling took her turn. "Rivkele," she said, her eyes flashing, "you have to accomplish, you have to do, nothing should stand in your way!"

One summer, on a visit to the Drillicks' bungalow in the Catskills, she took in the sight of the vacationers relaxing on their lounge chairs, chatting casually in the sunshine. "You should know," she told her grandson Mendy, "that if I would sit and do nothing, I would feel like I'm wasting the talent Hashem gave me. Imagine a master tailor sitting idle, never creating anything with his gifted hands. I know Hashem gave me certain talents — I can push, I can get things done, I'm a doer. To sit and do nothing is not what I was created for."

In fact, when a newly married grandchild and spouse came to wish her goodbye before moving to Eretz Yisrael, she showed them a stack of index cards scrawled with notes from her phone calls and said, "See, it's 11 a.m. All these appointments I made just this morning."

But ask her grandchildren and great-grandchildren, and they will all describe a woman whose burning sense of duty never came between her and her family.

In the late 1980s, Reb Yaakov was robbed while on his way to work in Manhattan. His hand was injured during the robbery, and he was brought to Bellevue Hospital. The routine bloodwork that the hospital performed came back with strange numbers. The doctors realized that their patient had an underlying disease unrelated to his injury. More testing was conducted, and they discovered a malignant growth in his stomach.

In a sign of their great devotion and concern for one another, both Reb Yaakov and Mrs. Lubling valiantly tried to shield one another from the dreadful truth. Reb Yaakov cautioned the doctors not to reveal his condition to his wife. Mrs. Lubling, who had learned of the results on her own, beseeched the doctors not to tell her husband the diagnosis. And each warned the children not to dare disclose the information to the other parent.

The children weren't sure whether to laugh or cry at the double ruse — but they couldn't help but marvel at the efforts both parents made to protect one another from anguish and grief.

"Don't tell Ima what the doctors found." Reb Yaakov Lubling tried to shield his wife from the devastating knowledge of his condition. He didn't realize that she had likewise warned her children not to tell him the dreadful news.

Mrs. Lubling reached out to Dr. Yashar Hirshaut, who fought determinedly to save Reb Yaakov. But the disease soon spread to his liver. In 1988, he passed away, just seventy-three years old. Masses of friends, relatives, and admirers turned out to escort him on his final journey back to his beloved Eretz Yisrael, where he was buried on Har HaZeisim.

After that, Mrs. Lubling's careful balance of home, work, and hospital disappeared. While she continued to make time for weddings and *simchos* almost every night, her hospital advocacy seized the lion's share of her time and attention, as she became an address for Jews across the world.

Chanoch and Rachel's teenage son Aryeh moved into the apartment two weeks after the *petirah* of Reb Yaakov, so that Mrs. Lubling wouldn't spend her weeknights alone. He maintained the arrangement for the next three years, while attending Yeshivas Novominsk in Boro Park (the yeshivah attended by all her grandsons).

No matter what time Aryeh returned to the apartment after night *seder* — including well past midnight on Thursday nights — Bobby always had a hot, freshly cooked meal waiting for him, complete with a finely diced Israeli salad and sliced fruit for dessert. She would even rush home early from weddings so as not to keep him waiting.

She sat with him while he ate and often shared some details of the cases she was working on. If she had attended a *simchah* of a former patient that night, she shared her joy too. "*Baruch Hashem, baruch Hashem, mammesh a neis,* literally, a miracle," she would inform him.

When he finished eating, she urged him to get to sleep, but she herself remained at the table with her planner and Post-it notes, organizing the appointments and follow-up tasks for the next morning.

"When are *you* going to sleep, Bobby?" he asked.

"After one hundred twenty I'll sleep," she said.

"But aren't you tired?"

She shrugged. "So everyone has to know about it?"

Apparently, no one else did know about it. Her phone rang at all hours of the night — some of the callers from Israel must have been unaware of the time difference. "I take care," she reassured them all. And sure enough, when morning came, she got straight to work, using her well-honed connections to schedule appointments, scans, or surgeries for her patients.

One particular morning, Aryeh heard Bobby arguing with a secretary who simply refused to schedule an appointment for one of her patients. "But I need it today," Bobby insisted.

"I'm sorry, Mrs. Lubling, but we're fully booked," the secretary responded.

"Let me speak to the doctor. I'm sure he can fit in my patient," Bobby tried again.

"The doctor is busy."

Bobby tried again, but the secretary would not budge. Finally, Bobby put down the phone.

Two minutes later, Aryeh heard the telltale ring.

"Mrs. Lubling?" It was the doctor she'd been trying valiantly to reach. "You can bring in your patient, I'll figure it out. Just one thing — come during lunchtime, when my secretary is on her break. And please don't tell her that I called you!"

After Reb Yaakov's passing, Mrs. Lubling was rarely home, and she didn't spend much time in the kitchen. But she still managed to fit in regular visits to her married children and grandchildren.

Mrs. Lubling at a great-grandchild's graduation. She never missed a party or performance, somehow finding time in her packed schedule for every event.

She was present at every *siddur* play and preschool performance. She found or finagled rides to Lakewood for every graduation. And come Shabbos, her hospital advocacy was set on a back burner. Shabbos was for family — for savoring time with her children, grandchildren, and even great-grandchildren.

Mrs. Lubling spent virtually every Shabbos with her children and grandchildren. Up until the moment Shabbos began, she was busy on the phone, speaking to the ER staff about test results, room assignments, and discharge papers. But when Shabbos began, all that disappeared and Bobby Lubling fully embraced her role.

She wasn't the type of Shabbos guest who sat back in a chair waiting to be served. She was a hands-on grandmother in the most literal sense of the word. During the meals she was busy in the kitchen, slicing fish or plating chicken. And the busier and noisier the home, the more boisterous the children, the happier she was.

She loved hearing a full chorus of voices during the Shabbos *zemiros*, and avidly followed and participated in the table talk. Somehow she managed to contribute to every conversation without ever saying a word of *lashon hara*. She had no time or patience for pointing out negativity; she had too many important tasks on her to-do list for such pettiness.

Mrs. Lubling was extremely discerning. She quickly noticed when a granddaughter was expecting and couldn't prepare her usual spread, or if a child hadn't made his bed. But even if she noticed, she never criticized. She only had positive things to say — a spill or a rip or a quarrel between overtired children was waved away with her refrain of "*Gornisht geshein,* nothing happened — it's nothing."

After the Friday night *seudah*, she relaxed with a cup of hot tea and a square of chocolate, and invited the younger children to play Rummikub. During those games, she somehow manipulated the pieces so the little ones would win. "Shh, shh, it's okay," she said conspiratorially as she slipped them the exact pieces they needed.

Then she stayed up late — completing her *Tehillim* allotments and then conversing with the adults, recounting stories of her early life late into the night. Somehow, even after a week of running from the kindergarten to the hospital to *simchos*, sleep was the furthest thing from her mind.

Her grandchildren remember one time when Mrs. Lubling's Shabbos oasis was breached for bikur cholim. A family friend in Boro Park had a stroke on Succos, and his children went running to the Drillicks' succah, searching for Mrs. Lubling. But Mrs. Lubling was in Lakewood for the *bris* of Rav Aryeh Lubling's newborn son, Yaakov.

The family consulted a *posek* who told them to do whatever they needed to contact her, even on Yom Tov. Peshi called Hatzolah of Boro Park, who contacted their colleagues in Lakewood. They tracked down Mrs. Lubling in Lakewood and within minutes, she was on the phone, arranging for the patient to be admitted to NYU, and then calling a top neurosurgeon at home and instructing him to hurry to the hospital, where the patient would be waiting.

For Chanoch's grandchildren in Ashdod, Bobby Lubling's visits were watershed moments. She came bearing handpicked gifts for each great-grandchild, perfectly suited to their ages and interests. During her stay, the children watched wide-eyed as a constant stream of visitors overtook their home. Some came simply to greet

Mrs. Lubling, while others brought X-rays, CT scans, or MRI results for her to deliver to doctors in the United States. All the major *chareidi* publications published large notices announcing her arrival, and several organizations held receptions to welcome the honored guest from America.

When asked how many grandchildren she had, Mrs. Lubling's answer was always "never enough" — and she knew the names and birth order of every single one. Not a single Erev Shabbos went by without speaking to each one personally. She was generous in every way — lavishing the children with gifts, time, avid interest — and was very effusive in expressing her love: each child was showered with her repeated "I love you, I love you, I love you" at the end of every phone conversation. And when the little ones had their birthdays, she sang "Happy birthday to you" line by line with them, her pitch rising steadily as she sang.

Many of the grandchildren attended her kindergarten. Even those who didn't live in Flatbush traveled from Boro Park every

Five generations of the Lubling family — Mrs. Lubling remembered the name of each child, and kept track of what they were learning in school.

The grandchildren and great-grandchildren who attended the playgroup got special treatment — but only in a side room, so the other children wouldn't feel bad.

morning. As an educator, she didn't want to show favoritism in public. But as a grandmother, she couldn't help but treat her grandchildren to an extra measure of love. So she pulled the *einiklach* into a side room and gave them chocolate, reminding them to finish it before rejoining the group so the other children wouldn't feel bad.

As immersed as she was in the high-stakes hospital world, she kept tabs on the dreams and fantasies of her little grandchildren. After one of the Travitsky boys showed her his drawing of a bear, she remembered to start their next phone conversation with an inquiry about the fuzzy animal: "How's your bear doing? What is it eating? Is it hiding?"

During her Erev Shabbos phone calls, she spoke to each child in birth order, and remembered to ask which *parashah* her granddaughters were learning and when the boys would be making their next *siyum*.

On random evenings, she would surprise the grandchildren with donuts or even a Chinese dinner. And one Sunday of every

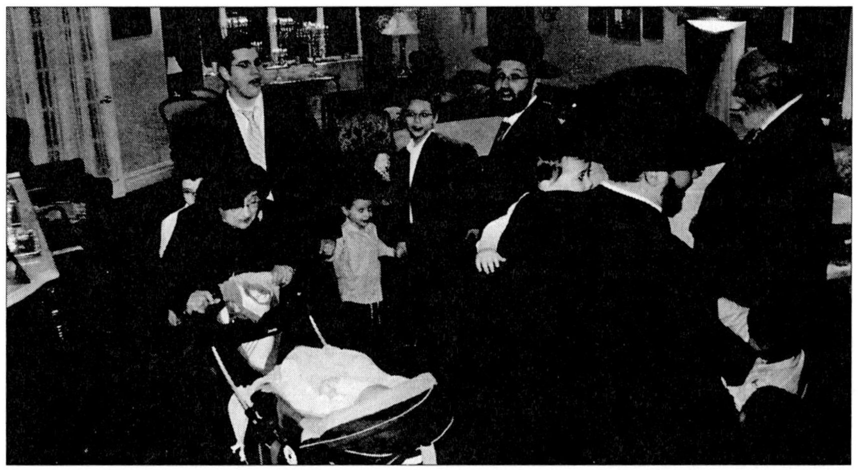

Bobby Lubling joining the dancing after menorah-lighting, pushing a stroller so the new baby could join too. You were never too old or too young to celebrate with family.

month, Mrs. Lubling hosted a grand birthday party for all the children who'd had a birthday during the previous four weeks. All the grandchildren were invited, and all relished the child-friendly menu: homemade crispy French fries and kielbasa.

When they arrived, her apartment was immaculate. The burgundy couches harbored not a speck of dust, and the throw pillows occupied their corners, plump and pristine. Each polished wooden chair stood in its exact spot around the dining room table, which

Bobby kept an immaculate home, with every photo, plaque, and plant fixed in place. But if the grandchildren left a mess, she didn't mind at all — these were the people she loved most.

was topped by a crocheted tablecloth with a silver vase at its center. The windows shone behind sheer curtains embellished with delicate embroidery. Every photo and plaque — and Bobby Lubling had received countless plaques over the years of luncheons, dinners, and fundraisers — was positioned with military precision on the wall.

When the grandchildren left, there were ketchup splotches and fingerprints everywhere. The toys had been removed from their spot in the spare bedroom and scattered about, and the kitchen chairs were left in a jumble around the white formica table. But Bobby didn't mind the mess for even a moment. Her home was crowded with the smiling faces of the people she loved most. What was a little mess?

In 2005, a fire broke out in the basement of the building where Mrs. Lubling lived, causing structural damage that required eight months of repair work. During this period, she moved into the home of her children Avrohom and Nechama Frankel.

Mrs. Lubling with (l–r) her daughters Peshi Drillick and Nechama Frankel and her daughter-in-law Rachel (Rhein) Lubling

The Frankels, who hosted her with dedication and grace, quickly discovered that their home would now be housing not just another individual, but an extremely consuming *chessed* operation. In short order, the phone was ringing at all hours of the day and night, drivers were pulling in and out, and Mrs. Lubling's round-the-clock activism and *simchah*-hopping set the tempo and schedule of the entire home.

But for the Frankel children and grandchildren, it was the most natural thing in the world to see Bobby Lubling juggling her beeper, cellphone, and address book even in temporary quarters. She managed to be wholly dedicated to her *cholim* and wholly dedicated to her *einiklach* — all at the same time.

When her grandson Menashe Frankel went to Eretz Yisrael to learn as a *bachur*, she fretted endlessly. "How are you going to manage to find your way to Yerushalayim? Where are you going to eat your Shabbos *seudos*?"

Finally she found a partial solution: she called Rabbi Asher Labin, one of the many family members of patients who'd become close family friends, and asked him to pick up Menashe from the airport. The Labins were more than happy to host Menashe — and many other Lubling grandchildren over the subsequent years — for Shabbos and Yom Tov meals during their stays in Eretz Yisrael.

One great-granddaughter remembers Bobby Lubling's trip to Eretz Yisrael during her seminary year. "She must have been 92, but she wanted to check out my seminary," she says. 'Bobby,' I told her, 'it's not going to work. There are too many stairs! If you have to see my seminary, just come see the outside of the building.'"

Mrs. Lubling wasn't deterred. She shlepped up two flights of stone stairs to the seminary office, where she charmed the

When the Labins married off a son, Mrs. Lubling attended the wedding as a full *machateineste*, posing along with her dear friends for a family portrait. An act of *chessed* performed years earlier had blossomed into a multi-generational bond.

Bobby Lubling visiting her granddaughters in Camp Bnos.
A trip to see the *einiklach* was never a shlep.

secretaries and met the principal. "You think I'm going to come all the way here and not check on my *einikel*?" she said.

After her granddaughter Ruchi married and made plans to move to Eretz Yisrael, Bobby Lubling called an Israeli friend to help find a rental apartment. She got there first — the timing coincided with her yearly trip every summer for her husband's *yahrtzeit* — and so she cleaned, set up, and stocked the apartment so the newlyweds would have a comfortable nest awaiting them.

When she realized that Ruchi hadn't yet mastered the art of challah-braiding, her inner kindergarten teacher came to the fore. She bought six colors of playdough, rolled out the strands, and patiently demonstrated how to form the braids.

When the grandchildren grew older and began to find *shidduchim*, they all knew that Bobby Lubling had to meet each new *chassan* or *kallah* before a *shidduch* was finalized (and once it was indeed "official," she thought nothing of hopping along in the car with the new *chassan* and *kallah* and asking them to expedite her bikur cholim travels).

"When I was dating my husband Mendy," remembers Chani (Frankel) Horowicz, the oldest grandchild, "Bobby kept track of the entire process. Shortly before we got engaged, we scheduled a date on Chol HaMoed Pesach to go to the West Point military academy. But our first stop was my grandparents — I knew they had to meet Mendy first. Bobby sent us back to the car with a homemade *kosher l'Pesach* lunch. When we got to the car, we opened it and found fresh latkes, matzah, hard-boiled eggs, and real silverware. As I settled into the seat, I saw her watching us through the window. She gave me a smile and a thumbs-up sign."

Every granddaughter knew that Bobby Lubling would help her choose a wedding gown and headpiece. And every child's *machateineste* became hers as well, joining her mental database of relatives who could help and be helped.

One new *machateineste* got a phone call soon after the engagement asking for help with bikur cholim. "I might have signed my life away," she confessed. "I have no idea what I just agreed to. All I know is that you don't say no to Mrs. Lubling!"

"The first time I married off a child," remembers Chani Horowicz, "Bobby gave me a list of people to invite. There were five hundred people on that list! And she made sure to host them properly. At all my *simchos*, she used to feed people — my husband's friends called her 'the fruit lady' because of the way she piled cut-up fruit on plates and serve them each individually."

Rivkie Lubling enjoyed watching Bobby host guests: she didn't just set out food, but actively shared it — cutting the cake and plating it, spooning out salad, making sure even the less assertive guests got to enjoy the *simchah*.

A granddaughter who married into the family introduced Mrs. Lubling to her aunt, then forgot about the encounter. Years later, the aunt set out in her car one Erev Shabbos to find some earrings. She noticed Mrs. Lubling and asked if she needed a ride. "Where are you going?" Mrs. Lubling asked as she entered the car.

"I was planning to go to the jewelry store, but I see it's closed," the woman said. "What a shame — I'm spending Shabbos with my granddaughters, and I was hoping to bring them each a piece of jewelry."

Mrs. Lubling opened her phone and selected the number of a jeweler she knew. "We're running over now," she told the jeweler. "There's a *machateineste* of mine who needs earrings before Shabbos."

Mrs. Lubling was very generous and showered all her grandchildren with gifts. Every new *kallah* received a necklace, every new couple got a sterling silver framed *tefillah* for candle-lighting, and when they settled into their apartment she bought them a custom-made breakfront or *sefarim* shrank.

She would visit the toy store and ask the proprietors for the latest toys: "What are all the kids playing with these days?" Then she'd buy the grandchildren their first dollhouses or magnetic tiles. She loved to give, and she loved to give gifts of real quality — "*di shenster un di bester*, the nicest and the best" was her motto.

But along with those items, she also offered the intangible gift of warmth and acceptance. Baruch Travitsky still remembers the first Yom Tov at his new in-laws, Chanoch and Rachel Lubling. "Bobby saw me looking uncomfortable, so she gave me a bowl of eggs to whip and put me to work," he says. He's still grateful for that casual gesture that said, without a word, "you're family."

Mrs. Lubling's involvement kicked into high gear whenever a granddaughter gave birth. Now she could fuse her two superpowers: her hospital advocacy along with her grandmotherly nurturing.

She always arranged for the new mother to have a private hospital room. One granddaughter remembers the hospital refusing the request. Mrs. Lubling, undeterred, grabbed the metal bars and wheeled her granddaughter's bed down the hall until she found what she was looking for. "Here, this is our private room," she declared as she maneuvered the bed into an empty room.

Before every *shalom zachar*, she cooked a pot of delicious peppery *arbis*. She purchased tiny knit ensembles for the new babies.

She hired baby nurses to help the exhausted new mothers and shared tips and tricks for newborn care.

She also made her naming preferences very clear. The family remembers the dreams that she providentially managed to have before every *kiddush* or *bris*. "Last night I had a dream," she told the new mother or father. "My brother (or sister, or uncle, or niece) appeared and told me he would like the baby named after him."

Whenever a granddaughter gave birth, Mrs. Lubling fused her two superpowers: hospital advocacy and grandmotherly nurturing.

At heart, the grandchildren understood her motivation. Most of her family had been wiped out during the war, without any remembrance whatsoever. "I have no *matzeivos*, I have no *yahrtzeits*, all I have is the name," she often said plaintively. Those names meant the world to her.

But if the new parents decided, for whatever reason, not to give the name she had requested, her reaction was remarkable — perhaps a greater *mofes* than any dream would have been. She simply accepted their decision without even a hint of a grudge and moved forward with the same love, warmth, and acceptance as always.

After every one of Chani Horowicz's six births, Mrs. Lubling accompanied her home from the hospital, holding the baby in a new outfit she had purchased expressly for the occasion. When the Horowiczes had a baby girl after the passing of Mendy's mother, Chaya Miriam, they knew they couldn't name her Miriam, since that was Bobby Lubling's name.

"So that's why we named her Chaya Leah," Chani explained to Bobby Lubling as they headed into the hospital elevator.

Bobby Lubling paled. "You know," she said as the elevator began its descent, "my middle name is Leah."

Chani was immensely grateful that Bobby was holding the baby, because she almost fainted. How could they have made such a terrible mistake, naming their new baby after her grandmother who was very much alive? And what were they to do now?

Mendy called Mirrer rosh yeshivah Rav Nosson Tzvi Finkel, who was a close cousin and confidant. "Should we change the baby's name?" he asked.

"Leave it," Rav Nosson Tzvi said. "It will be *segulah* for *arichas yamim*."

Mendy recounted the conversation to Chani. But she wasn't placated. "Rav Nosson Tzvi may have some Gerrer DNA [his maternal grandmother was a Lubling relative, from a Gerrer family], but he is Litvish," Chani said. "Bobby comes from a Gerrer family. I don't think that argument will work for her."

So Mendy called Rav Elya Fischer, the rosh kollel of Gur. He gave the same response.

Fingers trembling, Chani dialed Bobby Lubling and reported the conversation.

Bobby Lubling brushed it aside. "*S'git, s'git,*" she said. "It's fine. The main thing is that you should rest up so you have *koach* to take care of the baby."

When the great-grandchildren began to arrive, they were coached to call Mrs. Lubling "Bobby-Bobby," not Elter Bobby. She could not, would not, be called "elderly." That went against her grain. Ultimately, all her grandchildren and great-grandchildren remember her as a woman of strength and dignity, but more importantly, as an unusually vibrant and energetic giver and doer.

When Mrs. Lubling's grandsons got their drivers' licenses, some of them discovered that *bein hazmanim* was their time to drive Bobby around town — to the pharmacy, to the hospital, or even home from the wig stylist. The boys remember waiting at the wheel as Bobby Lubling descended the stairs holding myriad shopping

Mrs. Lubling surrounded by great-grandchildren. They learned to call her "Bobby-Bobby," not Elter Bobby — it went against her grain to be perceived as elderly.

bags. Following behind her was the *sheitelmacher*, gingerly balancing the freshly-set *sheitel* on a Styrofoam head.

Mrs. Lubling would nod in thanks and hurry into the car. "Come, we go," she told her grandson as she grabbed the wig and added it to the pile of bags teetering next to her. Other people her age might be slowing down, but Hashem had made her differently. She was a doer, and there were places to go and people to help.

CHAPTER 14
Self-Appointed Askan

Say the name "Miriam Lubling" in Brooklyn and beyond, and most people will envision a hospital. But Mrs. Lubling was one of those self-appointed *askanim* who intervened in many spheres and advocated for many different types of causes.

There were three traits that propelled Mrs. Lubling's varied *askanus* efforts. The first is simply that she noticed. A child in need, a family not quite coping, a teenager with an unfulfilled dream — it takes special powers of perception to intuit the story beneath the surface. She had those powers. Despite her busy schedule and very full life, her wise eyes and sharp brain picked up on the unspoken requests.

The second was her complete lack of inhibition. "So they'll say I'm a nudge," she brushed off anyone who questioned her persistence. "But what do I lose from asking?" Nothing could deter her from asking for help, be it a check for fifty thousand dollars or to get a promising young man accepted into Brisk.

The last trait that marked Mrs. Lubling as an unusually effective *askan* was the way she showered those who helped her with gifts and lifelong gratitude. If you helped her once, you were on "her team" forever — part of her network of benefactors and a cherished friend.

Back when she was a newly arrived immigrant in Crown Heights, she noticed that a fellow immigrant couple didn't quite seem to comprehend how the educational system worked. Their little daughter attended Mrs. Lubling's kindergarten at age two. She returned for the next school year, at age three. Then her parents sent her yet again for another full year, when she was four years old. At the beginning of the next year, Mrs. Lubling grew concerned.

"Tell me," Mrs. Lubling casually asked the mother, "what are your plans for Sarala next year?"

"She loves the kindergarten," the woman said.

Mrs. Lubling realized that the basics of school enrollment — something that most people picked up by osmosis — had bypassed this couple. She telephoned Rabbi Meir Levi, the pioneering principal who'd started a Bais Yaakov in Brownsville and was now heading it in Crown Heights.

"Rabbi Levi," she said, "I want to enroll a student in your school."

"A daughter?"

"No, someone else's daughter."

Rabbi Levi didn't quite understand.

Mrs. Lubling explained about the little girl who seemed fated to attend her kindergarten forever.

"Okay," he said tentatively. "What's her name? How old is she?"

Mrs. Lubling gave him the details.

"But she's already six years old," he said. "She'll be too old for first grade."

"You're taking her," Mrs. Lubling said.

And so he did. The little girl, now a grandmother herself, remembers her years in Bais Yaakov fondly. She was always half a grade older than her peers, but she fit right in.

During those years in Crown Heights, a devoted community *askan* died very suddenly. Mrs. Lubling, whose ears were always pricked up to the most delicate frequencies, heard that while the *niftar* would be buried in Eretz Yisrael, none of the children had plans to accompany the *aron*.

A few subtle inquiries unearthed the simple fact that the teenage boys didn't have valid passports. Between the lines, she realized that the expensive tickets were way beyond their budget.

To Mrs. Lubling, that was untenable. She never deemed the absence of money a valid reason to avoid a mitzvah. In the span of just a few hours, she contacted Reb Nachman Elbaum of the Upper West Side, owner of Ideal Tours, and purchased two plane tickets. Then she accompanied the boys to the passport office in Manhattan, where she arranged for them to receive expedited passports, so they could accompany their father on his final journey.

In the late 1990s, Rabbi Yechiel Kaufman, rav of Boro Park's Anshei Sfard (the "Sfardishe") shul, received a telephone call from Mrs. Lubling. At the time, Rabbi Kaufman also served as director of the Boro Park Jewish Community Council, a non-profit organization that provided Boro Park residents with access to a broad range of governmental services and benefits.

He had long known and admired Mrs. Lubling, but he never imagined that she would call him with an offer he couldn't refuse. "Rabbi Kaufman," she said simply, "I would like to work with you. Do you have an office for me?"

At that point, Mrs. Lubling was no longer involved with her kindergarten. Her afternoons were devoted to the hospital, but she had detected a real need for providing assistance to the local Holocaust survivors, and so she decided to spend her mornings helping them. The most efficient way to do so, she decided, was to join Rabbi Kaufman's staff and serve as head of the Holocaust Survivors' Project, which she expanded to include medical referral services as well.

On the surface, the new job title didn't spell much of a difference for Mrs. Lubling. She had helped survivors obtain medical care for decades, and she intended to continue doing so now. But an official title and office meant she'd be able to help in a more comprehensive way, because the Council had ready access to services and resources beyond her existing medical contacts.

Mrs. Lubling was always the consummate lady, from her freshly-set wig to her pearls to her heels — but she had big dreams and plenty of gumption to bring them to fruition. At the groundbreaking ceremony for a dedicated bikur cholim building.

For the next ten years, Mrs. Lubling showed up at the Council building on 14th Avenue promptly every morning, and made her way to her office. The Holocaust survivors of the neighborhood swiftly learned that here was a council representative who spoke their language and understood their background. They beat a steady path to her desk, and she delivered results.

Be it Medicaid, insurance, medication, nursing care, or physical therapy, Mrs. Lubling undertook to get it done. All she asked for was a desk and chair; she required no secretary or receptionist. Rabbi Kaufman put his resources at her disposal, assigning her a room adjacent to the Council reception area.

Within weeks, a pattern developed. A potential client would walk in and begin explaining their issue to the receptionist: "We have government funding for an aide for four hours a day, but since my husband's stroke we're not managing... we need more help..." Or, "We have to register our change of address for the Holocaust Claims Conference; do you have the form?" Then Mrs.

Lubling would scurry out of her office, from where she'd overheard the request. "Come here, come here, I help you," she said, beckoning them to her desk. Quickly and efficiently, she would provide them with the resources they needed before the Council staff had managed to isolate the issue.

Throughout that period, Rabbi Kaufman never once saw Mrs. Lubling frustrated or at a loss. She was a consummate lady, always professional and always polite. Even when she was under stress, she mustered her adrenaline and got the job done.

Rochel (Rozi) Hellman can't pinpoint exactly how she got to know Mrs. Lubling. As a resident of Boro Park, she knew both of the Lubling daughters, and as an innate *baalas chessed*, she became a dedicated volunteer for the Rivkah Laufer Bikur Cholim.

Early in their marriage, Rochel's husband Moishe learned of a small foster care agency called Ohel that sought to ensure Jewish children from unstable homes were placed in Jewish foster care. His initial interest grew into steady involvement, then a position on the board, and eventually a leadership role.

Partners in *chessed*. When Moishe Hellman introduced Mrs. Lubling to Ohel, he and his wife Rochel gained a lifelong champion and dear friend.

As the agency expanded its scope and ambition to an umbrella of mental health resources and resources for families dealing with developmental disabilities, Mr. Hellman's team began to build and administer group homes for adults with limitations and challenges. Knowing about Mrs. Lubling from his wife — Rochel described her as "dynamite with a heart of gold" — he decided to introduce her to the work of Ohel.

One evening, Mr. Hellman drove Mrs. Lubling to an Ohel group home for women with mental illness. With her usual charm, Mrs. Lubling introduced herself to all the residents and heard about their lives, their jobs, their shared responsibilities keeping their apartment in order. But one of the names had rung a bell; she was clearly emotional when she got back in the car.

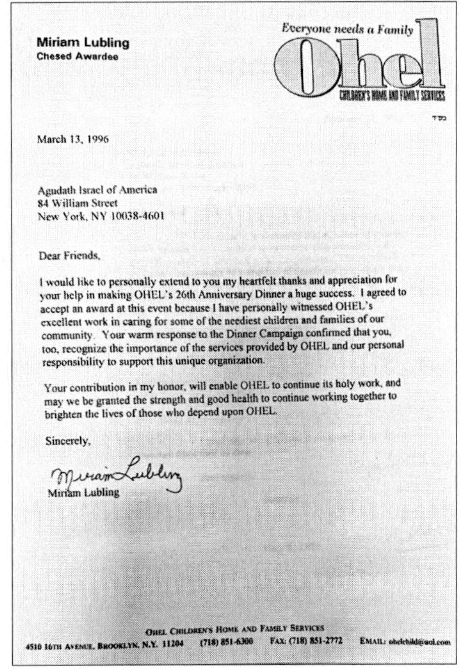

Miriam Lubling
Chesed Awardee

Everyone needs a Family
Ohel
CHILDREN'S HOME AND FAMILY SERVICES

בס״ד

March 13, 1996

Agudath Israel of America
84 William Street
New York, NY 10038-4601

Dear Friends,

I would like to personally extend to you my heartfelt thanks and appreciation for your help in making OHEL's 26th Anniversary Dinner a huge success. I agreed to accept an award at this event because I have personally witnessed OHEL's excellent work in caring for some of the neediest children and families of our community. Your warm response to the Dinner Campaign confirmed that you, too, recognize the importance of the services provided by OHEL and our personal responsibility to support this unique organization.

Your contribution in my honor, will enable OHEL to continue its holy work, and may we be granted the strength and good health to continue working together to brighten the lives of those who depend upon OHEL.

Sincerely,

Miriam Lubling

OHEL CHILDREN'S HOME AND FAMILY SERVICES
4510 16TH AVENUE, BROOKLYN, N.Y. 11204 (718) 851-6300 FAX: (718) 851-2772 EMAIL: ohelchild@aol.com

A thank-you letter from Mrs. Lubling for a contribution to Ohel

"One of the women in this home used to attend my kindergarten back when she was four years old!" she told Mr. Hellman after they left. "I remember her parents. What a difficult situation this must have been for them, to watch their daughter get sick, with so little for them to do."

Then she turned to Mr. Hellman. "And what a special thing you are doing, giving this woman a home, a place where she feels welcome."

From that moment on, Mrs. Lubling was a faithful partner of Ohel, eventually joining the board of the growing organization — and in a show of mutual appreciation, Mr. Hellman became a trusted partner and patron of her bikur cholim work.

One of the most strategic connections that Mrs. Lubling made was enlisting NYU chairman Thomas Tisch in the Ohel cause. Mr. Tisch, a son of billionaire businessman Laurence Tisch — CEO of the CBS television network and co-owner of Loews Corporation — sat with Mrs. Lubling on the NYU board of trustees, of which he was chairman. Watching this softhearted warrior in her modest dress and wig passionately advocate for "her patients," he developed deep-seated respect and fondness for Mrs. Lubling.

Mrs. Lubling realized there was a warm Jewish heart beating in the chairman, and she suspected he might be persuaded to contribute to some Orthodox initiatives. He had little exposure to the *frum* community of Brooklyn or the various *chessed* organizations under their auspices — but Mrs. Lubling thought she could change that. Yeshivah education might not speak to Mr. Tisch, but she sensed that the social service ethos of Ohel would resonate with him.

"Moishe," Mrs. Lubling called Mr. Hellman one day, "I need you should come drive me to Manhattan. We have an appointment to see Mr. Tisch."

Mr. Hellman picked her up and together they drove to Mr. Tisch's office on Manhattan's Upper East Side. Mrs. Lubling brought along an elaborate silver bowl; it was her practice to bring a gift to every benefactor she met. Privately, Mr. Hellman doubted whether an heir to billions of dollars would really appreciate the bowl.

But when Mr. Tisch saw Mrs. Lubling, his face lit up. He personally escorted her and Mr. Hellman to his office, asserting, "Mrs. Lubling is an angel" to Mr. Hellman. After the meeting, in which they explained Ohel's work, he wrote a generous check and then accompanied them to the elevator.

"Where did you park?" he inquired.

Mr. Hellman told him they'd parked in a lot just down the block.

"Okay, so let me help you get out," Mr. Tisch said.

He then walked the pair to the parking lot, stepped into the street, held up his hand, and personally stopped the traffic on 58th Street, between Madison and Lexington Avenues, so Moishe Hellman could pull out of the narrow spot.

He dismissed Mr. Hellman's shock with an easy wave. "This is what Mrs. Lubling taught me," he said.

After she introduced Mr. Tisch to the work of Ohel, he became a steady supporter, even agreeing to serve as co-chairman of one of their yearly dinners. Her delight when he donated significant sums spilled over the phone lines. "Moishe," she'd tell Mr. Hellman, "I got *'ah fifziger'* from Mr. Tisch — he gave a check for fifty thousand dollars!"

(At the time of Mrs. Lubling's *petirah*, Mr. Tisch's annual donation to Ohel exceeded one hundred thousand dollars.)

On Purim, Mrs. Lubling decked herself out in a costume, bringing laughter and cheer to everyone in her orbit.

And she enlisted other donors, too, for every major campaign, serving as a champion fundraiser who always came through for the causes she believed in. Dr. Antoine, the renowned obstetrician, proudly attended the Ohel dinner every year as a special guest of Mrs. Lubling, one of the many well-connected contributors she brought in.

But Mrs. Lubling didn't just help Ohel financially. She spent time with the residents and spread her warmth and personal concern at parties and functions. At the Ohel pre-Purim party, she went so far as to don an improvised costume — a flax-colored wig and face makeup, or a clown wig with a red nose — just to bring a smile to the precious souls at the event.

One day, a sick baby was admitted to the pediatric department at Maimonides Medical Center. When a baby is sick, the staff often gets a closeup view of the family's overall dynamic. In this case, the view was alarming. The baby had clearly come from a dysfunctional home, where money was lacking, fresh food was not a given, at least one child was a serial truant from school, and the parents lacked basic resources and tools to function as adults.

Mrs. Lubling spent most of her afternoons in NYU, but the Rivkah Laufer Bikur Cholim sent a steady cadre of volunteers to Maimonides, and she soon learned of the case. She swept in and took in the total picture with a keen eye that noticed everything

— and a warm heart that pulsed with compassion even where others would feel repulsion and disgust.

"She took care of this family as if they were England's Royal Family," Douglas Jablon remembers. Not only did she ensure that the baby received the best medical care, she also arranged for the family to receive freshly cooked meals. Then she reached out to the relevant communal organizations to set up long-term aid for the parents, tutor the struggling schoolchild, and ameliorate the family's financial straits.

The doctors saw a baby who needed treatment. The more observant staff members saw parents who weren't functioning well. Mrs. Lubling saw a family in need, and she wouldn't rest until they were on solid footing.

Once, Peshi Drillick overheard her mother working the phones with an unusual request: she was enlisting her contacts to get a young *bachur* accepted into the elite Brisk yeshivah in Eretz Yisrael, an institution known to be extremely selective.

"Ima," Peshi protested, "if you use your *protektzia* for him, what will happen when your own grandsons want to go to Brisk? Save it for us!"

"Right now I'm helping him," Mrs. Lubling replied firmly. "When you need something, someone will help you. That's how it works for us Yidden."

But even Peshi had her doubts when Mrs. Lubling decided to interfere in the seminary acceptance process — just days before the start of a new school year.

One of her granddaughters had an orphaned friend who made the decision, early in twelfth grade, not to attend seminary in Eretz Yisrael. As the year came to a close, and all her friends got busy shopping and packing for seminary, she had a change of heart.

"I can't believe I'm not going to seminary in Eretz Yisrael," she confessed tearfully. "I'm going to feel so alone the whole year. How will I survive?"

Just three days before the group flight to Israel, Mrs. Lubling heard her granddaughter ruing her friend's sad situation. Instead of clucking her tongue and moving on, she stopped and got to work. "She wants to go?" she said. "She's going."

She found out which seminary the young woman wanted to attend and tracked down the personal phone number of the principal. He listened politely as a woman with accented English told him a sad story about a girl who'd made poor decisions and now regretted them. "I'm so sorry," he said contritely. "It sounds like a very sad situation, but we literally don't have an extra bed."

"I want to tell you something," Mrs. Lubling answered vehemently. "This girl wants to go to seminary so badly. She is coming to your school. I am getting her a ticket, I am putting her on a plane, and I'm sending her to your dormitory. Make sure there's a bed for her when she arrives."

The principal took a deep breath. "Okay, Mrs. Lubling," he said.

The next day, the newly accepted seminary student boarded the plane along with her friends. And that Erev Shabbos, the principal received the most magnificent chocolate platter he'd ever seen.

CHAPTER 15

Even at Death's Door

Everyone wants to think of hospitals as bastions of altruism and good will. The reality is that hospitals have financial bottom lines, and they must remain profitable to stay in business.

Everyone wants to think of doctors as people who vanquish disease. The reality is that doctors have always been limited. While the modern medical arsenal is constantly growing and improving, there inevitably comes a point when doctors are powerless to heal.

Put those realities together, and you might begin to understand the sea change that began to sweep through the medical world in the 1980s. For decades, hospitals had been places where severely ill patients lingered and deteriorated until they died, and doctors saw their role as trying everything they could to stave off death.

But passage of new insurance protocols meant that many hospitals could not make a profit once a patient had spent more than four days in a bed. This meant that hospitals were effectively losing money if they could not vacate beds quickly. New admissions took priority.

At the same time, the increasing availability and sophistication of ventilators, which facilitate breathing when a patient's respiratory system can no longer supply adequate oxygen, made the financial calculations a lot more complex. Hospitals could technically keep very ill patients alive for months. But was it worth it for them?

Beyond the cost, many doctors began to grow uneasy with the power they now had. They'd always seen it as their mission to prolong life. But now that they could keep patients in a suspended state between worlds, sustaining their heartbeats and respiration through mechanical means, they wondered whether they were prolonging death instead of life.

When doctors and medical ethicists grapple with these issues, they tend to use terms like "quality of life" and "a good death." What kind of quality of life will my patient have if he makes it out of the hospital but can receive nutrition only via a tube? Will a ninety-three-year-old with a tracheostomy enjoy life if she can no longer communicate? My patient is suffering from untreatable cancer and likely has just months left to live. When he comes down with pneumonia, should I treat it with antibiotics or just let it shut down his systems? My patient is in her eighties and was just diagnosed with a rare type of brain tumor. Should I try an experimental drug, or just give her pain relief and allow the tumor to overtake whatever remaining healthy tissue she has left?

As these questions increased in number and intensity, the medical world began to embrace palliative and hospice care — two related approaches with a shared goal of submitting to disease and treating patients only for pain. In 1990, the World Health Organization recognized palliative care as a distinct specialty in medicine. Doctors and hospitals began recommending that fatally ill patients consider checking out of the hospital, discontinuing active care, and prepare to meet their demise in a hospice facility.

Mrs. Lubling watched as the change took root, and she did not like what she saw. The concept of the "good death" completely ignores the spiritual dimension of life in this world and the next; too often, it is not compatible with the halachic and hashkafic understanding of the value and purpose of life, death, pain, and of the reality of eternal reward.

Moreover, according to this calculus the lives of the elderly are worth less. If "quality of life" is the prime determinant of care, why spend time, energy, and resources on a ninety-year-old whose aged body will never regain full independence? Better transfer her to a hospice, and free up the hospital bed for a younger patient with a better prognosis.

For Mrs. Lubling, though, the first breath and last breath had the same value. She fought for every additional hour of an aging Holocaust survivor with the same grit she employed for a seven-year-old cancer patient.

"I saw it many times," Douglas Jablon remembers. "When a patient had a really dire diagnosis, and the doctor said there was nothing to do, she didn't accept it. 'You can't help me? Okay, so I will try another doctor,' she announced. And she did. She would transfer patients in dire conditions to other hospitals, or to doctors who were willing to try different drugs or procedures."

Mrs. Lubling found a powerful ally in Dr. Yashar Hirshaut, the Manhattan oncologist who is renowned for both his medical acumen as well as his willingness to take on cases other doctors consider hopeless.

During his many years interacting with Mrs. Lubling, Dr. Hirshaut found her to be a very bright and perceptive advocate. Her approach combined attitude with information: a determined optimism along with a constantly updated knowledge of the medical options. She did not dictate to doctors, but she did encourage them to keep trying.

And while she herself did not have all the answers — she did not read medical journals, consume new research, or attend conferences, and she never presented herself as a medical expert — she definitely had some idea of the possibilities. "When you're involved in enough cases," Dr. Hirshaut says, "you begin to get a sense of what the opportunities are. And when she heard about successes in specific areas, she followed through and obtained the knowledge. Then she was able to make suggestions, or ask questions, about new drugs or treatments."

As her intuition began to prove itself, the doctors came to value the quality of her suggestions. And as they followed her urgings to try just one more avenue, investigate that new procedure, or look into a different medication, they found themselves enriched and gratified by what Dr. Hirshaut terms "the ability to do G-d's work" — to give a desperate patient another chance.

It takes a certain shift in thinking to concede the seriousness of the situation the patient is confronting, to admit that there is nothing in your own toolkit that can help them, and still acknowledge that there may be a way out, and you have to explore that possibility.

When doctors find the humility and tenacity to look beyond the obvious and succeed in giving a patient that second chance, it's an unusually rewarding experience that expands their sense of both their abilities and the possibilities that medicine offers. "You get a certain lift," Dr. Hirshaut puts it, "from looking back and seeing how far you were able to push, how far you were able to go."

It wasn't only doctors whom Mrs. Lubling discouraged from giving up. Very often, it was the patients and their families who needed a surge of her indefatigable optimism in order to keep fighting their battles.

Hudi Silber still remembers the time she accompanied Mrs. Lubling into the ICU to visit a woman who was deathly ill. The doctors had already informed the family that they were out of options. Now the woman was lying pale and still in her bed. Her family was assembled in the room. Some were crying, many were reciting *Tehillim*. The time for *Vidui* seemed to be approaching; an aura of despair pervaded the scene.

Mrs. Lubling looked around. She straightened up to her full height. "Everyone leave, right now!" she ordered the family.

They looked at her, confused.

"Out, you heard me," she said.

No one said no to Mrs. Lubling. They all stood up and left the room.

Mrs. Lubling opened her bulging handbag and pulled out some of the cosmetics she kept stowed there. She approached the sick woman and touched up her face with blush and lipstick. Then she searched through the drawers, found a wig inside, and replaced the kerchief the woman had been wearing.

She stepped outside and beckoned to the family members hovering there.

"*Zi leibt noch,* she's still alive," she said. "Let her look and feel that way. Why are you behaving as if it's over?"

Several of her drivers remember Mrs. Lubling's visits to rooms where patients hovered close to death. Her refrain upon leaving those rooms was always "The *Ribbono shel Olam* will help," and her sincere belief in His powers to bring back a patient from the brink was apparent to everyone. Only in the darkest of cases did she exchange that refrain for "The *Ribbono shel Olam* should have *rachmanus.*" When they heard those words, her drivers knew that the situation was truly dire.

In 1998, during the final illness of Rabbi Moshe Sherer, the legendary chairman of Agudath Israel of America, Mrs. Lubling mustered the same defiant optimism. Even when he seemed to be fading into the next world, and the grueling treatments sapped him of his usual aristocratic air, she refused to give up.

Mrs. Lubling (far right) called Rabbi Moshe Sherer (center) "the president of Klal Yisrael." He, in turn, called her "the angel of mercy." During his final illness, she was a staunch champion for his *kavod.*

One day, she arrived in his hospital room carrying a shopping bag from a high-end Boro Park shop, Gentlemen's Boutique, and pulled out an expensive pair of silk pajamas and a matching dressing gown. "Reb Moishe," she said with esteem and affection, "you're the *melech*, the king, of Klal Yisrael! You're the *nasi*, the president of Klal Yisrael! You need to look dignified, even in a hospital bed."

She didn't just leave the bag at his bedside; she returned to make sure that he was in fact dressed in the princely robe and even fluffed up his pillows to perk him up and make him more comfortable.

Mrs. Lubling often fielded phone calls from patients afraid to commit to aggressive treatment plans. A woman once called her and said, "My mother is sick, and she's refusing to start chemotherapy. She said the doctors aren't all that hopeful anyway."

"She must take the chemo!" Mrs. Lubling insisted. "If it will give her more time, how can she say no? Let me speak to her. I take care."

Mrs. Lubling religiously attended every Agudah Convention. One year, she attended a session that focused on the need for a kosher hospice facility, geared to *frum* patients whom hospitals deemed no longer treatable. Mrs. Lubling loudly objected to the proposal. Discontinuing medication and focusing solely on pain relief is contrary to our beliefs, she explained. We *frum* Jews cannot give up on anyone, no matter what the doctors say.

A different concurrent session about end-of-life issues was led by preeminent *posek* and Mesivtha Tifereth Jerusalem rosh yeshivah Rav Dovid Feinstein.

During the session, Rav Dovid addressed extremely weighty and complex questions regarding the delicate halachic issues that arise during the final stages of life. As was his manner, he responded to the questions in a very concise style, focusing on the halachah with utmost clarity and brevity.

At one point, the presenter related a detailed scenario involving a critically ill patient whose internal systems had shut down.

He asked Rav Dovid whether the family of the patient would be permitted to sign a DNR (Do Not Resuscitate) Order, effectively abandoning any attempts at prolonging life. Rav Dovid ruled in a very brief few words that in this particular scenario, there was no halachic obligation to maintain life support. (This ruling is in no way intended to be followed by any reader — it was specific to that situation.)

The session then opened up to a Question and Answer segment, where the audience was invited to speak up. Mrs. Lubling rose, bristling with passion.

Without fear or hesitation, she questioned Rav Dovid's ruling. "We must preserve life!" she insisted, blazing with fervor. "Every moment of life is precious! How can you sign a DNR and lose the chance to give someone more life?"

Rav Dovid sat quietly through her rebuttal. When she finished and returned to her seat, he took the microphone, inclined his head toward her, and in his mild manner said, "Well, now you've heard another opinion on the matter."

Mrs. Yuttie Frankel, one of Mrs. Lubling's longtime bikur cholim partners, decided at some point to volunteer for the *chevrah kaddisha*. When Mrs. Lubling heard about the decision, she was visibly disturbed.

"Why are you going to do that?" she asked.

"Dodah Miriam," Mrs. Frankel explained, using her term of endearment for Mrs. Lubling, "some people have to take care of the living, and some people have to take care of the *niftarim*."

Mrs. Lubling couldn't argue with that, but it still hurt. She was so intensely focused on life that the very thought of death upset her.

And that unapologetic focus on life spilled over into all her interactions with the medical staff. "If you begin with the assumption that because a patient is seriously ill, they don't have much to look forward to, it affects all the medical decisions," Dr. Hirshaut says. But Mrs. Lubling didn't see patients — even seriously ill patients — as just steps away from the end. Her destination was always life; the question was just how to get there.

"She wasn't willing to accept that something couldn't be done," Dr. Hirshaut remembers, "or that just because someone is a leading physician, his word is the final word. When you're determined to do the best for an individual and you realize how complex the situation is, sometimes you realize there are other options."

Mrs. Lubling didn't denigrate the doctors or accuse them of not caring or striving enough. But she did raise the possibility of other options. And she made it clear that she was on their side, sometimes even funding professional travel or consultations with doctors who had different backgrounds or training that might expand existing medical horizons.

Mrs. Lubling expended significant effort in getting patients admitted to the Rusk Rehabilitation Institute, a top-ranked physical therapy center under the NYU umbrella, and the world's first university-affiliated center devoted entirely to rehabilitative medicine. Often the director, Dr. Bruce Grynbaum, would push back. "Why should I admit this patient?" he asked. "I'm a clinical rehabilitation specialist, and I know full well that he's too sick for what we have to offer."

Mrs. Lubling always answered, "Come on, Dr. Grynbaum, give him a chance." And more often than not, he acceded.

In an ironic twist of fate, later in his life Dr. Grynbaum suffered a stroke and was admitted to his own institute for rehab. Mrs. Lubling was circling the wards when the staff wheeled him in. He met her eye and offered a lopsided smile.

"Give him a chance, right?" he said.

CHAPTER 16

What Mrs. Lubling Can Do

Every night in the hamlet of New Square, the waiting room of the Skverer Rebbe, Rav Duvid Twersky, fills with a pulsing mass of humanity. Some of the visitors make the trip to seek the Rebbe's advice in matters of *chinuch*; others want his blessing before finalizing a *shidduch* or business deal. And many broken Jews come for guidance and encouragement after receiving a serious medical diagnosis.

Over the years, the Rebbe grew well acquainted with Mrs. Lubling and her web of connections. He also intuited something else about her, something more otherworldly than pure logistics and practicalities.

"I just got a terrible diagnosis," one petitioner asked. "The first *askan* I spoke to recommended a specific doctor. But then we called Mrs. Lubling and she told us to see a different doctor. What should we do? Whom should we listen to?"

"Listen to Mrs. Lubling," the Rebbe said. "She has *siyata d'Shmaya.*"

So many patients attest to the Heavenly Hand that seemed to accompany Mrs. Lubling in her advocacy. Though she had no medical training or official degrees, she often displayed an uncanny intuition.

The women who accompanied Mrs. Lubling on her hospital rounds all describe the same scenario. After visiting the admitting office, she would stand in front of the elevator bank and muse, "Where should we start today?"

Then, seemingly at random, she would say, "Let's try the sixteenth floor," or "Let's start on the maternity floor today." Inevitably, when she exited the elevator at whichever floor she randomly selected, a person who just "happened" to be right there would say, "Mrs. Lubling! How did you know? I was hoping I would find you here today. I need your help..."

When Chanoch Lubling's children Baruch and Tova Travitsky moved to Passaic, one of their first priorities was registering their sons in the local school. After filling out an application, they were invited to meet with Rabbi Heshie Hirth, executive director of Yeshiva Ktana of Passaic.

Rabbi Hirth greeted the couple and began to peruse their application. As he read Tova's maiden name, he stopped. "Are you related to Mrs. Miriam Lubling?" he asked.

"Yes," Tova answered. "I'm her granddaughter."

Rabbi Hirth rose to his feet. "Your grandmother gave my mother ten more years of life," he said, voice trembling with emotion. "My mother was scheduled for a very delicate stomach surgery. Somehow your grandmother sensed that this was the wrong course of action for her. She canceled the surgery, pulled her out of the hospital, and arranged for her transfer to NYU. They treated her with medication instead and she had ten good years afterward."

On August 29, 1986, during the First Intifada, Rav Moshe Meir Prag, a brother-in-law of Rav Shlomo Zalman Auerbach and the rosh kollel of Shomrei HaChomos, took his regular walk to the Kosel. Just outside Shaar Shechem, an Arab terrorist approached and stabbed him violently. The terrorist knifed him in two crucial spots: a lung, and the upper portion of his spine.

Rav Prag was rushed to the hospital, where the doctors tried valiantly to reverse the damage. But they quickly realized that they were outmatched. The stabbing had mutilated crucial areas of Rav Moshe Meir's spinal cord. He was paralyzed and soon slipped into unconsciousness.

The medical advisors who took on his case told the family that his only hope was a complex surgery performed by a top neurosurgeon in the United States. The family consulted with their uncle Rav Shlomo Zalman Auerbach, who advised them to set out at once.

Within twenty-four hours, the patient, lying on a stretcher, was loaded onto a plane along with his son Rav Yehuda Leib and son-in-law Rav Dovid Shapira, rosh yeshivah of Yeshivas Beer Yaakov. Neither Rav Yehuda Leib nor Rav Dovid knew English, or how to get to the hospital, or even what kind of surgery Rav Moshe Meir needed. All they knew was that a *heimishe* woman named Mrs. Lubling would take care of everything.

Rabbi Zelig Prag, a nephew of Rav Moshe Meir who lived in Boro Park, still remembers the surreal experience. Early Thursday morning, he traveled in a Hatzolah ambulance to John F. Kennedy Airport to meet his uncle and accompany him to the hospital. The ambulance took them directly to NYU, where the distinguished patient immediately underwent an MRI. The family was then invited to a consultation with the surgeon — and that is when they met Mrs. Lubling for the first time.

"*Shulem aleichem*," she greeted them warmly in a friendly Yiddish that set them at ease. "*Bruchim haba'im*, welcome to America. How can I help you? Can I get you something to eat? Maybe a drink? You're going to be here for Shabbos, I will make sure you have a place to sleep, don't worry. Now we will meet the doctor, then we will talk some more."

Mrs. Lubling had arranged for the injured Rav Moshe Meir to be seen by Dr. Joseph Ransohoff, a third-generation surgeon who was internationally acknowledged for his expertise in brain and spinal surgery. Dr. Ransohoff was at the cutting edge of his field, and personally involved in the development of a pioneering device, the Cavitron Ultrasonic Surgical Aspirator, to treat deeply embedded tumors the medical world had previously considered invincible.

(His mentee Dr. Fred Epstein took the innovation a step further by adapting the device to treat spinal growths in children as well.) The Harvard-educated physician was also a Jew — and one of Mrs. Lubling's favored doctors.

Dr. Ransohoff analyzed the MRI, and then Rabbi Zelig Prag watched in amazement as this elite professional, over six feet tall, turned to the *heimishe* woman from Boro Park to discuss his findings.

"I'm seeing some sort of blockage in the spinal column as a result of the stabbing," he said. "We'll need to operate, and we'll have to do so very soon. First thing on Saturday morning."

"Who will do the operation?" Mrs. Lubling asked.

"I will," Dr. Ransohoff said.

"But Dr. Ransohoff, you never work on Saturday," she said in surprise.

The celebrated doctor squared his shoulders and looked directly at her. "For this, of course I'll come in." Then he faced Rabbi Prag and remarked offhandedly, "It's true, you should know. I never come in on Saturday. But you can't say no to Mrs. Lubling."

Then he grew quiet. "There is one thing," he finally said. "Saturday is the Jewish day of rest. I would like you to ask your rabbi and see if he agrees with the timing. If the rabbi gives his blessing, then I will operate, even on Saturday."

Rabbi Prag turned to his cousins and translated the curious request of the bareheaded, extremely secular doctor.

"We will ask Rav Shlomo Zalman," they said. "Whatever he says to do, we will follow."

Rabbi Prag assured the doctor that the family would procure the guidance of a great rabbi in Jerusalem and only then proceed with the surgery.

"And how much will you charge?" Mrs. Lubling asked.

The doctor bowed his head. "Whatever money you can come up with will be fine."

On Shabbos morning, Rav Moshe Meir was taken into surgery, still completely unconscious. His son and son-in-law waited for hours until he was finally released from the recovery room, then ushered into an elevator to be taken to the neurosurgical unit on the twelfth floor. There in the elevator, still attached to multiple tubes and monitors, he opened his eyes.

"Tell me, Yehuda Leib, where am I?" he asked. "Where is Ima?"

"Abba!" Reb Yehuda Leib could barely contain his emotion at finally hearing his father speak again. "Ima isn't here. She's still in Eretz Yisrael."

"What do you mean, in Eretz Yisrael? And where are we?"

It took some time for Rav Moshe Meir to process his son's explanations of all that had happened since the stabbing outside Shaar Shechem. The last time he'd been conscious, he had been thousands of miles away, very close to death's door. It was hard to assimilate the details of just how critical the situation had been, and just how transformative a role this unknown woman from Boro Park had played.

But during the next seven weeks, as his recovery proceeded, he got to see her in action. Soon enough he moved from post-op to rehab, where skilled physical and occupational therapists were charged with helping him regain mobility.

During rehab, Mrs. Lubling stayed intimately involved in every detail of his treatment. She even managed to find two therapists who knew Hebrew and would be better able to communicate with the Prags. (The therapists hung a blackboard over Rav Moshe Meir's bed with both Hebrew and English versions of all the common requests the patient and his children might make; when the Prags had to communicate with English-speakers, all they needed to do was point. Rav Yehuda Leib did, however, learn to instruct the nurses in English that he preferred "cup of cola, no ice," unaccustomed as he was to cold drinks in the wintertime.)

After seven weeks in NYU, Rav Prag asked his children to arrange a flight home. His youngest child, a *ben zekunim* born close to eighteen years after the nearest sibling, would soon be celebrating his bar mitzvah. Rav Moshe Meir was determined to be there for his son.

Amazingly enough, the same person who seven weeks earlier had been escorted onto the plane unconscious, strapped onto a stretcher, now sat in a regular seat.

Upon his return to Eretz Yisrael, he continued the rehab process with local therapists. The paralysis still affected his entire right side, but he was eventually able to walk with the aid of a walker. He wasn't able to write properly, however, and was very pained at the thought of not being able to record his *chiddushim*. Then he found a solution: he bought a typewriter and managed to type instead.

During the next fifteen years, Rav Moshe Meir often had to strain to breathe, due to the damage the terrorist had wreaked to his lung. But he forged on, and managed to write two *sefarim*, *Neiros Aharon* and *Neiros Bnei Moshe*, both on the Rambam.

Until today, his family credits Mrs. Lubling — the woman they hadn't even known, but who made their father's plight her greatest concern — for those fifteen extra years and the *harbatzas Torah* generated during that time.

In January 2001, after suffering from weeks of splitting headaches and nausea, nineteen-year-old Yehuda Kamenetzky was diagnosed with a brain tumor. The scans indicated an enormous mass, the size of a golf ball. Time was of the essence.

His parents, Rabbi Mordechai and Mrs. Sora Kamenetzky, were suddenly faced with an array of dizzying decisions, with almost zero time to research and consider their options. They learned of two brain surgeons with the skill and experience to take the case. One was Dr. Patrick J. Kelly, who studied under Dr. Joseph Ransohoff and served as chairman of the Department of Neurosurgery at NYU School of Medicine. But how would they get an appointment with the doctor, whose waiting list was months long?

Then Rabbi Kamenetzky received a phone call from his friend Rabbi Shimshon Sherer. "I heard that you need an urgent appointment with a top doctor at NYU," he said. "The person you need to speak to is Mrs. Miriam Lubling — she's the 'Queen' of NYU. I'm going to set up the phone call, and she will take it from there."

The phone call was perfunctory and Rabbi Kamenetzky barely understood Mrs. Lubling's English. But he followed instructions and brought his wife and son to the parking lot at First Avenue and

34th Street. There they saw an elderly woman with an oversized handbag and umbrella. She greeted them warmly and let loose a stream of reassurances: they were in a good hospital, they would soon be seeing a top doctor, and of course, the ultimate Healer would surely help their son.

Then she whisked them to Dr. Kelly's office and finagled an immediate appointment from the secretary. Dr. Kelly greeted them and asked to see the scans.

He studied them carefully, then turned to face the terrified teen and his parents.

"I can operate," he said. "I can even do it tomorrow. But I don't think you will get more than fifteen months, two years at most. And that's with chemo and radiation."

Utter dejection overcame the Kamenetzkys. It seemed like the end of the road — for a son who had barely begun to live. But Mrs. Lubling showed no such emotion. Instead, she bristled.

"Dr. Kelly," she said firmly, "you may be a very good surgeon, but you are not G-d." Then she pointed upward. "One thing you forget: the real doctor is the One Above."

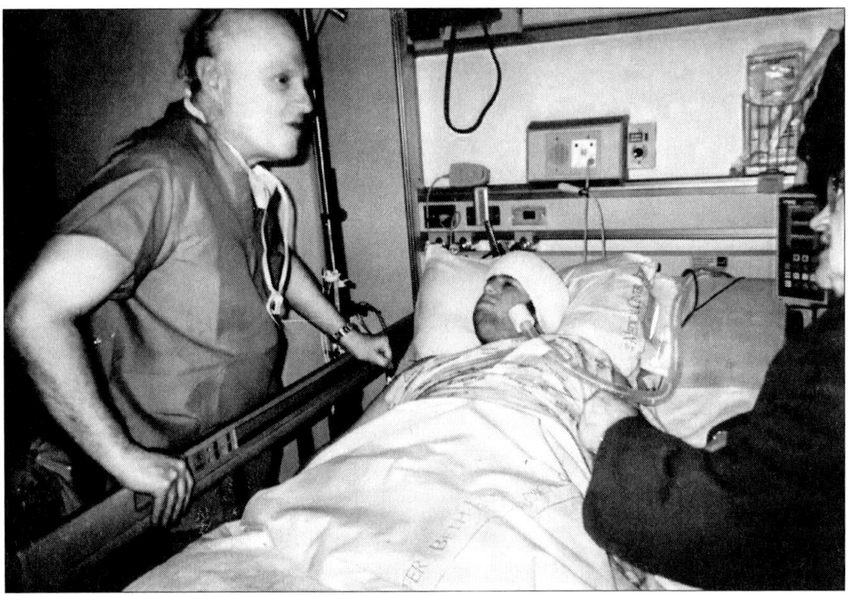

After Yehuda Kamenetzky (center) underwent a complex brain surgery by Dr. Fred Epstein (left), Mrs. Lubling (far right) was waiting at his bedside, clutching her *Tehillim*.

She motioned to her guests to follow as she swept out of the office.

Mrs. Lubling encouraged them to see Dr. Fred Epstein, who had left NYU to open a private practice on Manhattan's Upper East Side and subsequently joined Beth Israel Medical Center. Dr. Epstein performed the surgery and successfully removed the tumor. Nearly a quarter of a century later, Yehuda Kamenetzky is enjoying a productive life as a husband and father, fully healed from the massive tumor.

And he still has a distinct memory from that time: when he finally came to after the long, complex surgery, he noticed three faces waiting anxiously at his bedside. His father, his mother, and an elderly woman clutching a *Tehillim*. It was the woman he'd just met but who clearly saw herself as his champion: Mrs. Miriam Lubling.

Mrs. Lubling enjoyed an especially close relationship with her downstairs neighbors, the Weinbergs. During one visit to the United States, Rabbi Weinberg's father stumbled and fell down the stairs a few times. His children were alarmed and asked Mrs. Lubling what to do. In a matter of minutes, she arranged for him to see NYU neurologist Dr. Govindan Gopinathan on East 38th Street on Manhattan's Upper East Side.

"You will need an MRI," the doctor ruled after examining his patient. "But appointments are hard to get. You'll probably have to wait two weeks."

"Two weeks?" the Weinbergs asked, dismayed. The stakes were way too high for such a long wait.

The doctor nodded. "Maybe Lubling — you know her? — can get it done a little faster."

"Yes, we know her," Mrs. Weinberg answered, and she swiftly called Mrs. Lubling.

About five minutes later, the phone rang at Dr. Gopinathan's office.

"Is there a Weinberg here?" the secretary asked. "Someone wants to speak to you."

Mrs. Weinberg took the phone. It was Mrs. Lubling. "Take a taxi to 32nd Street," she commanded, "straight to the MRI machine. They're waiting for you and they'll do it right now."

An hour later, they were back at Dr. Gopinathan's office holding the scans.

"I can't believe it!" he said. "You did it today? How did you get an appointment?"

"It's all because of Mrs. Lubling," Mrs. Weinberg said. "She arranged it."

Dr. Gopinathan shook his head in awe. "What she can do, I can't."

Late one evening in 2007, Mrs. Sally Lamet, a good friend of Mrs. Lubling, underwent a medical crisis. As soon as Mrs. Lubling got the call, she sprang into action. She came along with the Lamets to the emergency room at Maimonides Medical Center and waited with them until Mrs. Lamet was examined.

At 2 a.m., the medical staff decided to admit her. Mrs. Lubling marched right along as her friend was settled into a room.

To their dismay, the roommate was blasting the television at full volume, making it impossible for Mrs. Lamet to sleep.

"Can you please turn it down?" Mrs. Lubling asked politely.

"No," the patient said.

Mrs. Lubling walked briskly to the nurses' station. "My sister is exhausted," she told the nurse on duty. "She has to sleep. But her roommate won't turn down the television. Can you help us?"

The nurse shook her head. "Sorry, we can't get involved," she said laconically. "It's on her side of the room."

Mrs. Lubling thought for a moment, then returned to her friend. She sat down next to Mrs. Lamet and very loudly, albeit not quite tunefully, began to sing. Her determined warbling along with the blasting television made for quite a cacophony, and it wasn't long before the formerly blasé nurse hurried into the room.

"Please!" she said. "We need quiet here!"

Mrs. Lubling cocked her head. With a mischievous smile, she responded, "Oh, but this is my side of the room!"

Within minutes, the television was silenced, and Mrs. Lubling happily ceased her serenade so Mrs. Lamet could finally get some sleep.

Miriam Hendeles is a daughter of Mrs. Lubling's faithful friend and chauffeur Mrs. Eva Stern. She married and moved to Los Angeles in 1980, and therefore did not have a front-row seat to Mrs. Lubling's bikur cholim work. Still, she kept tabs on her mother's forays to and from Manhattan.

When one of her children was just two years old, he was referred to an ophthalmologist due to a severe case of strabismus (cross-eye). "This doesn't look like a typical case," the ophthalmologist said. "I want you to take him for an MRI before I make a decision whether to operate."

The MRI uncovered a cyst in the optic region. That would have been frightening enough, but some of the medical staff suspected that the mass might be a tumor. The Hendeleses began a grueling round of doctors' visits, seeking a second and then third opinion.

Opinions they got, but clarity was elusive. Some doctors said the cyst had to be removed immediately, because of its proximity to the optic nerve. Others advised watching and waiting; perhaps it would resolve on its own.

It was a difficult and confusing time. One day, Miriam unburdened herself to her mother. "I'll call Mrs. Lubling," she promptly said.

Miriam doubted whether her mother's feisty immigrant friend could do more than the doctors at Los Angeles's top hospitals, but when Mrs. Lubling phoned and asked her to send the scans to NYU, she followed her orders. The next thing she knew, her phone rang. "Miriam," said a heavily accented voice, "Dr. Fred Epstein from NYU wants to talk to you."

"I still remember where I was standing — the exact spot in my kitchen," she says. "I remember his voice. He was so confident as he told me, 'It's a tumor. A benign tumor.'"

"Wait," Miriam interrupted, "isn't it an arachnoid cyst?"

"Yes," Dr. Epstein said patiently, unruffled. "And that's a tumor.

"But," he went on, "you shouldn't touch it. I'm an aggressive surgeon and I wouldn't touch it. He can live with it for one hundred twenty years. Many of us have cysts like that and just don't know it. All you have to do is keep an eye on it and do a follow-up MRI every three or four years."

For the first time since this long odyssey had begun, Miriam began to breathe again.

"I'm going to refer you to Dr. Gordon McComb at Children's Hospital of LA," Dr. Epstein said. "He's the doctor you need to see."

Dr. Epstein, it turns out, had made the right call. Dr. McComb agreed with his plan and monitored the cyst, which never caused any trouble.

But Mrs. Lubling had the last word. After Dr. Epstein finished reassuring Miriam, she took the phone and said, "You hear, *mammele*? Listen to Dr. Epstein. He knows!"

Mrs. Lubling first met Mrs. Gutta Sternbuch at a wedding in Switzerland. Both were Polish Jews who had studied in Sarah Schenirer's Krakow Bais Yaakov and had endured immense hardships with unyielding strength and a passion for helping others. Mrs. Sternbuch, a survivor of the Warsaw Ghetto, settled in Switzerland after marrying Eli Sternbuch, a man dedicated to saving Jewish lives during the Holocaust.

Despite living continents apart, Mrs. Lubling and Mrs. Sternbuch nurtured a deep and enduring friendship that extended to Mrs. Sternbuch's children. When Reb Aryeh Leibush (Leon) Weinreb, a *mechutan* of Mrs. Sternbuch, suffered a severe stroke, Mrs. Lubling stepped in with her characteristic determination and resourcefulness. She worked tirelessly to secure his rehabilitation at Rusk Rehabilitation Institute, overcoming administrative resistance with grace and persistence.

Over the following months, she not only supported the Weinreb family with frequent visits, heartfelt encouragement, and joyous celebrations, but extended her care to countless others, always bringing light and comfort to those in need.

Mrs. Lubling often visited Mrs. Sternbuch at her children's home for Shabbos, infusing the atmosphere with her warmth, kindness, and uplifting presence. Her love and devotion were so deeply felt that she became like a cherished family member, invited to share in their most intimate celebrations and milestones.

More than forty years ago, Rabbi Dovid Mendlowitz hosted a guest named Reb Yisroel Levine. At first glance, Reb Yisroel's life seemed a litany of suffering. He grew up in Communist Russia, but managed to hold on to his Yiddishkeit by his fingernails. Though his marriage dissolved when he was young and he had little in the way of material possessions, he clutched tightly to the hope that he would one day move to Eretz Yisrael and bring up his only son to keep Torah and mitzvos.

His son, however, received permission to leave Russia before him, and joined a secular kibbutz on his arrival. Whatever feeling he had for religion was extinguished by the rabidly anti-religious kibbutz ethos.

When Reb Yisroel finally made his way to Eretz Yisrael, he reunited with his son — and was crushed. His dream had finally come true, but it had morphed into a nightmare instead. The hope he'd held onto for years had been snuffed out. What was there left to live for?

The State offered the newly arrived immigrant basic furniture and some sort of low-cost living quarters, but he bristled and refused their offers. "You took away my child!" he said. "You took away my future! Why would I want to receive anything from you?"

Reb Yisroel found a place to live in Jerusalem's Shmuel HaNavi area and a calling in the nearby Mir Yeshivah. He helped out in the yeshivah kitchen and forged close relationships with several longtime Mirrer *talmidim*, spending virtually every Shabbos with his new friends. The Mir became his adopted family and home, and he found his place as an essential thread in the fabric of its community.

Then the toughened Reb Yisroel began, uncharacteristically, to complain of weakness and pain. The doctor who examined him realized he was gravely ill with an advanced form of lung cancer. He was so precariously weak, his body so ravaged by disease, that the doctor wasn't sure whether there was anything to be gained by attempting to treat him.

The medical *askanim* involved in the case contacted Mrs. Lubling, and true to form, she refused to submit to the medical establishment's dismal prognosis. Instead she arranged for Dr. Yashar Hirshaut to treat Reb Yisroel in New York.

Rabbi Dovid Mendlowitz still recalls his stalwart guest with awe. When waves of pain hit Reb Yisroel, he looked up and spoke directly to his Maker. His words were simple but noble. "*Ribbono shel Olam,*" he said, "You've given me so much pain my whole life. I want to thank You for everything — for all the pain — I know it was meant for my good. But please, *Ribbono shel Olam*, it's been enough already. I'd be grateful if You don't give me any more, please."

Rabbi Mendlowitz drove Reb Yisroel to many of his medical appointments, and Mrs. Lubling joined them. Even though she was usually very even-keeled, something about this man — so utterly alone, with no one in the world save for a son who'd severed their connection — moved her, and her emotions quivered just below the surface on those trips to Manhattan.

The medical team tried their hardest, but after a few months of grueling treatments, they conceded defeat. They had tried every avenue and explored every possibility, they told Reb Yisroel, but this was the end of the road.

Reb Yisroel, his body frail and battered from the metastasized tumor and the rounds of toxic treatment, still retained his strength of spirit. "I want to go back to Eretz Yisrael to die," he declared. "That's my place."

Mrs. Lubling made the arrangements for him to fly home. She joined Rabbi Mendlowitz in the car on that last trip with Reb Yisroel, quiet and pensive. She had done all she could, and now there was no way she could help this principled Jew who had asked for so little and suffered so much.

Wait; there *was* something she could still do. As they entered the check-in area, Mrs. Lubling found the El Al flight manager. She pulled the uniformed woman into a corner and described Reb Yisroel's travails and the reason for his trip.

"I want him to fly first class," Mrs. Lubling said. "His bones are so brittle at this point, and he's suffered terribly. He needs a comfortable seat, so he can finally get some rest."

The manager shrugged. "You want first class, you have to pay," she said.

Mrs. Lubling tried again, this time with tears.

The manager wouldn't budge. "The plane is full, and I have work to do," she said, turning back to the counter.

Mrs. Lubling reacted almost as if by instinct. In one smooth motion, she reached to her neck and unfastened the string of pearls she always wore. Seconds later, the flight manager was beckoning to Rabbi Mendlowitz. "Here, bring the passenger over, we have a first-class seat for him!" she said.

Only someone who'd been watching the entire exchange would have noticed the gleaming strand of pearls now providing the finishing touch to the manager's El Al uniform.

Rabbi Yitzchok Gottdiener, executive director of Yeshivah Torah Vodaath, still remembers the yeshivah *melaveh malkah* that coincided with a historic blizzard. The yeshivah had no choice but to cancel the event.

He hoped and prayed that all the attendees would realize the *melaveh malkah* was not taking place that night — but just in case someone had made the trip in the driving snow, he took his front-wheel drive vehicle to the Menorah Hall on Boro Park's 14th Avenue so he could greet them and send them back home.

The hall was quiet and empty. Rabbi Gottdiener waited there. A sum total of two people showed up; he apologized for their trouble and told them the event had been canceled. Then he headed out into the empty streets of Boro Park, draped in white. And there he noticed a small figure plowing valiantly through the snowdrifts.

"Mrs. Lubling!" he exclaimed as he approached and recognized the woman. "What are you doing outside in this weather?"

"I have to get to NYU," she said calmly. "There's a patient I have to check on. I'm looking for a ride to the hospital."

It was far from the only time she made a nocturnal outing to check on a patient.

During one of their routine hospital visits, Mrs. Lubling and her devoted bikur cholim partner Judy Klein arrived at their first stop of the day: the operating rooms. "There's a woman here whose husband is having major brain surgery," Mrs. Lubling said. "We need to check on them."

They scrubbed up and entered the operating area. There they found a woman standing tensely, swaying as she cried through chapter after chapter of *Tehillim*. Mrs. Lubling introduced herself and gently asked how things were going.

"It's been hours since they took him in," the woman said, her anguish spilling out with her tears, "and I still didn't hear anything. I have no idea what's going on in there."

Without hesitation, Mrs. Lubling took Judy Klein by the hand and pushed open the OR doors. The two women marched inside. There on the operating table lay a man, his head swathed in bandages.

"Surgery's over," the nurse announced. "They were able to remove the whole tumor — it was a big one, somewhere between the size of an orange and a grapefruit."

"Why didn't you tell the wife?" Mrs. Lubling asked accusingly. "Very nice that you do your job here in the operating room, but you know she is waiting outside, so worried. How can you keep her waiting like that?"

They then went out to the waiting area. "I checked, the surgery just finished," Mrs. Lubling told the woman. "It went well and they were able to remove the tumor. The doctors are very happy."

"Thank you so much! Thank you!" the woman said. The tears kept coming, but her forehead seemed a little less furrowed. "Thank you for telling me. I was so worried — it was taking so long and I was terrified that something had gone wrong in there."

"Come, sit down," Mrs. Lubling said, patting the chairs. "You still have a long wait until they bring him into the recovery room, you might as well sit."

Then she and Judy sat down too, and stayed with the trembling woman until she regained her composure. They wished her well and headed up to make their usual rounds of the hospital for a long, exhausting afternoon.

That evening at 10:30, Judy's phone rang.

"*Mammele*, Judele, I can't sleep," Mrs. Lubling said. "Please let's go back to the hospital and check on this *veibel* and her husband, the one with the brain surgery."

"What?" was all Judy could manage.

"I beg you."

"But Mrs. Lubling, it's so late!"

"Okay, but I am dressed and ready. When can you come?"

Judy envisioned the eighty-something-year-old Mrs. Lubling standing fully dressed at her phone, consumed by worry for this couple she barely knew. She grabbed her car keys and left the house.

The streets were quieter now, and the trip to Manhattan was swift and smooth. They headed back down to the operating rooms, where Mrs. Lubling ascertained that the woman had not yet been allowed to see her husband. It may have been close to midnight by then, but there was nothing sleepy about her righteous indignation.

"This woman is waiting since the morning to see her husband!" she protested loudly to the nurse manager. "You have to let her in already!"

There was no saying no to Mrs. Lubling, and within minutes the woman was permitted into the recovery room to see her husband. Her relief was palpable. Finally, after so much fear and uncertainty, after so many hours shut out by the barrier of the OR door, she had made it to the other side.

Judy had hoped to go to sleep early that night — it had been an exhausting afternoon — but she didn't make it home until after 1 a.m.

"But you know what?" she told her husband as she recounted

the woman's endless wait and Mrs. Lubling's sixth sense — from miles away — that she was needed. "Mrs. Lubling was right. She always is."

CHAPTER 17
Power and Prestige

During the course of a single day, Mrs. Lubling could exhibit many emotions. She could be concerned, impassioned, comforting, enthusiastic. Those who spent time with her on the floors occasionally saw her give way to sadness. But no one who knew Mrs. Lubling can remember a time she was ever intimidated.

"*Mammele*, I'm afraid of no one except the *Ribbono shel Olam*," she repeatedly told the women who accompanied her on her rounds. And it was clear — from her plucky attitude and courageous actions — that she meant every word.

New York Mayor Michael Bloomberg poses alongside Mrs. Lubling. She may have been petite, but power didn't intimidate her.

After Mrs. Lubling underwent surgery for spinal stenosis, the hospital staff wanted to ascertain whether the anesthesia had worn off and if she was fully cognizant of her surroundings. They began to ask her the usual questions: What day is it? What city are you in? Do you know who the president is?

To the last question, she answered tartly, "Do you know who the president of this hospital is? Because I do, and I can bring him here into the recovery room right now."

It was true: She worked with some of the most imperious administrators and doctors in New York City, whose education, experience, and bank accounts far outranked hers. But she never felt inferior and her bearing never broadcast any insecurity.

One of her mottos was, "They won't shoot you, they won't kill you. Worse comes to worst, they'll tell you no." Buoyed by that confidence, she could approach anyone of any rank without a modicum of trepidation.

Rabbi Moshe Sherer, the longtime legendary chairman of Agudath Israel of America, enjoyed a close relationship with Mrs. Lubling. As a public servant who devoted every ounce of his talent, intellect, and resources to Klal Yisrael, he recognized a fellow "Klal Yisrael Yid" and harbored extraordinary admiration for her grit and passion. He regularly referred to her as the angel of mercy, a moniker that was later adopted by many of the medical professionals and communal activists who saw her in action.

Mrs. Lubling's background as a PAI activist left her with a finely-honed sense of organizational savvy. She was a faithful Agudist who often offered advice to Rabbi Sherer, and later to Rabbi Chaim Dovid Zwiebel, who currently serves as executive vice president of Agudath Israel of America. "Stay away from this person," she warned. Or, "This person will be a good contact for you, try to form a strong connection." Invariably, her advice was on target.

Rabbi Sherer valued Mrs. Lubling's life experience so greatly that he invited her to join Agudah's national leadership mission to Washington, DC, several times. During these missions, a select group of activists and influencers travels to America's capital to discuss shared areas of concern with elected officials and politicians. The schedule is packed with meetings, discussions, presentations, and at least one official luncheon, and each event is conducted with formality and utmost respect.

During one mission, Mrs. Lubling was escorted into the White House along with the Agudah team for a session with several high-level Cabinet members. The organizers seated her in the front row, a sign of Rabbi Sherer's abiding admiration, and then introduced the first elected official on the agenda. The Agudah representatives all listened attentively as the guest began to speak. Then a cellphone began to ring.

Mrs. Lubling didn't particularly care that she was in the White House, the locus of American executive power. Nor was she intimidated by the fact that a prestigious elected official was sharing his valuable time with the Agudah representatives. Her phone was ringing, and that meant that someone needed help. She reached into her large handbag, pulled out the phone, and took the call right there in the White House.

(After the session concluded, the Agudah organizers approached the official and explained that Mrs. Lubling dealt with medical emergencies at all hours of the day and night, and that she'd meant no disrespect by taking the call.)

During another mission, then-Senator Hillary Clinton addressed the Agudah team during a luncheon in the Senate. Mrs. Lubling, with her sharp nose for potential allies, approached Senator Clinton as soon as she finished her speech, and began to describe one of her *chessed* projects — perhaps the Senator could help obtain funding.

That unplanned conversation developed into a warm relationship, and a year later, when Agudah's mission arrived in Washington, Senator Clinton greeted Mrs. Lubling with familiarity and respect.

But that wasn't their last encounter. During the time that Mrs. Lubling worked for the Boro Park Community Council, Council Executive Director Rabbi Yechiel Kaufman received funding to hold a special tribute luncheon for Holocaust survivors on Chanukah of 2002. Since Mrs. Lubling handled the Holocaust Survivors' desk, she was charged with organizing the event.

It was clear that most of the attendees would be women, and Mrs. Lubling decided to bring in a fitting guest speaker who'd make her guests feel honored and prestigious. Who better than

"No one in the world can walk into my office and tell me where to go on what day — except Mrs. Miriam Lubling." Then-Senator Hillary Clinton with Mrs. Lubling, who arranged for her to speak at a Holocaust Survivors' event in Boro Park.

New York Senator Hillary Rodham Clinton, a powerful and influential woman who had once been the First Lady of the land?

When the afternoon of the luncheon came, the Khal Chassidim *simchah* hall in Boro Park was packed. The tables were set and the kitchen staff was at work, putting the final touches on the menu, when suddenly their quarters were overrun by Secret Service operatives. The cook came running to Rabbi Yechiel Kaufman. "What did you do?" he demanded. "How can I cook like this?"

Rabbi Kaufman soothed the man and watched as the Secret Service gave the all-clear for Senator Clinton to enter the hall. Suddenly scores of elderly women, dressed in their best weekday suits with matching scarves, brooches, and earrings, surged around the visiting dignitary. Everyone wanted to get close to her, share a word with her, shake her hand. The Secret Service operatives had no idea how to cope with an invasion of genteel *heimishe* Holocaust survivors eager to get hold of their client; this definitely had never been part of their training.

Finally the crowds returned to their seats and the program began. Senator Clinton made her speech paying tribute to the survivors, the families they'd built, and the community they established upon the ashes of a shattered world. Then she turned to Mrs. Lubling.

"You're probably wondering why I'm here," she said. "The truth is that no one in the world can walk into my office whenever they want without an appointment and say, 'Hillary, you're going to be in this place at this and this time' — except Mrs. Miriam Lubling.

"A few weeks ago, Mrs. Lubling marched into my office. She told me, 'Hillary, I'm making a luncheon for Holocaust survivors, I want you to be there at this and this time.' And then every week since, I got a phone call: 'Don't forget, Hillary, December 8 at 12 noon in Khal Chassidim.'

"So of course, here I am."

In September of 2002, Mrs. Lubling received a phone call from the New York Public Library. "Is this Miriam Lubling?"

"Yes, how can I help you?"

"I'm calling from the New York Public Library, and I want to let you know that you've been chosen to receive the Brooke Russell Astor Award for Unsung Heroes."

Mrs. Lubling was rarely at a loss for words, but this time she was truly confused. "What is this? What do you mean?"

"The Astor Award is an annual award that honors an unsung hero or heroine who has contributed to the betterment of New York City. You've been chosen as this year's winner, and we want to invite you to the awards ceremony on October 22."

Brooke Russell Astor was a legendary New York socialite and philanthropist who distributed millions of dollars over the course of her lifetime — not just to museums, universities, the botanic gardens and the zoo, as is typical of donors of her social standing, but also to homeless shelters, city-run nursing homes, schools, and youth centers.

In 1987, an award in her name was established as part of a generous endowment gift to the New York Public Library. The annual winner would be given ten thousand dollars at a highly publicized ceremony, attended by the famous Brooke Astor herself.

Mrs. Astor's guiding philosophy was "power is the ability to do good things for others." In that sense, though she hailed from a very different world with very different values, there was some cosmic logic in Mrs. Lubling winning an award bearing her name.

Nominations for the 2002 Brooke Russell Astor Award were solicited from over four hundred individuals and organizations,

Lady Brooke Russell Astor, who believed that "power is the ability to do good things for others," at the awards ceremony honoring Mrs. Lubling. Imagine her surprise when Mrs. Lubling refused to accept the prize money.

including cultural groups, universities, foundations, elected officials, community groups, and social service agencies. One of those elected officials was then-New York City Council Member Simcha Felder, of the 44th District, Brooklyn, who had nominated Mrs. Miriam Lubling.

To one of the journalists who covered the ceremony, Mr. Felder described Mrs. Lubling as both modest and forceful, and explained how she could get anyone an immediate appointment with NYU's top doctors — even those whose schedules were booked solid for months.

"You can't refuse her," he said. "You know she isn't getting paid. You know what she's been through. How can anyone possibly say no?

"She's a living lesson," he went on. "Even when she was sick, she was on her cellphone from her hospital bed making appointments for other people. She never stops."

Apparently the selection committee — comprising representatives from the cultural, academic, government, and social service communities of New York — was impressed, because they chose Mrs. Lubling from the hundreds of nominees.

The official ceremony was held at a fashionable cocktail reception in the Trustees Room of the New York Public Library at Fifth Avenue and 42nd Street, a majestic New York City landmark whose exterior boasts soaring arches and two marble lions dubbed "Patience" and "Fortitude."

Mrs. Lubling and her family were ushered through the massive building to an exquisitely decorated drawing room paneled in walnut, with an elaborate marble fireplace and floor-to-ceiling seventeenth-century Flemish tapestries. There, surrounded by celebrities and politicians, she formally accepted the personal congratulations of Mrs. Astor and addressed the gathering.

Her words were simple and her unpretentious immigrant diction was worlds away from the introductory speeches of the upper-crust assemblage. But the accented speech, coming straight from her heart, touched everyone in the room.

"I feel very blessed to have been chosen," she said. "My childhood and family were taken away from me in Europe during the Second World War. As long as I can, I will do whatever I can to make people's lives better."

The ceremony's crowning moment was the presentation, to flashing cameras, of a decorative plaque along with a ten-thousand-dollar check made out to Mrs. Lubling. Mrs. Astor smiled graciously as she extended the check toward Mrs. Lubling, waiting for the evening's guest of honor to accept it with a smile in return.

But Mrs. Lubling had other plans. "I don't want the money. Give five thousand dollars to Rivkah Laufer Bikur Cholim," she said, "and the other five thousand to Ohel."

"Don't you understand?" Mrs. Astor insisted. "This check is made out to you — it's a personal gift!"

Mrs. Lubling shrugged. "What would I do with it?"

The moment stretched on awkwardly. Mrs. Lubling motioned to her son Chanoch.

"Come here, Chanoch," she said. "You have to explain it to her — I can't take the check, it's not for me. I don't do this for myself, it's all for other people."

There was a tense moment as Chanoch approached Mrs. Astor. But ever the lady, she rebounded within moments, and swiftly prepared two new checks. When Mrs. Lubling finally accepted them, the audience responded with a rousing standing ovation.

At a critical juncture for the administration of NYU, the board was summoned to a meeting. The hospital was considering a merger with another major medical center, and its board members needed a full picture of the proposed merger in order to decide whether to move ahead. They filed into the boardroom, sat down around the table, and listened attentively as a leading board member guided them through an intense forty-slide presentation prepared by the financial analysts, crunching all the projected numbers — profits, synergies, increased revenues and rewards, and expected timeframes.

Then the floor was opened to questions. One board member asked about the finer details of the projected earnings. Another had a complex question about insurance coverage. Another asked whether there was a plan in place for any necessary public relations expenses related to the merger.

Then Mrs. Lubling raised her hand.

"In the entire presentation," she said defiantly, "all I saw was information about money. There was nothing — nothing! — in any of those forty nice pictures about patient care."

The room went very quiet, and everyone averted their gaze from the board member who'd confidently shepherded them through his presentation. No one dared look him in the eye.

Mrs. Lubling, however, had no compunctions about speaking truth to power. "Isn't the whole point of a hospital to treat patients?" she demanded. "How can you talk about the benefits of a merger and never once consider what it will mean to your patients?

"Too big is no good," she went on, shaking her head in disapproval. "Think about your patients and you'll realize what's best for the hospital."

In the end, the merger did not go through.

Illness does not discriminate when it comes to class, influence, or social standing. It is a universal reality that when newly diagnosed patients face the bewildering world of medical treatment, they feel vulnerable and alone — even if they are pedigreed, prestigious, and powerful.

Mrs. Lubling left no door unopened in her quest to help ease Rav Nosson Tzvi Finkel's medical condition. Years after his *petirah,* the family still feels the warmth of her concern.

During the course of her work, Mrs. Lubling helped many prominent community members, rabbanim, and Rebbes. She had an innate understanding of the right formula to deploy in these cases: she displayed exceptional deference and respect for Torah leaders, but at the same time she never lost her equanimity and down-to-earth sensibility. Even as she worried for their honor, she utilized her usual toolkit of quick wit and a fine eye for the little details that can make a big difference. No matter how prestigious the patient, she never lost her equanimity.

The family of Mirrer rosh yeshivah Rav Nosson Tzvi Finkel still remembers the novel way Mrs. Lubling related to him.

Rav Nosson Tzvi suffered from Parkinson's disease, a disease of the nervous system that progressively inhibits movement. Mrs. Lubling was immensely pained by his condition and determined to find the right doctors and treatments to help him. There was no door she left unopened in this quest.

Rav Nosson Tzvi's mother was a distant relative of the Lubling family, and during his annual trips to the United States, he was hosted by Mrs. Lubling's grandchildren Mendy and Chani Horowicz in their Boro Park home.

During those visits, Mrs. Lubling stopped in regularly to check on the eminent guest. Along with the utter deference and respect she evinced for the rosh yeshivah, she shone with vitality and good cheer, sharing witty jokes and amusing stories with his wife, Rebbetzin Leah Finkel.

Even after the rosh yeshivah's passing, she maintained a warm relationship with the family. Whenever she visited Eretz Yisrael, she stopped in at the rebbetzin's home just outside the Mir Yeshivah, loaded with gifts.

Years later, Rebbetzin Finkel still remembers Mrs. Lubling as a powerhouse: a woman brimming with warmth and vitality who couldn't sit still while others needed help. She was well aware of each patient's standing in the *frum* world's spiritual hierarchy, but cared for even the simplest Jew with total devotion. Most of all, Rebbetzin Finkel remembers, she was a woman who lived with Hakadosh Baruch Hu.

The Belzer Rebbetzin on one of her visits to Mrs. Lubling's apartment — a testament to her admiration and appreciation

Throughout her life, Mrs. Lubling maintained close relationships with the Rebbetzins of Gur: the Beis Yisrael's wife Rebbetzin Perel, the Lev Simchah's wife Rebbetzin Yuta Henna, the Pnei Menachem's wife Rebbetzin Tziporah, and the current Rebbetzin Shoshana.

The Belzer Rebbetzin, Rebbetzin Sura Rokeach, is another grateful admirer of Mrs. Lubling, who devoted much time and effort to the medical care of many Belzer chassidim as well as to the care of her sisters, the Rebbetzins of Skver and Satmar.

One of the Rebbetzin's visits to New York coincided with Mrs. Lubling's ninetieth birthday, and Mrs. Hudi Silber, who has a close relationship with the Rebbetzin, brought her to Mrs. Lubling's apartment for a special birthday surprise. There, the women joined hands and began to sing and dance, an expression of admiration and appreciation for this angel of mercy who dared to wage battle with the Angel of Death.

Chanoch remembers when the son of a major Israel-based chassidic Rebbe arrived in the United States to raise money for his father's *mosdos*. Shortly after the esteemed guest settled into his lodgings, he fainted. Hatzolah was summoned to the scene, and the medics feared that their patient had just experienced a stroke.

They rushed him to NYU, where he was examined and admitted. That afternoon, Mrs. Lubling — who'd been alerted to his admission — made sure to visit. She found the patient in a drab, thin hospital gown.

"You don't have a proper bathrobe?" she asked in dismay.

"I have nothing," he admitted. "I was only planning to stay in America for two days."

Mrs. Lubling left the room and called Chanoch at work. "I want you should go to Gentlemen's Boutique right now," she said, dispatching him to a high-end men's clothing store in Boro Park. "The Rebbe's son is here in NYU, with nothing respectable to wear. Go buy him nice pajamas and *ah sheine chaluk*, a nice robe, and everything else he might need."

A few hours later, Chanoch arrived in NYU with a suitcase in hand. He made his way to the room and unloaded a full wardrobe so the Rebbe's son would be properly outfitted for the duration of his unplanned stay.

That Erev Rosh Hashanah, Mrs. Lubling received a phone call from the Rebbetzin in Eretz Yisrael. "Thank you so much for taking care of my son," she said tearfully. "You didn't just think about what he needed medically — you thought about his *kavod* too."

After the passing of Rebbetzin Meisels, the daughter of the Beirach Moshe of Satmar, Mrs. Lubling paid a *shivah* visit to the family. First she consoled the women. Then, since she had been extremely involved in every detail of Rebbetzin Meisel's care, she decided that she simply had to offer her condolences to the Rebbe and his son-in-law as well.

As she approached the location where they were sitting *shivah*, about a block away, she saw a long line of chassidim waiting for a chance to walk by the Rebbe and offer condolences. So she went to a side door and knocked softly. The Rebbe's *gabbai* opened the door slightly.

"I am Miriam Lubling," she said. "I would like permission to wave to the Rebbe and wish him a *nechamah*."

The *gabbai* approached the Rebbe and whispered in his ear, pointing to the open door.

"*Alle arois*, everyone leave!" the Rebbe shouted.

The chassidim may have been curious and confused, but they all obeyed. When the room was empty of all men, the Rebbe motioned to Mrs. Lubling to come in for her own private audience.

Two other "royal patients" Mrs. Lubling helped were a married couple, scions of a prominent chassidus. The couple waited many long years for children, then embarked on fertility treatments. Mrs. Lubling helped them through the process with dedication and discretion.

When they were blessed with twins, she made sure to visit regularly to "see her *nachas*," as she put it. She would bring treats and gifts and soak up the joy that filled the once-empty home.

When the twins were four years old, she noticed that they were still using pacifiers. "Do they really still need the pacifiers?" she asked. "They're getting older, and you know that their teeth might be affected."

"I know," the mother said, shrugging hopelessly, "but I just can't get them to agree to throw them out."

"Why don't you leave the room for a bit," Mrs. Lubling suggested, "and let me talk to them."

When the mother returned to the room a few minutes later, she saw her children scurrying around, collecting all their pacifiers. "We're giving them to Mrs. Lubling!" they announced proudly.

"What's the biggest present you can dream of getting?" she had asked them. The little girl wanted a dollhouse, her brother a Cozy Coupe riding toy.

"Bring me all your pacifiers and you'll have the presents waiting for you in a week," she promised.

The twins knew they could trust this woman with the soft eyes and ready smile. Sure enough, they gave up their pacifiers, and Mrs. Lubling had the gifts delivered to their home. Years later, the family still called that Cozy Coupe "Mrs. Lubling's car."

Another home that Mrs. Lubling made sure to visit repeatedly was that of Rabbi Moshe Sherer, the illustrious president of Agudath Israel of America. After his passing, his wife Mrs. Devorah Sherer encountered a suddenly quiet existence. No longer did her home pulsate with that sense of urgency and purpose for Klal Yisrael.

But Mrs. Lubling would not allow Mrs. Sherer to retreat into a shell of solitude. She visited regularly, cajoled her to dress up and join her on outings, and brought friendship and succor to the "forgotten queen of Klal Yisrael," as her son Rabbi Shimshon Sherer put it.

Mrs. Lubling maintained her warm family ties with the Sherer family for the rest of her life. Rabbi Shimshon Sherer remembers the time she swept into a 2000 Agudah Convention before the Motzaei Shabbos keynote session, which he'd been asked to deliver, and made a special point of seeking him out and giving him a *berachah* before his speech.

"My Shimshi!" she said fondly. "I came back especially to hear you speak!"

Just a month or two earlier, the Associated Press had run a story about the religious values of vice-presidential candidate Senator Joseph Lieberman, a practicing Orthodox Jew. The story raised questions about the Senator's fealty to feminist principles, considering that Orthodox men recite the daily blessing *"shelo asani ishah,"* expressing thanks to the Creator for not fashioning them as females.

As the AP piece put it, "The Liebermans are struggling to square some of their faith's teachings with modern life." Many outlets picked up the story, and a public debate erupted about the daily *berachah*. Did Orthodox women feel sidelined? Was Senator Leiberman's wife Hadassah a second-class citizen? Did the blessing cause resentment and bitterness among observant women?

With the indomitable Mrs. Lubling standing there before him, Rabbi Sherer seized those few spare moments before his speech. "I have to ask you one thing before I start speaking," he said. "Does it bother you that I make a *berachah 'shelo asani ishah'* and you make a *berachah 'she'asani kirtzono'*?"

Mrs. Lubling didn't miss a beat. "Shimshele, *du bist meshiga*? Did you fall on your head?" she retorted. "Why should it bother me? I'm proud that this is the *berachah* you make, and that this is the *berachah* I make."

Rabbi Sherer proceeded to deliver his speech, but the exchange remained sharp in his mind. The next Shabbos he addressed the men who davened in his shul, and repeated Mrs. Lubling's words.

"There was something I wanted to tell her in response, but there was just no time," he confided. "When the press fixated on Joseph Lieberman and the disparity in the *berachos*, one of the antireligious Jewish periodicals decided to expand on the story. They had a reporter phone my rebbi, Philadelphia rosh yeshivah Rav Shmuel Kamenetsky. The reporter asked Rav Shmuel to explain the fact that Orthodox women recite a different *berachah* than do men.

"Rav Shmuel told the reporter that the phrasing of a woman's *berachah* in fact underscores her elevated spiritual nature. In his *sefer Derech Hashem*, the Ramchal often describes the Creator with the words '*retzono l'heitiv*, His desire is to benefit others.' Look at the phrasing of the woman's blessing and you will find the same word — *retzono*. This means that the Jewish woman was created in G-d's image, with the same innate desire to benefit others. Surely that description is the furthest thing from denigration of women."

Rabbi Sherer called Mrs. Lubling to mind and mentally replayed her completely unapologetic response. If there ever existed a woman who emulated Hashem's unceasing desire to give, it was she.

In 1998, when the previous Novominsker Rebbetzin, Rebbetzin Yehudis Perlow, was diagnosed with a fatal illness, Mrs. Lubling served as much more than a medical advocate. She felt a deep

Reb Yaakov Lubling dancing with the Novominsker Rebbe. The families had long been close, and when the Rebbe's wife was ill, the bond only deepened.

personal connection to the Perlows. Not only had her grandsons attended Yeshivas Novominsk, she had collaborated discreetly with the Rebbe and Rebbetzin many times over the years to help local families facing medical crises. Now, with the Rebbetzin in a precarious state, she tirelessly lobbied the administration of Lenox Hill Hospital to provide her with the best possible care.

"This is the wife of a very big rabbi," she said. "One of the biggest rabbis in America! I want you should give her the penthouse" — referring to the expanded suite on the top floor, which was reserved for dignitaries and VIPs.

The admitting office wasn't impressed by her honorifics. But Mrs. Lubling insisted.

"If the pope would be hospitalized here, which room would you give him?" she asked doggedly.

"We'd give him the penthouse, of course."

"So this patient, she is like the pope's wife!" she said triumphantly. Did Mrs. Lubling know that no pope in the history of Christianity ever had a wife? Whether she did or didn't, her point had been made. Rebbetzin Perlow was admitted to the VIP suite, where Mrs. Lubling made sure she received the most reverential treatment.

During the period when the Rebbetzin was recovering from surgery at home, Mrs. Lubling visited regularly. She knew she was visiting royalty and related to the Rebbe, Rebbetzin, and their children with obvious esteem. At the same time, she didn't allow her abiding respect to cloud her sense of practicality.

When the Perlows' youngest daughter, Mrs. Sarah Chana Treger, arrived from Eretz Yisrael to spend some time with her ailing mother, she brought along her small children. Mrs. Lubling came by to visit, lugging a selection of toys to keep the little ones occupied while the adults focused on their sober reality.

And even in those elevated surroundings, she retained her sense of humor. She sat and entertained the family with witty stories and jokes.

"Yesterday we were getting the children ready to leave the kindergarten," went one story. "It was pouring outside, and we had to fit all those little feet into their rubber boots. It was a big job.

"I sat there with one little boy, squeezing and pushing and pulling up those rubber boots until his toes were in the right place. 'Okay, Shloimy, you have your boots on now, let's go to the bus,' I told him.

"'But Morah,' he said, 'these are not my boots!'

"So there I sat, huffing and puffing, as I pulled and pushed and squeezed again. Finally I got the boots off. 'Okay, Shloimy, now bring me your boots,' I said. He pointed to the boots I had just taken off.

"'I thought you said those aren't your boots?'

"'They're not,' he explained. 'They're my sister's boots, but my mommy said I should wear them today.'"

The Perlow family shared a laugh together as Mrs. Lubling concluded the hapless tale. "So what did I do? I started again — pulling, pushing, squeezing..." and so she injected the serious atmosphere with her trademark sunshine.

Rabbi Yechiel Kaufman remembers the time he brought several VIP visitors — Israeli Knesset Members who were visiting the United States — to the Boro Park Community Council office. As he took them through the office, explaining the work he did, he introduced them to the various staff members. Mrs. Lubling's desk, of course, was one of their first stops.

"Wow, so nice that a woman of your age is so active, still working every day," one of the politicians commented condescendingly to this great-grandmother in her glasses and twinset.

Mrs. Lubling straightened her shoulders. "*Adoni chaver haKnesset*," she said, her voice uncharacteristically sharp, "what time did you wake up today?"

"I don't know," he shrugged. "Maybe around 7 o'clock?"

"Let me tell you something," she said. "Every day, I wake up at 5 a.m. and sit by the telephone waiting for someone in need to call me, just so I can help them. And you're telling me it's *nice* that I'm here at 10 o'clock?"

In 1992, Mrs. Lubling arranged for a young Israeli cousin of hers, a descendant of the Imrei Emes of Gur, to undergo a cutting-edge laparoscopic procedure in New York. The young woman arrived with her mother, and they received the classic Mrs. Lubling treatment: personal accompaniment to the hospital, a surgery slot first thing in the morning, and a private hospital room. Mrs. Lubling even "gowned up" and stole into the OR mid-surgery to check how it was proceeding.

The two women stayed in her home after the surgery, and she lavished them with attention and love. When the patient recovered sufficiently, she told her two visitors, "Now I am going to show you New York." She planned an itinerary that would do a professional tour guide proud: the skyscrapers of Manhattan, Times Square, a ride through Central Park in a horse-drawn carriage, and a pampering shopping experience in a high-end boutique.

"Now you've seen one side of New York," she told them as they tried to catch their breath, "but there's another side you should see. You are Gerrer chassidim, and I know that you'd appreciate a *berachah* from a Rebbe. I want to show you a different kind of Rebbe — something you can find only here in New York."

She called a car service and instructed him to head to 770 Eastern Parkway in Crown Heights. With practiced ease, she ushered her visitors into the large building, where they were dazed to see a line of hundreds of people of all ages, stripes, and types — men, women, children, even some non-Jews.

"They're waiting to see the Lubavitcher Rebbe," Mrs. Lubling explained. "Every Sunday, the Rebbe spends hours seeing visitors. His room is open to everyone, and he greets each visitor personally with a dollar and a *berachah*."

(The Rebbe once explained the reason why he gave out dollars: His father-in-law, Rav Yosef Yitzchak Schneersohn, used to say, "When two people meet, something good should result for a third." The Rebbe intended for that dollar to be used as *tzedakah*, to benefit yet a third Jew.)

Mrs. Lubling's two guests eyed the long line warily. But she was not fazed in the slightest. "Come with me," she commanded them

The Lubavitcher Rebbe, like every Rebbe privy to personal sorrows and medical sagas, knew and respected Mrs. Lubling.

as she headed past all the waiting petitioners and headed straight to the small wood-paneled room where the Rebbe stood for hours every Sunday. Other people might have time to wait, but not Mrs. Lubling.

The *gabbaim* — who recognized and respected Mrs. Lubling — let her right through; this was not her first visit, and her reputation preceded her. She nudged the two women into the room and stood right before the Rebbe.

"Lubling," she said in her hoarse voice. The Rebbe nodded in recognition. Like every Rebbe who was privy to people's personal sorrows, dilemmas, and medical sagas, he knew Mrs. Lubling.

"Rebbe," she introduced them, "these are two women from Eretz Yisrael, two *chashuveh* descendants of the Imrei Emes. One just had a surgery and needs a *refuah sheleimah*."

The Rebbe nodded and presented each woman with a dollar and a personalized *berachah*. His *gabbai* then tried to usher Mrs. Lubling out, so the line could keep moving.

"Wait." Mrs. Lubling wasn't intimidated. She stood firmly in place and kept talking with full confidence and aplomb. "They have a cousin in Eretz Yisrael who has been married for years and is still waiting for a child."

The Rebbe pulled out another dollar from his pile. "Here, this is for your cousin," he said.

The two women emerged dazed and trembling. They knew Mrs. Lubling was bold and determined, but they had never dreamed she could be so forthright as to push her way past hundreds of people right into the private room of a prominent Rebbe. But she brushed off their amazement with a laugh. "I told you I was going to show you something different," she said.

In the spring of 1991, Binyomin and Nechie Berry's three-year-old son Naftoli was diagnosed with a fatal illness. With shaking hands, Binyomin dialed the first person he could think of: his rosh yeshivah, Rav Aharon Schechter.

"Where are you?" asked Rav Aharon, the aristocratic leader of Yeshivas Rabbeinu Chaim Berlin.

"I'm at NYU," Binyomin said.

"Did you speak with Mrs. Lubling?" Rav Aharon immediately asked.

Binyomin knew Mrs. Lubling — his children had attended her kindergarten — but he couldn't quite comprehend her connection to the dire news he was trying to absorb.

Rav Aharon must have intuited his confusion through the phone line. "Let me handle it," he said.

Apparently Rav Aharon had his ways of contacting Mrs. Lubling. He sent a message to her, and she swiftly tracked down the shattered Berrys. During the ensuing months, she proved a Heaven-sent angel. For the duration of their terrifying hospital journey, she extended love, tenderness, and hand-picked gifts to the little patient — along with constant, steady support to his entire family.

One evening in the early 1990s, Ohel president Moishe Hellman was approached by an elderly Israeli man soliciting *tzedakah* funds.

"I have two grandchildren who were born with impaired hearing," he said. "We just learned about an innovative technology that can help them, called a cochlear implant. Our Israeli insurance will compensate an Israeli hospital for performing the surgical procedure to implant the device. But the actual devices are developed in the United States and we'll have to pay for them out of pocket."

"How much money do you need?" Mr. Hellman asked.

The man bit his lip. "They're telling us it will be ten thousand dollars for each child," he said. "It's a very new device, something that's being used by doctors in NYU Hospital." (NYU was in fact the first facility in the region to implant a multichannel cochlear prosthesis in an adult, and soon developed expertise in helping children as well.)

"Wait," Mr. Hellman said. "If NYU has experience with this device, why don't you do the entire surgery there? The doctors will know the technology and procedures better than the doctors in Israel."

The man's shoulders sagged. "You're right. Of course, that would be ideal. But if we do the implants in NYU, it will cost fifty thousand dollars for each boy — because we'll have to pay for the hospitalization and the surgery too. There's no way I can ever dream of collecting one hundred thousand dollars."

"Wait a few minutes, let me see what I can do," Mr. Hellman said. He took out his phone and began dialing the number of a trusted friend and generous donor. Then he stopped. Why not call Mrs. Lubling and ask her to donate funds from the Rivkah Laufer Bikur Cholim reserves?

"Listen, Mrs. Lubling," he said. "I have a Yid sitting with me. He has two hearing-impaired grandsons, and there's a new technology that can help them hear. I would prefer that they do the surgery in NYU. Can you arrange that?"

Mrs. Lubling took the details, but she didn't immediately jump on the case. Mr. Hellman turned to the anxious grandfather. "Mrs. Lubling is a Gerrer chassidiste," he said. "Do you have any connections to Ger?"

"Yes!" The fellow brightened. "One of my neighbors is the *gabbai* there."

"Call your neighbor," Mr. Hellman instructed him, "and tell him that you want Mrs. Lubling to arrange the operation for one of your grandsons in NYU. Don't mention my name."

The next day, Mrs. Lubling called Moishe Hellman. "You won't believe it," she said, her voice a mixture of wonder and awe. "You remember those boys who need a cochlear implant? The Gerrer Rebbe's *gabbai* called and said the Rebbe himself wants me to arrange the surgery for one grandson in NYU. Can you believe it?"

The next week, she called with another update. Dr. J. Thomas Roland, a leading ENT and neurological surgeon at the cutting edge of this new field, had been moved by her description of the little boy and agreed to do the surgery pro bono. Not only that, when he learned that there was another child in the family with the same impairment, he said, "Bring the kid's brother, we'll do him too!"

Mr. Hellman still has the handwritten letter of thanks that the grandfather sent after the two little boys had returned home with a new world of communication, conversation, and connection open to them. "Every time I looked at my grandsons, knowing they couldn't hear, knowing they'd be shut out from so much of our world, it was a dagger in my heart. You removed that dagger and patched up the wound."

Mr. Hellman called up the man. "You wrote a beautiful letter," he said, "but you should be sending it to Mrs. Lubling, not to me!"

The man obligingly wrote another letter and sent it to Mrs. Lubling.

It took some time for Mrs. Lubling to learn of the little subterfuge that Moishe Hellman had employed. They had long been faithful partners in *chessed*, and she took it with good cheer. "Just one thing I ask you, Moish," she said. "Don't send the Gerrer Rebbe after me ever again!"

CHAPTER 18
Spine of Steel, Heart of Gold

It was the morning of Erev Yom Kippur, and a blanket of solemnity was slowly settling over Boro Park. The last few rounds of *kapparos* were completed and the residents turned their minds to preparing for the holiest day of the year.

The third-floor apartment at 1369 51st Street was ready for Yom Tov, with a white tablecloth spread on the dining room table and a simple but filling meal cooking on the stove. Reb Yaakov's *kittel* had been freshly ironed and two *machzorim* rested on the crocheted lace tablecloth, ready to be transported to shul.

Mrs. Lubling, however, was not home.

Just that morning, she'd received a phone call from her fellow bikur cholim activist, Mrs. Yuttie Frankel. Mrs. Frankel had been contacted by a family whose new son-in-law — reputed to be "the best *bachur* in yeshivah" — spent the months since his wedding lying listlessly on the recliner. He deteriorated to the point where he fainted and was transported to a local hospital.

Now, on Erev Yom Kippur, his family had realized the hospital was not equipped to deal with the severity of his condition. "Can you help us get him admitted to NYU?" they asked. "Something is seriously wrong, and we need a top hospital."

With Mrs. Lubling's help, the transfer was arranged. But that wasn't enough for her. She asked Mrs. Frankel to drive her to the hospital, so they could offer personal support to the young couple as they dealt with the bewildering and frightening world of the ER.

An initial examination revealed that the young man had suffered a stroke. He was admitted immediately — and his newlywed wife was utterly shattered.

"We just started our lives together," she sobbed. "We haven't even started a family. Now we have no future."

"I am going to call the best neurologist," Mrs. Lubling reassured her, "and we will make sure that your husband gets the right care."

Even though Dr. Epstein was a pediatric neurologist, Mrs. Lubling decided that he was the right physician for this patient, who wasn't more than twenty years old in any case. More importantly, Dr. Epstein's gentleness and compassion would relay a sense of security to the devastated family.

"Dr. Epstein," Mrs. Lubling said when he picked up his home phone, "I have a patient for you, a cousin of mine, waiting in NYU. He had a stroke and the family needs a good doctor to examine him. You have to come now. We're waiting for you."

"But Mrs. Lubling," he protested, "It's Sunday morning and I'm working in my garden in a pair of shorts and a plaid shirt. I can't come to the hospital dressed like this."

"It doesn't matter what you're wearing," she countered. "Can you come right now?"

Soon enough a man in shorts came striding into the hospital room where Mrs. Frankel was standing alongside the patient. Despite his casual clothing, Dr. Epstein was clearly in his professional element as he took a keen look at the patient, assessing his color, function, muscle tone, and response time.

"He's going to recover," he pronounced firmly. "At most, he'll have a hard time with some fine motor skills — like buttoning his shirt. But there's every reason to expect him to lead a normal life."

At that point, the word had gone out about the couple's plight, and a small group of the young man's friends arrived in the hospital, prepared to spend Yom Kippur with the couple. Mrs. Lubling and Mrs. Frankel bid the couple a gut Yom Tov, then hurried to the parking lot.

They arrived back in Boro Park less than half an hour before *Kol Nidrei*. The *seudah hamafsekes* (meal prior to the onset of the fast) was long over. Each grabbed a bite to eat and changed into Yom Tov clothing. They met again in the Gerrer *shtiebel* as the hushed strains of *Kol Nidrei* began.

Mrs. Frankel took deep breaths as she tried to regain her equilibrium. Surely no one in shul could imagine the type of day she and Mrs. Lubling had just experienced — the urgent drive to the hospital that morning, the exhortations to Dr. Epstein, the frantic rush back home. Other people might have conducted their advocacy from afar. But Mrs. Lubling had to be on site, at the hospital, with the young couple. Even before the onset of Yom Kippur — when all Jews resemble angels — she was an angel of mercy who transcended time, space, and logic to soothe and encourage her patients.

Mrs. Lubling was once making her hospital rounds when she encountered a woman in terrible pain from cancer treatments.

"Let's ask the nurse to get you a painkiller," she said.

"She won't agree," the patient said hopelessly. "It's still too soon since my last dose."

Mrs. Lubling marched briskly to the nurses' station. "I want you should give my cousin some pain relief," she said. "She is suffering terribly. We need to help her!"

The nurse shrugged at the request. "It's still too early to give her another dose," she said.

Mrs. Lubling bristled. "Do you know what it means to be in pain?" she asked. "Do you understand what this woman is feeling? She is lying there suffering and there's nothing you can do? There must be some way to help her!"

The nurse thought for a few moments. "Okay," she said as she stood up. "Let me go see what we can do."

Tzippy, a Boro Park native, grew up knowing Mrs. Lubling as a determined, insistent woman who had no problem issuing orders to New York's top doctors. But she encountered a completely different side to Mrs. Lubling when her own husband contracted a serious infection that did not respond to oral or even intravenous treatment.

The doctors told Tzippy and her husband that he would need a surgical procedure at the site of the infection. Her husband categorically refused. "I will not allow you to operate," he said brusquely. "Just keep the IV in for a few more days."

Tzippy was inclined to support her husband. Surely the infection just needed additional antibiotics, and then her husband would be strong and healthy again. But maybe the doctors were right? What was her role here?

Then her phone rang. "Tzippy, this is Miriam Lubling. How is your husband? What is going on?"

The voice on the phone was soft, sympathetic, and so understanding — the voice of a caring friend. Almost instinctively, Tzippy unburdened herself and described her husband's situation.

"I hear you, I understand. He doesn't want to have the surgery," Mrs. Lubling said warmly. "But *mammele*, you want him to get better. We all want him to get better. He must have the surgery. You can convince him. I know you can do it."

Tzippy had always known Mrs. Lubling as an iron-willed doer who gave orders that everyone couldn't help but follow. Now she found herself following orders too, from a woman overflowing with empathy and emotion.

A top dermatologist once received an angry phone call from Mrs. Lubling on a Sunday morning. "I can't believe you didn't tell her until now!" Mrs. Lubling said.

"Tell who? Tell her what?"

Mrs. Lubling named a patient, a woman she'd referred to the doctor for a suspicious growth.

"I did tell her," the doctor said. "I called her this morning to let her know the pathology report came back — and it was good news, the growth wasn't malignant."

"Yes," Mrs. Lubling said indignantly, "but how could you let her go through a whole Shabbos waiting and worrying? What kind of Shabbos do you think she had?"

One of Mrs. Lubling's steady volunteers visited her at home and found her extremely agitated. "What's wrong?" the volunteer asked.

"I just got back from a *levayah,*" Mrs. Lubling answered. It was the funeral of a patient for whom she'd invested extraordinary effort, resources, and hope. At the end, though, she felt that the doctor had not invested likewise — because, she believed, of the patient's advanced age and diminished mental aptitude.

The volunteer listened in awe as Mrs. Lubling got the doctor on the phone and delivered the most passionate and pained dressing-down she had ever heard. "We trust you! We refer our patients to you! We expect you to give your best!" The tirade went on and on.

What the doctor couldn't see is that through the entire conversation, hot, angry tears streamed from Mrs. Lubling's eyes. That was how much it hurt her to lose a patient.

During the time that his uncle was hospitalized in NYU, Rabbi Zelig Prag often gave Mrs. Lubling rides to Boro Park. One night, he was on his way out of the hospital with Mrs. Lubling when a receptionist beckoned.

"There's this woman crying," she said, pointing toward sagging couches in the lobby. "Maybe you can help her."

Rabbi Prag and Mrs. Lubling approached the couch and discovered a distraught Italian woman weeping aloud. Mrs. Lubling sat down, introduced herself, and softly asked what was wrong.

"My husband is here in NYU, dying of cancer," the woman said. "I want to spend as much time with him as I possibly can, but I have a small child to support, and no extra money. My only time to visit him is at night — and now I have to leave him here alone."

Mrs. Lubling leaned over to Rabbi Prag. "Do you have any money on you?" she murmured.

Rabbi Prag pulled two hundred dollars out of his pocket and handed them to Mrs. Lubling, who promptly pressed the bills into the woman's hand.

"Why are you giving this to me?" she asked, startled.

"Because I want to help you."

"But I can't pay you back," the woman said.

"That's fine. Keep it," Mrs. Lubling told her. "You need help and we want to help you. Go find a hotel nearby and check in for the night. Then you can come back here and spend time with your husband."

Ezra Erani, a veteran member of Brooklyn's Syrian-Jewish community, first met Mrs. Lubling in the 1980s. He was davening in the Ateret Torah flagship building on Ocean Parkway when he noticed an unusual pair entering the building: a man who was obviously blind, dressed in a stained white suit, holding tightly onto the hand of a boy who looked around six years old.

Mr. Erani approached them, introduced himself, and asked who they were and what had brought them to Brooklyn.

"My name is Eliyahu," the man said in Hebrew, "and I'm here because my son Elchanan needs medical treatment for a tumor in his head. They told us to come to Brooklyn and find a woman named Mrs. Lubling — she'll help us through the process."

"And where will you be staying?" Mr. Erani asked.

The man shrugged.

"Okay, so you're invited to my house," Mr. Erani announced, and escorted the pair to his home.

After settling them in, he had a hurried, whispered conference with his wife Joyce.

"Did you ever hear of a woman named Mrs. Lubling?"

No, she hadn't.

"Well, we're going to have to track her down. This child is sick — he has a growth in his head. Mrs. Lubling, whoever she is, is supposed to be arranging his medical treatments. How are we going to find her?"

Ezra and Joyce sent out feelers and made some phone calls. Eventually they were connected with the Rivkah Laufer Bikur Cholim — and with the angel at its head.

"Mrs. Lubling really was like a *malach*, an angel," Mr. Erani says wryly. "Angels don't speak our language, they don't live in the same sphere that we do — but when they give you a command, you listen. That's how it was with Mrs. Lubling. She spoke very quickly, she had a heavy accent, but when she told me to do something, I knew I had to do whatever she said."

The first command came very quickly: Mrs. Lubling had arranged for young Elchanan to be seen by Dr. Fred Epstein, and she wanted Ezra to escort him to his appointment.

Ezra followed Mrs. Lubling's instructions. He drove the young patient and his father to NYU and led them through the building until they reached Dr. Epstein's waiting room. There he saw a small woman in a dark suit and gleaming jewelry scanning the entrance. It was Mrs. Lubling.

As soon as she noticed them, she approached and took charge, ushering them into Dr. Epstein's examining room and explaining their case to the doctor. But she didn't stop there: she made their next appointment and even instructed Dr. Epstein how much he should charge this patient who had no financial resources.

For the duration of Elchanan's treatment, he stayed at the Erani home. His father Eliyahu found solace and purpose in the Ateret Torah *beit midrash*, attending Rav Yosef Harrari-Raful's Gemara *shiur* every morning before davening. The other participants were awestruck by his incredible command of *Shas*: he knew Bavli, Yerushalmi, Rashi, Tosafos, and Rambam by heart, with total clarity and recall, even though he'd been blind since age two.

Unfortunately, despite Dr. Epstein's determination to help Elchanan, he was not able to excise the tumor. After months watching Elchanan deteriorate, Eliyahu realized it was time to go back home. At that point, Elchanan's head was so swollen and his balance so tenuous that he had to make the trip on a stretcher.

But Eliyahu had long been accustomed to miracles, and he

didn't give up. Upon his return to Israel, he found a natural healer. That healer proved the right *shaliach* to help Elchanan.

The Eranis' relationship with Mrs. Lubling didn't end with the close of that story. It only became stronger. From then on, Mrs. Lubling involved Ezra and Joyce in her bikur cholim on a regular basis and grew close to the entire family, attending their *simchos* and bringing handpicked gifts for all the children. And she knew that whenever she needed their help, she could call the Eranis and they would come through.

"She got me involved in great things," Ezra says, his voice laced with fondness and reverence.

Every year, before the holiday season, Mrs. Lubling visited Mr. Erani at the Manhattan office of his business, Enchante Accessories. There, with keen insight, she selected items from his stock of home accessories as gifts for the doctors and nursing staff.

"These vases are very pretty, the nurses will like those; can you give me twenty of them, please?" she instructed his assistant. "And the candy dishes will be perfect for the secretaries; we'll take eight of those. And then, for the ER staff, I think they'll like the tea sets..."

Mr. Erani always marveled at the way she kept a running catalogue of the staff — and their likes and dislikes — in her very sharp mind. Maybe that's why he wasn't surprised to see her finely honed insight employed in a completely different area.

It happened in the late 1990s, when he got a phone call. "*Bubbele*, do you hear me?" the voice said.

Mr. Erani knew it had to be Mrs. Lubling on the phone. No one else in the entire world would call a Syrian businessman *bubbele*.

"*Bubbele*, I need your help. There's a boy from Yeshivat Porat Yosef in Israel who flew in for treatments. He has Hodgkin's disease and he'll be here for a while. He's staying with a wonderful family and they're doing what they can to make it easier, but I want you to visit him and cheer him up — he feels very alone."

Mr. Erani quickly took down the address of the family that had graciously offered to host the young man and his mother. Then he drove to the Kensington neighborhood bordering Boro Park, knocked on the door, and was led to a comfortable basement unit. There he met Nissim — a thin, frightened sixteen-year-old — along with his mother.

It took just a few minutes for Ezra to realize that beyond the intimidating medical treatments and pain of being so far from the rest of the family, the pair was suffering from something else: the utter foreignness of their surroundings. They didn't understand the language. The food provided so generously by their hosts may have been delicious by Ashkenaz standards, but it was completely unfamiliar to their Sephardic taste buds. The davening in the local shul sounded so different from their own *nusach*. What should have been a welcome haven felt like a prison.

Mr. Erani realized, not for the first time, how smart Mrs. Lubling was. She had realized that this patient of hers needed something he wasn't getting.

He quickly called his wife Joyce and asked if she'd be willing to host a mother and son from Israel. She agreed at once, and he told Nissim and his mother to pack up their belongings.

One of the Eranis' young sons vacated his room and doubled up with his brother, and Joyce quickly prepared the room for the new guests. Nissim didn't know it then, but he would ultimately stay in the Erani home for almost a year.

During that year, there were many more calls from Mrs. Lubling to Ezra. "*Bubbele*, I need you to drive Nissim to the hospital tomorrow morning." "*Bubbele*, Nissim has a scan, can you take him?" "*Bubbele*, the doctor wants to see Nissim next week, will you be so good and drive him to the appointment?" He was even enlisted to discuss specific concerns regarding Nissim's treatment plan with preeminent *posek* Rav Dovid Feinstein.

During that year, Nissim became something akin to an adopted son of the Eranis, and a big brother to their children. When he eventually married and built a family of his own, he never forgot the family in Brooklyn that had welcomed him and accompanied him through his cancer journey.

And throughout Nissim's stay, despite the pressures of Ezra's growing business and his multiple communal commitments, he never once considered saying no to Mrs. Lubling's instructions. She was an angel, after all. And when an angel gives you a mission, you wouldn't dream of turning it down.

Dovid worked as a guidance counselor in a public school in Brooklyn's Brighton Beach neighborhood, where he developed a cordial relationship with the non-Jewish assistant principal. Somehow, word got out that the Orthodox Jew on staff had "connections" in the medical world.

One day, the assistant principal visited his office.

"David, I heard that you know doctors," he said. "If you can help me out, I will be forever indebted to you."

"What's wrong, Victor?" David asked.

Victor spilled out the story: a close friend's new baby had just been diagnosed with a brain tumor. They'd been referred to a pediatric neurosurgeon in NYU, but the first available appointment was in three months. They couldn't afford to wait an extra day — but the doctor's schedule was fully booked.

"They say you have connections to doctors," the assistant principal beseeched. "Can you help my friend?"

Dovid's "connections" actually consisted of a relationship with Mrs. Lubling; he and his wife were friendly with the Lubling children and his wife often drove Mrs. Lubling home from the many *simchos* she attended.

So he dialed Mrs. Lubling. "Bobby Lubling," he said, "I have this friend at work who needs help." He described the situation.

"I will call you back in twenty minutes," she said briefly, leaving him with a dial tone.

Sure enough, twenty minutes later his phone rang. "Dovid," she said with no preamble, "can he get there this afternoon?"

"What?" Dovid stammered.

"The friend — the one with the baby who needs brain surgery. Can he get to NYU this afternoon?"

Dovid swiftly dialed his colleague on the other phone. "Victor," he asked, "can your friend get to the hospital for an appointment this afternoon?"

That very afternoon, the baby was seen by a surgeon who scheduled emergency surgery at once.

A few days later, Victor stopped in at Dovid's office again. "David," he said, shaking his head in wonder, "I still can't believe what happened yesterday."

"What happened?"

"I went to NYU, to visit my friend and see how his baby's recovering. So he gives me the room number, I go up there, I walk inside, and I see a little woman — a Jewish woman, dressed all modest, with a wig, you know? — and she's holding the baby, humming to him, so gentle, so caring.

"I went to the nurse and told her, there's this strange woman holding my friend's baby. Do you know what's going on? It is okay?

"The nurse peeked inside the room and smiled. 'That's Mrs. Lubling,' she said. 'Of course it's okay. Whatever she says to do, we jump and do it.'

"David," the assistant principal said, eyes welling, "I always knew that Jews help each other. But I'm Italian through and through! I still can't believe what you — what this woman — did for my friend. The baby's going to be okay, and it's all because of her."

Mrs. Lubling long enjoyed a warm and fruitful relationship with the family of the Munkatcher Rebbe, Rav Moshe Leib Rabinovich. His wife, Rebbetzin Nechama Perel, heads a bikur cholim organization, and therefore they collaborated on many projects.

In 2008, when the Rebbe required shoulder surgery, the medical interaction became more personal — almost familial.

Mrs. Lubling intervened to ensure that the most qualified surgeon would perform the operation. Not only that, she met the family in the hospital early on the morning of the surgery, and stayed with them in the waiting room for the duration of the procedure.

While the family waited and wondered, she straightened her shoulders, pulled herself to standing, and with the help of her walker, proceeded directly to the OR. "I need an update for the rabbi's family," she said commandingly. "They're waiting to hear how the surgery is going."

The Rebbe's daughter, Rebbetzin Frimi Horowitz, still remembers how reassured they all felt with Mrs. Lubling there in the room. They knew they had a fearless advocate and champion at their side.

She also remembers the fly that kept circling around the waiting room, buzzing ceaselessly and grating on their already frayed nerves. "I wish I had a fly swatter here," she commented as she swatted at it in irritation.

"Leave it, leave it!" Mrs. Lubling said in response. "Why would you kill a living creature that isn't hurting you? It isn't bothering you, it isn't bothering me — it's flying around, having a nice day. Let it live."

Rebbetzin Horowitz was floored. Their family had long known of Mrs. Lubling's boundless compassion for ill patients, but here she had shown her compassion even for a fly.

Douglas Jablon's daughter was just a few years old when she climbed onto the kitchen counter one Shemini Atzeres during the 1980s. Her dress got caught on the hot water urn, and it tipped over, sending cascades of scalding water over the little girl.

At that time Douglas was a social worker on the staff of Maimonides Medical Center, but the Boro Park hospital was not equipped to handle such serious burns. He rushed his daughter to the burn unit at Cornell — where they waited in vain for a doctor to address their case, frantic with worry and fear.

"I need Dr. Jerome Finkelstein, he's the burn expert," Douglas kept begging the staff. "I need him to see my daughter. Can someone call Dr. Finkelstein? Please help me!"

But no one paid him any attention.

On Motzaei Simchas Torah, Douglas reached out to a friend. "Call Miriam Lubling," he was told.

"My Yiddish was like your Chinese," he says with his

self-deprecating humor. "I could barely communicate with Mrs. Lubling, but I told her the gist of the story."

In less than an hour, Mrs. Lubling was there in the room with Dr. Finkelstein — known as "The King" for his expertise in burn wounds. (In 1997, Dr. Finkelstein inaugurated the famed burn unit at Staten Island University Hospital, which he led with great distinction to become one of the top burn units in the region.)

Now Dr. Finkelstein leaned over the bed and began to examine his new patient as Mrs. Lubling looked on.

He gave instructions to the staff and then turned to Douglas. "I'll be back tomorrow to check on her," he said. "She's going to be okay, we'll make sure she gets good care. Just one thing: if you need me, just phone me directly. Whatever you do, don't call Mrs. Lubling — she'll pull me out of bed and bring me here herself!"

That was Douglas Jablon's first encounter with the uncompromising commander who had doctors quaking in their boots. But then the doctor left the room, and Douglas saw the other side of Mrs. Lubling. With the warmth of the quintessential Bobby, she smiled at the bandaged little girl. "You're behaving so nicely that I'm going to bring a present," she said. "Whatever present you want. So tell me, *mammele*, what should I get you?"

"A big doll!" the patient said.

The next time Mrs. Lubling entered the room, she was carrying a doll almost as big as she was. "You said you wanted a big doll, right?"

As her downstairs neighbor, Mrs. Malky Weinberg enjoyed a privileged view of Mrs. Lubling's practical nature. She marveled at how quick and efficient Mrs. Lubling was, how neat she kept her home, and how nonchalantly she turned out such large quantities of traditional Polish Shabbos delicacies — only to greet Shabbos several hours later with a spotless kitchen.

"To me, it was clear that her mind was so orderly because she knew her priorities," Mrs. Weinberg says. "She didn't get involved in petty issues like *machlokes* or *lashon hara*, so her mind was free to focus on the truly important things. She never let herself be derailed by the kind of minor annoyances that could irritate and occupy other people. She said, 'Let it go, let it go,' and just moved on. That attitude played a big role in her incredible efficiency."

But Mrs. Weinberg also marveled at the feeling heart that coexisted with Mrs. Lubling's very orderly mind and gifted hands. Once, when Rabbi and Mrs. Weinberg were packing up to attend a *simchah* in England, Mrs. Lubling learned that they weren't planning on taking their son, a new bar mitzvah *bachur*, with them on the trip.

"Take him," she told Mrs. Weinberg. "He's going to feel bad, you really should take him."

Then she tried to slip Mrs. Weinberg a pile of dollar bills. "You see, now you have enough money for his ticket."

Years later, the Weinbergs got a phone call from a family of Slonimer chassidim living in Eretz Yisrael. Their baby had just been diagnosed with neuroblastoma, a form of pediatric cancer that develops in the nervous system. They had been told the best place to treat him was in New York. Unfortunately, the mother was not able to travel. Could Mrs. Weinberg host the baby and care for him during the treatments?

When Mrs. Lubling learned of this plan, she was very upset. "You have a big family of your own," she remonstrated. "Why did you agree to such a crazy thing?"

Soon after the father and baby arrived, Mrs. Lubling knocked on the Weinbergs' door. She looked at the patient, all of nine months, her lips pursed disapprovingly. "I'm not getting involved," she said, shaking her head. "It's not my case. Don't ask me for any referrals or opinions — I'm staying out of this one."

The implication was clear: she didn't approve of the plan to transport such a sick baby for treatment without his mother; had she been consulted, she would have mapped out a different arrangement for his care.

Still, she couldn't keep her instinctive compassion locked inside her heart. She looked again at the baby, then approached Mrs. Weinberg and pulled out a pile of dollar bills. "When is the appointment? Tomorrow, yes? Here." She gestured toward the pile.

"I'm sure they need money, this family, to pay for the treatment. Here is one thousand dollars to help pay the hospital bill. You tell me if you need more, and I take care."

About a decade after Reb Yaakov Lubling's passing, one of Mrs. Lubling's supporters decided to gift her with a break from her frenetic schedule. "Mrs. Lubling," he said, "you work too hard. You need a vacation. I know that your friends, the Friedmans, are making a wedding in Switzerland. Here, I bought you tickets to the kosher hotel in St. Moritz. First you'll attend the wedding, and then you can check in to the hotel for a few days to relax and recharge. It will be good for you and good for the *cholim*."

Mrs. Lubling wasn't entirely sure about the plan, but she packed her suitcase and took the flight to Switzerland. The day after the wedding, she made her way to the hotel. She deposited her suitcase in the hotel room and then went to the lobby, where she found an old friend.

"Miriam!" The friend was delighted. "It's so good to see you here! Would you want to join me for a walk in the mountain air?"

Mrs. Lubling nodded. She got a sweater and her bulky cellphone from her room, and headed out into the beautiful Swiss mountainside.

The women chatted comfortably about this and that — until Mrs. Lubling's cellphone began to ring insistently.

Mrs. Lubling took the call. On the line was a young woman whose voice was choked with sobs. "Mrs. Lubling, where are you? Where are you?" she asked repeatedly. "Everyone told me that I need to speak with you, but you're not here!"

Mrs. Lubling swiftly extracted the story. The young woman had just been diagnosed with cancer, rudely catapulted onto a new planet with a new and hostile language, foreign terms, procedures and prognoses she could barely decipher. She had no idea what her next step should be. All she knew was that Miriam Lubling was the one with the knowledge, resources, and empathy to help her through the unfamiliar terrain.

"Don't worry, *mammele*. I'll meet you in ten hours at the hospital," Mrs. Lubling said. "I will find you the best doctor, and Hashem will send you a *refuah sheleimah*."

She bid a quick goodbye to the Swiss mountains and to her friend, hurried back to her room, grabbed the still-packed suitcase, and asked the hotel concierge to order a driver to transport her to the airport. That was the beginning and end of her Swiss vacation.

In June 2002, Rabbi Motty and Mrs. Malkie Katz were on their way home from a vacation in Vermont when they got a call from Rabbi Yaakov Pollak, rav of Boro Park's Shomrei Emunah shul and Mrs. Lubling's handpicked hospital chaplain.

"Motty," he said, "I'm looking for another rabbi to join the chaplaincy staff at NYU, and my son Avraham told me you'd be perfect for the job."

Avraham's intuition was right on the mark: Rabbi Katz was a beloved educator and gifted communicator. He was fluent in Yiddish and Hebrew, and experienced in leading davening and *leining*. Perhaps most importantly, he had a talent for bringing sunshine and solace to Jews suffering on the sidelines.

But there was a very important prerequisite to this job.

"Mrs. Miriam Lubling is a trustee at the hospital and they take her recommendations very seriously. Can you go to her apartment in Boro Park on Friday morning? She wants to meet you."

That Friday morning, the Katzes proceeded to Boro Park and Reb Motty went upstairs to the Lubling apartment while Malkie waited in the car. All it took was that one conversation for Mrs. Lubling to pronounce Rabbi Katz her chosen candidate. She must have sensed his unconditional *ahavas Yisrael* — to her, that was the most crucial quality for this job.

"The pay isn't too good," she warned him, "but the benefits are fantastic."

At first, he thought she was referring to the health insurance package that came along with the job. But soon enough, he realized that Mrs. Lubling was referring to what she saw as the true benefits: the ability to help Jews every hour, every day.

And she did, in fact, expect 24/7 devotion from Rabbi Katz. Though his official shift lasted about eight or nine hours, she could and did call him for help around the clock. She'd begin each phone call with a characteristic "Rabbi Katz, Rabbi Katz!" and then list the names of patients who needed help. She demanded a lot of her chosen chaplain — a lot of effort, a lot of hours, a lot of devotion — but he took up the mission willingly. He knew that every Jew in the hospital was so important to her, and the feeling resonated within him too.

On Fridays, Rabbi Katz stayed in the hospital until the last possible moment, making sure every patient had what they needed and that all the Shabbos resources were in place. Often he didn't arrive home until twenty minutes before Shabbos.

In order to be as available as possible, the Katzes kept their travels to a minimum. After spending the first days of Pesach with Malkie's family in Chicago, they hurried right back to New York, so Rabbi Katz could return to the patients.

And during the single week that the Katzes took off during the summer, Mrs. Lubling called and berated him, "Rabbi Katz, Rabbi Katz, how could you go away? There are people who need you here in the hospital!"

"One week, Mrs. Lubling," he responded goodheartedly. "Just one week!"

One year, Mrs. Lubling insisted that Reb Motty lead the Rosh Hashanah davening in NYU. He and Malkie slept in an apartment across the street, and spent all their waking hours in the hospital.

Malkie still remembers that davening: the words of the *tefillah* had never seemed so intense and immediate as they did in that room, surrounded by patients staring their mortality in the face. After the davening, they walked along the corridors, and Reb Motty offered to blow his shofar for those who hadn't made it to the minyan.

In the ER, they saw an elderly *frum* man who'd just arrived in an ambulance from Williamsburg. "Would you like to hear the shofar?" Reb Motty offered in Yiddish.

Rabbi Motty Katz, one of the hospital chaplains hand-picked by Mrs. Lubling, constantly got calls from her asking him to check on patients, explain halachah and *minhagim* to staff, and even to lead the Rosh Hashanah davening.

The man's eyes lit up. He pulled himself up to a sitting position on his stretcher, and Reb Motty raised the shofar.

"*Nein*, not yet," the man said.

He gestured to the Hatzolah volunteer who'd brought him in. "I need my hat and *reckel*," he said.

The volunteer helped the elderly patient don his Yom Tov clothing. Then he took his *machzor* and paged through it until he found *Perek* 47, *Lamenatzeiach livnei Korach mizmor*, which is recited seven times before hearing the shofar.

As the Katzes waited patiently, the man sat there on his stretcher, slowly and intentionally reciting the *perek*, his finger inching along the page with each word. All around him, nurses talked into phones, monitors beeped, doctors gave orders — but in that one little corner, the world halted while a man prepared to hear the shofar.

A hospital chaplain's duty is to provide spiritual and religious counseling and support, but Rabbi Katz's job encompassed much more than that. He became an unofficial translator for overseas patients; he used Yiddish to communicate with Russian immigrants and Hebrew for Israelis. Before Pesach, he spent an entire day supervising the preparation of the section of the kitchen used to heat up kosher meals. He organized minyanim, and when necessary, he davened and *leined*.

The chaplains on staff divided the hospital into different areas, and each would visit the Jewish patients on "their" floors. Of course, whenever Rabbi Katz visited a Jewish patient, he'd greet any non-Jewish roommates graciously and ask if they needed any help. Not only was that his personal instinct, Mrs. Lubling had made it clear that this was important to her as well. But his focus was the Jewish patients. Every day, the hospital provided him with a list of patients who'd registered as Jews, and he made his way from room to room, checking whether they could use any resources or support.

Over the years, Rabbi Katz became a bridge between the well-meaning but sometimes clueless staff and the religious patients they served. To help educate the staff, he held in-service sessions, explaining the laws of *kashrus*, *chametz*, and *chalav Yisrael*. After a nurse, trying to be helpful, shaved off a patient's *peyos*, he delivered a talk explaining the sanctity of beards and sidelocks in Jewish tradition. He also explained the special sensitivities of Holocaust survivors — a typical comment like "We're going to take you into the shower now" could evoke trauma and fear in these patients.

Soon the nurses knew that if they faced any misunderstandings or miscommunications with *frum* patients, they could call Rabbi Katz, and he would swiftly resolve the issue.

In October 2012, NYU suffered a blackout and went into emergency mode. Family members were asked to leave and crucial staff members had to put in extra time. Rabbi Katz was informed of a patient left alone, without his wife or any close family, who was refusing to eat.

He approached the bedside, leaned over, and spoke to the man in Yiddish. He quickly learned that the patient was a Holocaust survivor, and the forced separation from his wife had left him traumatized.

"Look, there's nothing wrong with the food," Reb Motty reassured him.

The patient kept his mouth tightly shut.

"Reb Yid, you have to eat. We want you to get your strength back so you can go home."

The patient didn't respond.

"Look," Reb Motty suggested. "I'm going to taste the food and make sure it's good. Then you'll take a turn."

The eyes glinted with interest.

Reb Motty took a spoon of the food and swallowed it. "Hmm, that was fine. Now you try." Then he offered a spoonful to the elderly man, who opened his mouth.

And so they continued, alternating spoons, until Reb Motty had finished feeding the lonely and terrified man.

Rabbi Katz was very discreet and never shared the names of his patients with his wife Malkie. But every now and then, she heard through the grapevine that a prestigious Rebbe or rav had been hospitalized in NYU. "*Nu*, I hear you have a VIP patient in the hospital. So did you visit the Rebbe?" she would ask her husband.

"The Rebbe has plenty of visitors," he would tell her. "I need to go to the people who won't have anyone checking on them."

Mrs. Lubling often asked Rabbi Katz to check on *frum* patients in the psych ward; she knew that they desperately needed his support and encouragement. Though the ward could be depressing and lonely, it was a fitting assignment for Rabbi Katz: he had an acutely honed sixth sense for the abandoned, the forgotten, the less glamorous or "pretty" cases, and they tugged at his sensitive heart.

Years after Mrs. Lubling's passing, he maintained that mandate, devoting extra time and care to those forgotten patients. Even during his last day at work, on Purim of 2020, he exerted himself to visit the psych ward and read the *Megillah* to the Jewish patients there.

Though he didn't know it at the time, Rabbi Katz was already ill with the mysterious virus that was about to lock down the world. At the Purim *seudah* that afternoon, he was so weak that he could barely muster the strength to cut his meat. The next day, he went to the ER and was officially diagnosed with Covid-19. He never returned home; he passed away on Erev Pesach.

The Covid regulations meant there were no appreciative crowds at the *levayah*, but the *zechus* of Rabbi Katz's myriad *mitzvos* performed in the hospital and beyond surely accompanied him to his eternal rest.

Maya Schneyer was born in the Russian city of Ufa, in the Ural Mountains, in the 1970s. Her parents, who'd grown up in Communist surroundings, knew nothing about Judaism. Still, their passports stated that they were Jewish, and everyone knew it. Her teachers knew it, her neighbors knew it, and Maya knew it as well, although at first it didn't make any difference.

As she grew older, however, the children in school began to persecute Maya, calling her names, telling her to move to Israel, and even beating her on the way home. The persecution spurred Maya to talk to the G-d Whose existence — so emphatically denied by the Soviet regime — she innately sensed. She also realized that she had a different identity and destiny than the Russians who surrounded her.

When Maya was thirteen years old, her family was granted permission to leave Russia. During a stop in Italy, they met representatives of the Vaad L'Hatzolas Nidchei Yisroel, an organization that helped draw Russian Jews to Yiddishkeit. "These are Jews and I belong with them," Maya thought when she met the visibly observant representatives.

Her parents had a different vision for their gifted daughter, but assumed that Maya's infatuation with "the cult of Torah and mitzvos" was just a passing phase. They finally arrived in Brooklyn, hoping to enroll Maya in public school so she could pursue academic excellence and the American dream. But right before the summer began, Maya met Rabbi Mordechai and Mrs. Alice Neustadt, heads of the Vaad, who arranged for her to attend Camp Chayl Miriam, Agudath Israel's camp for teenage girls located in the Catskill Mountains.

The Neustadts were a heroic couple who were the pioneering activists behind the Vaad L'Hatzolas Nidchei Yisroel. While Russia's Jews were trapped and denied access to religious connection and practice, the Neustadts made multiple trips behind the Iron Curtain, offering hope and faith to the forgotten Jews of the Soviet Union and doing their best to galvanize support for them among American Jewry.

In Camp Chayl Miriam, Maya found friends who genuinely cared for her, and she soaked up some Hebrew and the rudiments of halachah. This was her place, this was the lifestyle she wanted, and nothing would stop her from keeping mitzvos.

The first night back home after camp ended, Maya refused to eat the nonkosher supper her mother had lovingly prepared. The next morning, she spent a full hour davening. Her parents panicked.

"Either drop this religious nonsense or you leave the house now!" her father commanded.

Inconveniently for her father, Maya had inherited his strong backbone. She did indeed leave the house. Then she promptly called a *frum* woman who'd shared her phone number during a visit to camp, and moved in. A few days later, Maya's parents brought her back home — and shortly enrolled her in Bais Yaakov Academy, known as BYA for short.

Maya's new schoolmates and teachers invited her for Shabbos meals, helped her master the new curriculum, and facilitated her acclimatization to religious life. Even though her parents still hadn't made peace with losing their daughter to the "opiate of the masses," she was happy and thriving.

Maya was fifteen years old and had just started tenth grade when the accident happened. On the Shabbos between Yom Kippur and Succos, she was walking on the streets of Brooklyn with some friends when a car lost control and rammed into the sidewalk, driving over Maya's legs and hitting a streetlight. The streetlight collapsed onto Maya's left arm, amputating it just below the shoulder.

She was flown by helicopter to Bellevue Hospital and rushed into emergency surgery to reattach the arm. But the surgery was unsuccessful. Thousands of Jews in Brooklyn were devastated to hear that Maya Schneyer — the teenager who had triumphed over Communist Russia, an American immigrant experience, and a valiant battle for Yiddishkeit — had been thrown into a new challenge, one that would change the contours of her life.

Maya doesn't remember her stay at Bellevue; she was sedated and then treated with powerful painkillers for the duration of that month. She first began to take in her surroundings when she was transferred to the Rusk Rehabilitation Institute. And one of the steady visitors at her bedside was a small woman she would come to call Bobby Lubling.

Mrs. Lubling may have been short, but she was a fierce warrior who had no compunctions about fighting for the best care for Maya. "This is what needs to be done for Maya," she said, and even the chief of the therapy department — a powerhouse in her own right — didn't dare contradict her.

Every time Mrs. Lubling entered Maya's room, she related to the entire family with warmth and personal interest. She may have been a busy activist with a long list of patients to check on, but when she stepped into that room at Rusk, she was a grandmotherly figure who cared. "I felt like I was the only person she was busy with," Maya says. "I was important. The only thing on her list. I knew she was fighting for me to get the best possible care and the most up-to-date therapies. She gave me the feeling that she had all the time for me."

It wasn't only Maya who got that sense from Mrs. Lubling. Her parents, the Schneyers, were still fairly new immigrants who hadn't mastered the American language and culture — Maya had been their translator until her accident — and now they were more lost than ever. Mrs. Lubling helped them navigate not only the medical aspects of Maya's care, but also the logistics of her hospitalization — she arranged for them to stay in the Rivkah Laufer Bikur Cholim apartment during those many Shabbosos in Manhattan — and the emotional blow of seeing their injured daughter in life-altering straits.

"A lot of people were good to me," Maya clarifies. "The entire community rallied to help me. There were constant visitors, so many people bringing food and balloons and gifts. Someone came every morning with coffee and donuts — my nutritionist wasn't so happy about that. A dear friend managed to visit every single weekday, for six months straight. Friends came and made impromptu parties there in my room, to keep things upbeat and hopeful. But I don't know what we would have done medically without Mrs. Lubling — my parents really didn't know what to do or who to talk to. With her on our side, we knew that we'd get the right care."

It took six surgeries and half a year of hospitalization until Maya was able to return home. During that time her parents gained a new respect for her commitment to Torah. "If Yiddishkeit can produce people like this," her father commented, "then there must be something there."

Maya eventually returned to school, camp, and full functioning. During those years, she didn't see Mrs. Lubling often, but whenever they met, Mrs. Lubling offered her a warm hug. Maya knew with certainty that she wasn't a number or an item on a list — she was a real person.

After marrying and building a beautiful *frum* family, Maya was once invited to speak about her personal journey at a community function. As the room began to fill up, she noticed an elderly woman walking slowly but determinedly into the room. It was Mrs. Lubling — she had made the effort to attend in person, even though she was quite weak by then. Once again, she was going to be there for Maya.

"Mrs. Lubling had two sides to her personality, two qualities that don't usually go together," Maya muses. "She had this warm and loving side along with a powerhouse element, an iron will that no one could refuse. But maybe that was the secret of her success — you couldn't say no to her precisely because she was so caring, so warm, so good. Just to know that there's a person like that in the world is tremendous. It makes the world a better place."

Every time Mrs. Lubling visited her at Rusk, Maya saw a calm, composed woman in total control of her emotions. "You can't get emotional in the hospital," she acknowledges. "Emotions aren't helpful in a medical setting, and it wouldn't have been helpful for me to see her cry. I knew she cared — but she stayed upbeat and smiling."

But Maya didn't know about Mrs. Lubling's very first visit to her bedside.

Mrs. Alice Neustadt, who helped so many Jews from Russia, became Maya's lifelong mentor, accompanying and encouraging her on her journey to Yiddishkeit. When Maya lost her arm, Mrs. Neustadt was summoned to the hospital. Naturally, she called Mrs. Lubling. Bellevue Hospital was not Mrs. Lubling's territory, but when she heard about the horrific medical status of this courageous *baalas teshuvah*, an only daughter of antagonistic parents, she came to visit.

Mrs. Neustadt still remembers escorting Mrs. Lubling into Maya's room. Maya was lying in a haze of sedation and painkillers. As she drifted in and out of consciousness, she clutched her wound and moaned.

"Maya, it's me, Mrs. Neustadt," her mentor said softly. "I'm here to visit you. Maya, do you hear me? It's Mrs. Neustadt."

"Mrs. Neustadt," Maya moaned, "tell me, it's almost Succos. How will I *bentch lulav* and *esrog* with one hand? How? Tell me, tell me!" Then she fell back into her unconscious haze.

During the following months in Rusk, Maya got to know Mrs. Lubling as a woman who never showed emotion, a woman who remained calm, controlled, commanding. But Mrs. Neustadt still remembers Mrs. Lubling breaking down at Maya's Bellevue bedside.

"Did you ever see anything like this in your life?" she asked plaintively as she sobbed. "*Mi k'amcha Yisrael*, who is like the Jewish people?"

Several of Mrs. Lubling's steady drivers waited many years to find a *shidduch*. For the most part, she didn't mention their single status; she just encouraged them in their work, complimented their appearance, and thanked them profusely for helping her out. But there were a few times when she let them know how deeply she cared about their long search.

Every now and then, she would pull out lovely pieces of jewelry for her drivers and present them with delight and deep gratitude. More significantly, every year, during the Elul pre-Yom Tov season, she made a special trip to the Skverer Rebbe and ushered her drivers into the waiting room along with her. The room was full, but she announced her name and the *gabbaim* led her right in to see the Rebbe. "You come too, girls," she said, and the drivers obeyed.

Mrs. Lubling with Rebbetzin Sarah Pam

Once inside the Rebbe's chamber, she asked for *berachos* for herself, her children, and her grandchildren. The Rebbe, who was a faithful admirer of hers, issued a steady stream of *berachos*. "Now for these girls," she said. "They need *berachos* too."

One of her drivers remembers the time Mrs. Lubling brought her into the Sadigerer Rebbe, whose wife had been Mrs. Lubling's kindergarten partner back in the Crown Heights days. "I didn't understand what

Mrs. Lubling was saying — she was talking in this quick Yiddish — but I watched her get all choked up as she explained how fiercely she wanted me to find a *shidduch*. Soon enough she was crying, and I was crying too. I could see her heart spilling over with concern and love."

Another driver remembers Mrs. Lubling taking her to visit Rav Avrohom Pam, the rosh yeshivah of Yeshivah Torah Vodaath. "Rav Pam," Mrs. Lubling said, "these girls need *shidduchim*. Please give them a *berachah*."

Rav Pam looked up. His wise eyes surely saw straight into the heart, because in his sweet, humble manner he said, "Mrs. Lubling, *you* give them a *berachah*."

CHAPTER 19

With Every Breath

Mrs. Lubling embraced all of life's experiences with intense vitality. She was fully present in all the roles she filled, pulsing with energy and purpose whether she was exhorting a doctor to provide an appointment or dancing at a wedding.

Often, when she was personally acquainted with a newly bereaved family, she would join the inner circle of mourners at a *levayah*. She may not have been a blood relative, but she had accompanied them through all the stages of their loved one's illness. Her heart beat in sync with theirs, and her presence itself brought them comfort and support.

Even after her best efforts in the hospital failed, she devoted the same effort and attention to the bereaved families. She never showed up empty-handed to a *shivah* home. And she thought not only about the adults, but also the children. Long before there were any official organizations for orphans, Mrs. Lubling tallied the ages and interests of each child in the home, and made sure to arrive with appropriate toys for each one — dolls, kitchen sets, Matchbox cars, sticker albums, handheld electronic games.

But her vitality — the way she threw herself so fully into life's experiences — came to the fore most markedly when she attended a *simchah*. And that happened virtually every night.

At the end of a long afternoon of hospital rounds, most people would be tired — certainly most octogenarians. But when her drivers pulled out of the hospital parking lot, Mrs. Lubling rarely directed them back to her apartment. Instead, she reached into her handbag, touched up her lipstick, and then consulted her mental list of community events and *simchos*. As the sky grew dark, she began her nightly parade of bar mitzvahs, dinners, *vorts*, and weddings.

She could attend three weddings in one night, handily finagling rides from one to the next with her typical request: "*Zai azoi git,* would you please be so kind and take me to…?" A distant family connection or fourth-degree friendship was enough to deem someone her designated driver.

And she didn't just step into the hall, find the *baal simchah*, and wish a hearty mazel tov. She threw herself fully into each *simchah*, joining the center circle of dancers and performing her trademark *kazatzke* dance, beaming with joy and radiating a sense of utter belonging. Then she settled in and stayed until the end of the *mitzvah tantz*, like true family.

Mrs. Lubling performs her famous *kazatzke* dance at a granddaughter's wedding. She exhibited the same enthusiasm for friends, relatives, and former patients, throwing herself fully into every *simchah*.

At Bobby Lubling's eightieth birthday party. She drew strength from *simchos* for her battles in the hospital.

At close to ninety years old, she was still attending the Stoliner Lag BaOmer bonfire on 16th Avenue in Boro Park at 10:30 p.m., even after putting in a long, exhausting day. "I think that she needed to feel," muses her neighbor Mrs. Weinberg. "Even though she dealt with so much pain, she never got desensitized. She always retained her intense capacity for emotion."

Her grandchildren theorize there's a different reason for her nightly *simchah* rounds: those injections of happiness, the music and well-wishing and spirited dancing, are what gave her the endurance to visit room after hospital room shadowed by disease and depression. Maybe other people would have craved a cup of hot tea and comfortable bed, but after so many hours battling on behalf of her patients, something inside of her sought the pulsing joy of a *simchah*. She sensed that it would fortify her with the emotional strength to face the next day's challenges.

One winter when Mrs. Lubling was in her early nineties, she casually mentioned to the Hellmans that she'd never been to Florida.

"Would you want to come along with us?" Moishe Hellman offered. "We're flying there soon, and we'd love to host you in our vacation apartment in Miami."

Mrs. Lubling was always open to new experiences, and she readily agreed.

She brought the Hellmans a creative gift: a doll that was a perfect reproduction of her, down to the poufy dark wig and glasses. "Keep the doll right here on your couch," she instructed her hosts. "That way even when I'm not here, you'll remember me."

Rochel Hellman remembers Mrs. Lubling as the easiest and most delightful guest. She gamely joined the Hellmans for all their excursions, brimming with curiosity and energy.

Apparently she was spotted during one of those outings, because one day she got a phone call. On the line were some friends spending the winter in Tower 41, a large building of condos that serves as a winter home for many *frum* Jews. "Mrs. Lubling, we found out you're in Miami," her friends said. "Wouldn't it be nice to have a get-together with the *chevrah*? You have to come join us for dinner!"

That evening, the Hellmans dropped off Mrs. Lubling outside Tower 41, where a group of friends had gathered in honor of their guest. They then headed back to their apartment.

About half an hour later, Mr. Hellman's phone rang. It was Mrs. Lubling.

"Moishe," she said, her voice laced with urgency, "*kim schnell*, come quick. You have to get me out of here!"

"What's wrong, Mrs. Lubling?"

"This place," she said derisively, "it's a *moishav zekeinim*, an old-age home. I can't be here another minute!"

Moishe Hellman got back into his car and hurried to pick up Mrs. Lubling — who was older than most of her friends, but had the youngest heart of anyone he knew.

But at some point even that preternaturally young heart began to show signs of age. As Mrs. Lubling approached her nineties, her body began to weaken. The stairs up to her apartment became a challenge. Her children installed a chairlift. "Why?" she protested. "Why do you treat me like an old lady?"

Posing with a great-great-grandchild just a few months before her final illness, fully dressed and in her *sheitel*. She may have been weak, but she never compromised on her regal appearance.

With time, she grew accustomed to the convenience, but she never made her peace with the indignity and frustration of a body that could no longer fulfill all the ambitions of her sharp mind.

As the years went on, she grew weaker and needed a wheelchair to get from her house to her children. She used to instruct her grandchildren, "*Loif, loif,* run as fast as you can!" as they pushed the wheelchair through the streets of Boro Park. She couldn't quite come to terms with anyone seeing her in that compromised position. One grandchild even remembers her putting a blanket over her head when she noticed a neighbor approaching.

During that period of increasing weakness, Mrs. Lubling's drivers still arrived faithfully every afternoon to take her to NYU. They maneuvered her wheelchair out of the car and watched her sit down, straighten her back, and steel her shoulders. Then she directed them to the elevators, her brain whirring at the usual pace as she ran through her mental list and Post-it notes of patients to visit and doctors to debate.

If Mrs. Lubling ever saw a doctor approaching, she sprang out of the wheelchair and stood upright. Her age-old ethos — "If you look right, you get treated right" — still drove her onward.

Later on, when she grew even more frail, she couldn't conduct her usual rounds. But even as her mobility decreased and her strength grew limited, she still felt the pull of NYU. After all those years, it was still her place.

So her devoted drivers embarked on the familiar route to Manhattan, pulled up in the parking lot, and escorted her to the bikur cholim room that had been her innovation and which bore her name. She scanned the shelves and opened the fridge to make sure it was well stocked, neat and clean, and then sat down in the recliner. Whenever a *frum* Jew stepped in, she straightened her back and the old vitality appeared once again in her eyes.

"Hello," she said. "I'm Miriam Lubling, and I'm a trustee at this hospital. How can I help you? Is there anything you need?"

The first time Mrs. Lubling was too weak to attend a wedding was a low moment. But her family and her many admirers often brought their *simchos* to her. When she was hospitalized in NYU after a procedure, she was visited by Reb Beinish Mandel, a widely known *baal chessed* and longtime member of Flatbush Hatzolah. Reb Beinish was a close friend of Mendy Horowicz — Mrs. Lubling's grandson by marriage — and had therefore come to know Mrs. Lubling well.

This time, however, he had brought along his daughter — and she was dressed for her wedding, in white gown, tiara, and veil.

"Beinish," Mrs. Lubling asked, startled, "what are you doing here? Aren't you making a *chasunah* in a few hours? And isn't it in Brooklyn?"

"Bobby," he answered firmly (all of Mendy's friends called his beloved grandmother Bobby), "my daughter is not going down to the *chuppah* without a *berachah* from you."

During that last period, Mrs. Lubling spent more time than usual in the Boro Park home of her daughter Peshi Drillick. "Whenever I think of Bobby during that period," remembers one of Peshi's

Mrs. Lubling with her famous *Tehillim* — even when she could no longer do regular hospital rounds, she still found a way to help the *cholim*.

daughters, "I think of a single image: Bobby sitting at the head of the kitchen table, in her *sheitel*, of course, with her lamp, her magnifying glass, and her *sefer Tehillim*. She was no longer visiting her patients, but the *cholim* were still in her heart and mind — and she was still taking care of them."

In February 2014, she contracted pneumonia. When the condition worsened and she seemed in real distress, the family called Hatzolah. Hatzolah arrived, ascertained her difficulty breathing, and decided to transport her to NYU.

"Wait!" she commanded as they began preparing her for the trip. "I can't leave the house without my *sheitel*!"

That was her last public appearance — at age 96, laboring to get in adequate oxygen — and she still made sure to adhere to her high standards.

The sad irony is that when she arrived at NYU, the institution where she'd waged so many battles, pressing doctors to explore just one more option and give her patients just one more chance, the doctors preferred to take the passive route and follow protocol: administer end-of-life care without the antibiotics so crucial to fighting off her infection.

"Your mother is 96 years old. She's so weak as it is," they told her children. "Why fight this infection? Her functioning will be so compromised, what kind of quality of life will she have anyway?"

True to their training, the children fought back. "Even if she won't be able to eat steak," Chanoch said, "she'll still value every minute that she's able to enjoy her family."

Some of Mrs. Lubling's famous fighting spirit must have lingered over that conversation. The doctors began treatment, and for the next four weeks Mrs. Lubling did in fact absorb the love and adoration of her children and grandchildren, who employed a round-the-clock personal aide and maintained their own steady rotation in her private room at the corner of the floor. Many of her faithful drivers made the trip to NYU as well, slipping into her room to recite a *perek* of *Tehillim* and bask one more time in her presence.

During that hospital stay, her pneumonia receded, only to be replaced by a staph infection. But by the middle of the fourth week, her white blood counts were back in normal range and she seemed to have turned the corner.

As Purim approached, the Lubling children tried to pull together a minyan for *Megillah-leining* in the hospital family room on the fifteenth floor. But their mother's energy and expertise were sorely missed. For the first time in three decades, there was no Purim party in NYU.

On Purim, March 16, a group of grandsons dressed in costume came to visit Bobby Lubling. They sang and danced in front of her bed, and noticed a slight smile hovering on her lips.

"Things are looking good," the doctors told her children.

Buoyed by their optimism, Chanoch decided to travel to his granddaughter's wedding in Israel. Peshi and Nechama began to dream about their mother spending the Pesach Seder with her children and grandchildren.

Then, early in the morning of Thursday, March 20th/18 Adar they received a call from NYU. "Her blood pressure is dropping," the doctors said. "Everything is crashing."

Mrs. Lubling always preferred to focus on life. She wouldn't have wanted her children to forever replay the frantic, futile efforts of those final moments. Instead, they remember her with open eyes and a slight smile, the lingering hope that better times were around the corner. Just as she would have wanted.

Mrs. Lubling was not a person for long, drawn-out ceremonies, and her *levayah* was no exception — but every person who attended felt utterly broken and bereft.

At 1 p.m. on that chilly Thursday afternoon, throngs of mourning Jews filled the Shomrei Hadas Chapel in Boro Park. Mrs. Lubling was not a person for long, drawn-out ceremonies. Whether it was cooking *galleh* for a crowd or arranging the removal of a brain tumor, she did everything quickly and efficiently. Her *levayah* was no exception. With a 6 p.m. flight to catch, the *hespedim* were short and succinct. But they were saturated with admiration and longing.

The Novominsker Rebbe described her as an *ishah gedolah*, a great woman, who wielded influence far beyond her immediate circle. "From her we can learn how much a single individual, a *Yiddishe tochter*, a daughter of Avraham Avinu, can do for Klal Yisrael," he said, as tears choked his voice.

Rav Dovid Olewski, Gerrer rosh yeshivah in New York, quoted the Sfas Emes: When a person trains himself to be so wholly attuned to his fellow man's grief that he can't possibly ignore his suffering, then he gains the power to lift his fellow man out of his pain. That is how powerful his empathy can be.

This was the power of Mrs. Miriam Lubling. Like Miriam HaNeviah, whose passing is linked by the Gemara to the *parah adumah* — which would be mentioned in that week's *parashah* — she would surely bring atonement to the entire Jewish people as she left this world. With her empathy, she could literally lift people out of their suffering.

"*Ribbono shel Olam*," Rav Olewski cried, "a woman is leaving this world, a *neshamah* that displayed so much dedication and caring for the *cholei Yisrael*. If one person can do so much for the ill, surely You can do so much more. Wipe away all the suffering and sickness, so no one should suffer anymore."

Menashe Frankel, Mrs. Lubling's grandson, noted that many public activists tend to be less involved with their family as their public involvement grows more extensive and demanding. "But in our family," he declared, "we knew that Bobby never forgot about us for even a moment. She carried us, each one of us, down to the last detail, with her concern."

He, too, compared Mrs. Lubling to Miriam HaNeviah, who began her "*klal* role" watching over a child, her brother Moshe. Bobby Lubling took so much pride in the fact that she ran a kindergarten for forty years. She invested her heart and soul in those children, and each "graduate" was imprinted with the indelible stamp of her *yiras Shamayim* and warmth for Yiddishkeit.

Mrs. Lubling's son-in-law Aharon Drillick remembered the time his business met with a company that was developing a cancer drug. During the course of their conversation, he learned that one of the doctors on the medical team worked in NYU, and he asked her if she knew Mrs. Lubling.

"Of course I know her," the doctor said. "She's that bossy woman who barges in to our offices, turns the doctors' schedules upside-down, makes demands and refuses to budge until we give in… How do you know her?"

"She's my mother-in-law," he had responded, with no small measure of pride.

Now he turned to the crowds that had gathered to bid a final goodbye to the woman who wouldn't ever give up when a Jew's life was at stake. "Bobby did so much — her entire life was a lesson in how much a single woman can accomplish. But she has a chance to do even more now," he said. "She is going up to *Shamayim*, and she can barge in to the Administrative Offices. She won't wait for an appointment. If the Doctor says no, she won't accept it.

"She knows better than we all do how much sickness there is, how many *tzaros*. Now she can go up there and do what she's always done down here. She can beg for healing and *refuos* — and she will refuse to take no for an answer."

Hundreds of friends, admirers, and beneficiaries of Mrs. Lubling's *chessed* accompanied her *aron* to the airport. The next afternoon, the El Al flight landed at Ben Gurion. It was a short Friday, but over one hundred Bnei Brak women joined Chanoch and his children in the airport, waiting to pay their final respects to Mrs. Lubling. Some of the women were friends or admirers; many were volunteers who shared her passion for bikur cholim and other *chassadim*. They had been brought to the airport by Mrs. Sarah Halpert, the Vizhnitzer activist and leader of Agudah's Avnei Noam sisterhood.

Mrs. Halpert led her own bikur cholim organization, and over the decades she had benefited from Mrs. Lubling's support and encouragement. Even the constraints of a short Friday couldn't hold her back from this final, albeit hasty, goodbye to a beloved mentor.

At 2 p.m., the procession arrived at the Shamgar funeral home in Jerusalem. It was Friday afternoon, just a few brief hours before Shabbos, and the Lublings were amazed and moved to see the sizable crowd that had gathered. They hadn't realized just how many people felt so deeply connected to their family matriarch.

One of the members of the *chevrah kaddisha* approached Chanoch and his children. "I want you to know," he warned them, "that we're going to be very tight for time. The Arabs have their day of worship on Friday, and they'll be leaving their mosques on Har HaBayis and choking up the entire area near Har HaZeisim. It will be a challenge to finish the burial in time for Shabbos.

"Not only that," he said, "the Jerusalem marathon is taking place today and half the streets of the city have been blocked off."

Yerushalayim is a city of steep slopes and forbidding hills, and the Jerusalem marathon combines topographical challenges with the tourist appeal of both ancient and modern landmarks. The course takes runners past the Knesset, the German Colony, the Old City, the Sultan's Pool — and, of course, the Mount of Olives, or Har HaZeisim. And those runners number in the thousands; the marathon is not just for the sports-minded, but also for the socially conscious, who run to raise money for a broad spectrum of non-profit causes.

"Thousands of marathoners are going to be passing Har HaZeisim today," the *chevra kaddisha* liaison explained, "so there's no way we can have any *hespedim* at this *levayah*. Just a *kapitel Tehillim* and then we're hurrying to Har HaZeisim."

Chanoch didn't know what to say. Could he really take his leave of his angel of a mother without any words of *hesped* at all?

"Please give us ten minutes," he begged, "so my two sons and I can say a few words."

"I'll allow you five minutes in total," the *chevrah kaddisha* liaison replied. "As things stand, there's a good chance the *chevrah* won't make it home in time for Shabbos."

After a quick consultation, it was decided that Chanoch and his son Aryeh would each speak for two minutes, while his son Mordechai, who lives in Ashdod, would speak at the *hakamas matzeivah*.

Aryeh recalled the years he was privileged to sleep in Bobby Lubling's apartment. "There were times when I came home from yeshivah and found Bobby crying," he said. "I asked why she was crying, and she told me it was because someone was *niftar*. Was it a cousin? Maybe a close friend? No, it was one of her patients. That's how strongly she felt their pain.

"But whenever a patient or their family asked Bobby how they could repay her, she had the same answer: invite me to your *simchos*. You know," he told the assembly, "Rav Mottel Pogromansky, the famous Litvishe *gaon*, famously said, 'Someone who doesn't feel another's grief is not a *mentch* — but someone who can feel another's *simchah* is a *malach*, an angel.' We all know that Bobby was a *malach*. It's no wonder that she came to be known as Klal Yisrael's angel of mercy."

Chanoch then turned to the *mitah* and implored his mother to advocate for Klal Yisrael before our Heavenly Father as only she could.

As the *mitah* was transported out of the funeral home, a stranger, a Yerushalmi man from the crowd, stepped forward. "You don't know who I am," he told Chanoch in Yiddish, "but you have to let me speak." Then he turned toward the crowd and raised his voice.

"Years ago, my child got sick," he said. "They told me to come to America, to one of the big hospitals in Boston, where a famous pediatric neurosurgeon named Dr. Michael Scott would operate. I had no money, no connections, no idea what to expect. When we got to Boston, the hospital refused to admit my son unless we could give them a fourteen-thousand-dollar deposit up front. I had no idea what to do. We had come all this way — for what?

"Then someone suggested that I call Mrs. Miriam Lubling. I had no idea who she was, but I called the number I'd been given. Mrs. Lubling listened to my story and took down the details. 'Wait there in the hospital, I will take care,' she said.

"Fifteen minutes later, the secretary in the admitting office waved me through. 'We're admitting your child right now,' they said. 'Miriam Lubling was in touch with us, and she promised to wire the deposit.'

"Later I found out that Mrs. Lubling had called four philanthropists and raised the money in about ten minutes. But I never had a chance to thank her.

"Mrs. Lubling," he choked out the words as he turned toward the *aron*, "thank you! You didn't even know us, but when we needed your help, we became your family."

A wave of unspoken agreement rippled through the crowd. Everyone in the funeral hall felt the same way. They may have been strangers — from different backgrounds, different communities, different cities — but they all knew what it meant to have a world upended by serious illness. And they had all tasted that sweet solace of Mrs. Lubling's "*Ich vel erleidigen,* I take care."

Twenty-five years earlier, Chanoch had brought a *kvittel* to the Pnei Menachem of Gur. "I want to be *mazkir meine mamme*, to mention my mother's name for a *berachah*," he said.

"*Deine mamme*," the Rebbe answered, raising his hands, "*iz der eim kol chai*. Your mother is everyone's mother!"

Is it any wonder the masses of unrelated Jews at the Shamgar funeral home considered themselves family?

True to the predictions of the *chevrah kaddisha*, the roads to Har HaZeisim were snarled by Arab worshipers streaming out of their mosques. The hearse inched forward and the tension rose as the sun slipped further west and the clock ticked closer to Shabbos.

Finally the road opened up and the van reached its destination. The group navigated the narrow path toward the Warsaw *Chelkah*, opposite the resting places of the Gerrer Rebbes. They hurried to the waiting gravesite, anxious to complete their holy mission.

Decades earlier, Friday after Friday, Reb Yaakov Lubling had sat on his Boro Park porch, waiting for his wife to return from her hospital rounds of mercy and join him for Shabbos. To the hum of his *Shir HaShirim*, as the honking of cars and pre-Shabbos clamor receded with the departing week, he waited for her to take a rest from six days filled with nonstop activity. Finally came the call, "Yankel, I'm coming, I'm here!" as her driver left

פ״נ
אמנו סבתנו אם כל חי
האשה החשובה טובת עין וחכמת לב
תפארת משפחתנו
מרת **מרים לאה** ע״ה
לובלינג
בת הרה״ח ר׳ **יונה** ז״ל הי״ד
אשת חיל עטרת בעלה
הרה״ח ר׳ **יעקב** ז״ל
קינצק, לובלין - תל אביב - ניו יורק

מסכת חייה היוותה שלשלת אחת
של נשיאות עול מתוך מסירות נפש
ללא הרף למען חולי ישראל
לבה הטוב סבל סבלם וכאב כאבם
רבבות הצילה ודאגה בלו״נ
לתומכם ולסעדם
חיזקה המוני שבורי לב ודכאי רוח
העמידה והחזיקה מוסדות תורה וחסד
בשארית כוחותה
יראת ה׳ אוצרה, חסד והטבה מהותה
מרוממות דרכיה השרישה
בלבות בני משפחתה

נלב״ע בשם טוב ובשיבה טובה
י״ח אדר ב׳ תשע״ד
ת נ צ ב״ה

מרת **מרים לאה לובלינג** ע״ה

The text on Mrs. Lubling's *matzeivah*

her off. Then she hurried upstairs, lit the waiting candles, and basked in the serenity that is the province of those who know they've used their week well.

Now, on a mountain in Jerusalem, silence slowly began to overtake the traffic that had strangled the city streets just an hour before. A gravestone stood proudly, patiently, marking the spot where Reb Yaakov Lubling had been laid to rest twenty-six years earlier. If you listened very closely, you might have even heard the echoes of that long-ago call: "Yankel, I'm coming, I'm here!"

Finally, his wife could take a rest from her lifetime filled with nonstop advocacy for her fellow Jews. Her eternal Shabbos was coming, and she could bask in the serenity that is the province of those who know they've used their time well.

CHAPTER 20
Irreplaceable

As the Lubling children prepared to sit *shivah*, a helpful relative suggested that they post a sign delineating visiting hours, so they could have some quiet time between visitors.

"For our mother's *shivah*?" they asked incredulously. "Ima never had hours. She was always available — morning, afternoon, long past midnight. She would go crazy if we were to limit visitors to specific hours!"

And in fact, the visitors kept coming, the entire day and much of the night. So many people had been helped and touched by the immigrant woman who saw every Jew as family. Rabbanim and rebbetzins, chassidic Rebbes and roshei yeshivah, politicians and community activists, and so many grateful beneficiaries of all types and stripes made the steady march to Mrs. Lubling's apartment on 51st Street.

Each one had a story, and each story starred the same pivotal character.

"Your mother likely saved my wife," one visitor said. "After she was diagnosed with cancer, she was admitted to the hospital, but treated like a nobody — the care was basic at best and anything other than that was ignored. Then Mrs. Lubling came and pulled two envelopes out of her pocketbook. She slipped one to the nurse, and when the doctor came by on rounds, he got one too. Suddenly the care changed. My wife became a VIP patient. They knew that Mrs. Lubling was on top of the case and it was a different world."

"If not for your mother, I don't know if I would be walking normally today," another man said. "I tore my ligament while dancing at a wedding. The top doctor that I saw told me I would need major surgery, a body cast, and months of rehab. Then Mrs. Lubling walked into the waiting room and asked me why I was there.

"'Not today, but tomorrow morning, a doctor is coming in from Switzerland to work in Joint Diseases Hospital,' she said. 'He spent three years perfecting a microsurgery procedure for skiing accidents. And you know what? You will be his first patient here in America.'

"The next morning, I was wheeled into the OR at Joint Diseases, where the newly arrived Swiss doctor was waiting. And just one day later, I walked through the door of my home on my own two feet. Today he's a celebrity doctor, treating sports stars and the rich and famous. But I was his first patient — all because of Mrs. Lubling."

Another visitor described the time his elderly mother fell while doing her shopping on the avenue. She suffered a major break in her hand — so severe that the bone actually protruded from her skin. From the ambulance, he called Mrs. Lubling. "I will be in the hospital in half an hour. Wait for me in the emergency room and I will have Dr. Charles Melone see her," she said.

"And within half an hour she came into the ER, in her fur coat, talking on her cellphone. And what do you know, just a few minutes later a doctor hurried down to us. When he saw Mrs. Lubling, he literally bowed to her. 'What can I do for your patient, Mrs. Lubling?' he asked."

Among the masses of *frum* Jews coming to the *shivah* house were some of the doctors who'd seen Mrs. Lubling at her finest. Some were fellow Jews familiar with the concept of *shivah*, but several non-Jews also made the trip to Brooklyn to demonstrate their abiding respect for Mrs. Lubling.

Haitian-born Dr. Antoine, OB-GYN, had learned from Mrs.

Lubling to respond to compliments with a modest "I'm just a *shaliach,*" and to reassure patients that "Hashem is with you."

Gastroenterologist Dr. Charles Friedlander told her children, "You know, not a day goes by that I don't miss your mother and her endless 'cousins.'"

Vascular surgeon Dr. Patrick Lamparello came too, speaking warmly of the woman who had turned his appointment book upside down, all for the sake of her fellow Jews.

"Who will take her place?" they all wondered. "Who can ever fill the shoes of Mrs. Lubling?"

In the ten years since her passing, no single person has managed to fill the enormous void this petite woman left. But that's not to say that no one is trying to fill at least some part of it. In fact, she inspired a mass movement of giving, caring, and advocacy — on both individual and organizational levels. So many men, women, and organizations owe their spark and drive to her trailblazing work.

On a personal level, many of the volunteers who drove Mrs. Lubling and who coordinated the fundraising events for the Rivkah Laufer Bikur Cholim have watched their children take on communal initiatives. The *chessed* they absorbed as they grew up — helping stuff envelopes, tally donations, cheer up the patients at the Purim parties, or sometimes even take the wheel of the family car to transport Mrs. Lubling to NYU — became an indelible part of their personalities and lifestyles. Giving to others is now their family legacy.

On an organizational level, much of the modern bikur cholim landscape was shaped by her trailblazing work. Step into almost any medical center patronized by a significant *frum* population, and you will find a fully stocked bikur cholim room. Spend a Shabbos in the hospital, and chances are good that you'll find a Shabbos elevator in service, and a dedicated apartment nearby will be available for family members of the patient. Visit any major New York hospital on Chanukah, and you will see menorahs freely distributed. Encounter a puzzling medical issue or a frightening diagnosis, and an army of skilled volunteers will utilize their hard-won connections to expedite appointments, speed up tests, and marshal the right doctor to the case.

All are continuing the work of that immigrant woman who couldn't stand the thought of a Jew alone in a hospital ward — and who possessed the determination and energy to set real change in motion.

Mrs. Pearl Pinter, who quietly and efficiently ran the original Rivkah Laufer Bikur Cholim fund since its initiation from her kitchen table, is still at it (albeit at a new table).

Over the decades, the fund has distributed millions of dollars to patients in need — not just locally, but across the world, from South America to Eretz Yisrael. And it does so with no overhead, no state-of-the-art office, no paid staff.

The bikur cholim still operates and funds two bikur cholim apartments near NYU. Its many volunteer drivers transport patients and their families to and from medical appointments throughout the New York City area and beyond. And under its auspices, a cadre of dedicated volunteers continue to visit the hospitals.

In Boro Park's Maimonides Medical Center, the volunteers operate a refreshment cart, loaded with cookies, snacks, and coffee for family, visitors, and even the hospital staff. As they distribute the goodies, they bring encouragement and succor to the patients' families, and no small measure of goodwill to the staff. Once a week, the volunteers also distribute Shabbos candles to the Jewish patients confined to the wards.

"People are more vulnerable when they're in the hospital," Mrs. Pinter says. "They're looking for spirituality. Even if they were resistant or just didn't know much before, when we connect with them in the hospital and offer them the chance to light Shabbos candles, they're much more likely to take the opportunity.

"You know," she observes, "back when Mrs. Lubling was *niftar*, a lot of people assumed it meant the end of the bikur cholim. But she had inspired so many women and built such a strong infrastructure that it kept going even without her."

Rabbi Boruch Ber Bender channeled some of Mrs. Lubling's determination when he built Achiezer, a celebrated communal organization that handles a massive number of medical, financial, emotional, or logistic crises. Every staff member of Achiezer knows that the organization operates on the foundation of a single, specific mantra: we never say no.

His father, Rav Yaakov Bender, the rosh yeshivah of Yeshivah Darchei Torah, often asks him in wonder and appreciation, "Boruch, you started your organization long after so many of the others — but managed to find the resources and connections to be incredibly effective in such a short time. What makes Achiezer so successful?"

Boruch Ber's answer echoes the first lesson he learned from Mrs. Lubling: "Because we're not scared to ask."

Embedded in the DNA of Achiezer are the openness and courage to make the effort and ask. "If a fellow Jew needs you to reach out to a doctor, a hospital, an insurance company — you don't lose by asking," he says. "Maybe they'll turn you down, maybe you won't get the answer you hoped for, but you have to try. As I built Achiezer, I always carried a vision of this short, determined lady walking up to a door that said 'Do not enter' and walking right in. Until today, that vision motivates me."

Mrs. Hudi Silber worked closely with Mrs. Lubling for four decades. She got to know Mrs. Lubling after catering several events for Nshei PAI. Then they discovered another area of mutual activity: bikur cholim.

Hudi and her husband, a transplanted Yerushalmi, hosted many Israeli Jews who traveled to the United States for treatment. They worked together with Mrs. Lubling to ensure the best care for these patients, and soon enough Hudi was learning the ropes of patient advocacy directly from Mrs. Lubling, building her own roster of sympathetic doctors.

Eventually Hudi helped the angels in human guise who founded the Rofeh Cholim Cancer Society. Even today, she helps expedite appointments, makes personal hospital visits, distributes delicious homemade food to patients, and eases the hospital stays of fellow Jews in need.

"Many things have changed since Mrs. Lubling's days," she says, "but the underlying principles are the same. When I need to discuss a case with a doctor, I don't send an email. I talk. From Mrs. Lubling I learned that success in this field comes from a personal, emotional connection. A few lines on the computer don't mean anything. When you speak to a doctor with passion, it has a whole different meaning."

Leah Horowitz, the daughter of Mrs. Lubling's kindergarten partner Rebbetzin Teitelbaum, is employed as a care navigator for the Chayim Aruchim end-of-life organization. She liaises between families of critically ill patients and the medical professionals providing their care. These cases inevitably involve wrenching halachic and hashkafic dilemmas, complicated further by volatile emotions and the highest of stakes.

Fighting for religious values in an increasingly progressive medical environment can be daunting — but Leah credits Mrs. Lubling, whom she saw as her "second mother," for gifting her with a master key that opens many doors.

"It's interesting," she muses. "I work in end-of-life. Fighting for every last breath is, in many cases, the opposite of what twenty-first-century medicine believes to be the correct course. Yet I still have a positive relationship with most doctors.

"How do I do it? I extend the doctors the respect they deserve for their medical expertise, and when I raise a different point, it's because I come from a religious perspective. Even if I disagree with their suggestions, they're the doctor and I'm not. I don't pretend to know more medicine than they do; my requests are about religious accommodation.

"Mrs. Lubling taught me to extend respect to everyone and make them feel valued — from a top doctor to the mailman. I think that's why she was so successful. She made every nurse, every orderly, every surgeon into a valued and necessary partner.

She made it her business to know everything about their personal lives, and would inquire with genuine concern each time they spoke. Most importantly, she turned every tragedy into a mission whose success depends on you. When you can convey that sense of respect — the sense that we are in this together and we need your input to get the best outcome — then even an adversary can become a partner."

Ask any of Mrs. Lubling's volunteers about her, and their eyes immediately brighten. They will describe a woman who taught them never to be cowed by human nature — or nature itself, to walk with pride and ask with courage for another chance, another drop of compassion, an earlier slot for surgery or a better bed for an ailing patient. They'll recall her *Tehillim* — recited aloud, as she must have learned back in the *heim*, at the bedside of her patients — and the single concern fueling every exchange, every effort, every encounter.

And they'll remember the way she interacted with the senior leadership of NYU. "How are you, Mrs. Lubling?" these powerful, moneyed board members would greet their oldest trustee.

"Thank G-d, thank G-d, thank G-d, I am fine," she would answer — then revert to her prime concern. "Now *you* tell me, how can we help the people here?"

Mrs. Lubling is no longer walking the halls of Manhattan's top hospitals. Her beeper no longer buzzes; her cellphone is finally quiet, after years of ringing throughout the day and night. But her spirit of genuine caring and indomitable action still hovers in the hospital wards, whenever and wherever good Jews echo her promise to "take care" of their sisters and brothers in need.

Approximately six years after Mrs. Lubling's *petirah*, Chanoch received a phone call from an unfamiliar number.

"Is this Mr. Lubling?" It was the voice of an elderly woman. "The son of Miriam Lubling?"

"Yes, it is," he said, wondering what this was all about.

"My name is Elizabeth Bruckstein and I want you and your

family to come to my home in Rego Park, Queens. I have something for you."

Chanoch had never heard the name before. "How did you get my number?" he asked.

"From the Lubavitcher *shliach* here in Queens," the woman said. "Will you come?"

"Yes, of course," he said. He took down her address and set a day and time.

Then he looked up the *shliach* and phoned him. "Do you know what this woman wants from me?" he asked.

"Actually, she probably has a check for you," the *shliach* said. "She asked me to come to her house last week, and she gave me a fifty-thousand-dollar check to deliver to Hatzolah. And then she asked me, can you track down the children of Miriam Lubling?"

On the appointed day, Mrs. Lubling's children drove to Queens. When they knocked at the door of the small private home, a medical aide answered. The aide was clearly very protective of her patient and tried to keep them out, but once they explained that Ms. Bruckstein had expressly requested that they come visit, she allowed the Lublings to enter.

There, resting in an armchair, they found an elderly woman with no overt signs of religious observance, frail and blind.

"Are you the children of Miriam Lubling?" she asked.

"Yes, we are," they said.

"There's something I want to give you," she said. She directed her aide to give them a check made out to Rivkah Laufer Bikur Cholim. Chanoch peeked at the amount and sucked in his breath. It was for two hundred thousand dollars.

"I have 'sugar,'" the woman said — a reference to diabetes. "You know that this disease comes with all kinds of *tzuris*. First my eyesight went. Then my leg got hot and swollen. The people from Hatzolah brought me to Queens General Hospital. The doctors said my leg was gangrenous and they would have to amputate. I thought that was it.

"Then a neighbor of mine came to visit and said, 'We can't let them cut off your leg just like that. We need a bigger hospital, we need better care. We need Miriam Lubling.'"

The woman's sightless eyes grew soft and moist as she unspooled her story. "That was the first time I heard your mother's name. Then I met her. She was a whirlwind. So strong, so determined. She came here, to Queens, and she fought those doctors. She brought me to NYU — and she made sure they saved my leg. She kept visiting me that entire time, checking on me and making sure I was recovering, that I had food and good care.

"That's why I'm giving you this check. It's in honor of your mother. Give it to her causes, her volunteers, so they can keep doing her work."

The Lublings thanked the woman warmly. She seemed tired and spent, so they prepared to leave.

"Wait," she said. "You're probably wondering, how did I know that it was your mother who kept checking on me? There are lots of volunteers there in the hospital, and remember" — she motioned at her milky eyes — "I can't see. So how did I know it was your mother who kept coming to my room?

"I'll tell you how I knew," she said. "A lot of volunteers came by, with food and drinks and encouragement and good wishes. But there was only one volunteer who held my hand. That was your mother. Every time she came into the room, she held my hand."

Epilogue

Power has an insidious way of causing its holders to forget their roots. After years of leading corporations, courts, or countries, receiving accolades and awards, or watching in satisfaction as obedient teams follow their orders, many if not most elites grow accustomed to their privileged positions. From their new stratum, the people on the "other side of the tracks" seem a lifetime away.

Not for Mrs. Miriam Lubling. Like the great leaders and *askanim* of Klal Yisrael, she never lost her capacity to empathize with the powerless or the poverty-stricken. She was honored at many a dinner and spent hours in Manhattan boardrooms and at exclusive black-tie events, interacting graciously and easily with the rich and famous. But she never became an elitist and she never lost her *heimishe* touch.

Even as she wielded the levers of power and influence, she always remembered the young woman who'd left behind everything familiar, drifting toward an uncertain future on a crowded boat — hungry, frightened, and utterly alone. Even after she amassed the private telephone numbers of New York's finest doctors, she never forgot the desperation of those early years in Tel Aviv, when her husband was facing a life of blindness and no doctor seemed able to help.

Every Jew was her cousin, every family facing illness became her favored relative, and she would exercise every earthly connection to get them the best possible care.

Fellow survivors merited a special spot in her heart, and perhaps none occupied a spot more tender than the one reserved for two distant relatives — Rabbi Shmuel and Mrs. Chana Wechsler, a couple who'd survived the Holocaust but had never been blessed with children.

"Who will visit us after one hundred twenty?" they once cried to this woman who'd absorbed so many worries and so much pain. "Who will come to our graves if we have no children or grandchildren in this world?"

Over the years Mrs. Lubling had raised millions of dollars, pried doctors from hard-earned vacations, and commandeered operating rooms for patients with no medical insurance — all with the promise of "I take care." Now she made the same promise.

Mrs. Lubling's *matzeivah* on Har HaZeisim. The inscription, as instructed by the Gerrer Rebbe, describes her as *eim kol chai*. Right behind it are the Wechslers' gravestones, in a spot strategically arranged to ensure there would be visitors.

"Trust me," she told them. "I will make sure that when the time comes, you will have visitors every year."

Even for the woman who could arrange emergency brain surgery in less than twenty-four hours, this seemed a very ambitious claim. But like so many of Mrs. Lubling's assurances, it proved well founded.

Sure enough, she contacted the Kollel Polin office in Yerushalayim, and bought two burial plots in the Warsaw *Chelkah* on Har HaZeisim — in a very strategic spot.

Twice a year, on 24 Tammuz and 18 Adar, the Lubling children and grandchildren visit their parents' final resting places on Har HaZeisim. Every visit without fail, they make a second stop at another pair of gravestones — one row back, in plots arranged with perfect precision by the woman who could never accept no for an answer.

"I take care," Mrs. Lubling promised, and though she can no longer schedule surgeries or expedite appointments, her promise is being kept. The angel of mercy is still showering down compassion from on High.